ICH

D0754584

NO LONGER PROPERTY OF
SEATTLE PUBLIC LIBRARY

5/96

MOBILE

SEATTLE PUBLIC LIBRARY

Wyatt Earp's Tombstone Vendetta

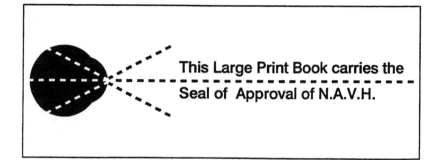

This Large Print Book carries the
Seal of Approval of N.A.V.H.

Wyatt Earp's Tombstone
Vendetta

Collected and Edited by
Glenn G. Boyer

G.K. Hall & Co
Thorndike, Maine

JUL 1 8 1994 MOBILE BRANCH

Copyright © 1993 Glenn G. Boyer

All rights reserved.

Published in 1994 by arrangement with Glenn G. Boyer.

G.K. Hall Large Print Western Collection.

The text of this Large Print edition is unabridged.
Other aspects of the book may vary from the original edition.

Set in 16 pt. News Plantin by Juanita Macdonald.

Printed in the United States on acid-free, high opacity paper. ∞

Library of Congress Cataloging in Publication Data

Wyatt Earp's Tombstone vendetta / collected and edited by
  Glenn G. Boyer.
       p.   cm.
    Includes bibliographical references.
    ISBN 0-8161-5959-9 (alk. paper : lg. print)
    1. Tombstone (Ariz.) — History — Juvenile literature.
2. Violence — Arizona — Tombstone — History — 19th century
— Juvenile literature.
3. Frontier and pioneer life — Arizona — Tombstone — Juvenile
literature.
4. Earp, Wyatt, 1848–1929 — Juvenile literature.
5. Earp, Morgan, 1851–1882 — Juvenile literature.
6. Holliday, John Henry, 1851–1887 — Juvenile literature.
7. Large type books. [1. Tombstone (Ariz.) — History.
2. Violence. 3. Frontier and pioneer life — Arizona — Tombstone.
4. Large type books.] I. Boyer, Glenn G.
    [F819.T6W88 1994]
979.1'53—dc20   94-739

TO ESTELLE and BILL, THE TWO TEDS,

AND ALL THE REST

*(And To The Wonderful Times
We Had Together)*

CONTENTS

INTRODUCTION

This volume by Glenn G. Boyer, the world's foremost authority on Earpiana, is the most informative and interesting work that has yet been written concerning the Earps and Tombstone. It is doubtful that it will ever be eclipsed.

Down through the years many books have been written about Wyatt Earp, his brothers, and their time in Tombstone. It seems that every few months yet another "true story" of Wyatt Earp besieges the reading public. Each, invariably, promises to reveal new facts but in actuality is simply a rehash of old information. In recent years, most of these have been embellished excerpts taken from Boyer's previous publications, for it is impossible to produce anything historically correct concerning the Earp family without consulting Boyer and his work. Unfortunately, few writers have given him proper credit for their use of his research and knowledge.

Now this man, who has the information and documentation to write the factual story, has produced the book that reveals all the pertinent information, the book that every western buff and Earp enthusiast has been waiting for: *Wyatt Earp's*

Tombstone Vendetta.

Glenn Boyer has spent his entire adult life (half a century) in **primary** research into personal diaries, unpublished manuscripts, family letters and photographs, as well as tirelessly conducting personal interviews — and perhaps more importantly, just having friendly conversations — with the Earp family and friends of that family. For many years Boyer has been a friend, associate, and confidante of these people. No other person has ever had access to such valuable information.

But these same people who provided this information — as well as many family heirlooms — placed strict requirements on Boyer. As they divulged their priceless knowledge, some restricted the use of it until after their deaths. Therefore, Boyer's previous publications could not reveal the entire story of the Earps and their sojourn in Tombstone. Boyer is now, however, free to reveal what he has known but could not tell.

Foremost in his mind is the promise he made to Wyatt's niece, Estelle Miller, who was as close as a mother to him, that he would tell the story as the Earp family knew it, thereby setting the record straight at last.

Glenn Boyer's *Wyatt Earp's Tombstone Vendetta*, reveals for the first time the secret lives of the Earps, and answers in detail the questions that, until now, have been answered with theory and conjecture only.

This fascinating volume tells why the Earps came to Tombstone; why they stubbornly stayed on, and who supported them and their actions; why Wyatt's wife, Josie, whitewashed his memory; why Democrat John Behan finessed appointment as sheriff of Cochise County from a Republican territorial administration, bypassing Republican Wyatt Earp; why robber and murderer Luther King was allowed to escape Behan's jail; who besides King, Crane, Head and Leonard was involved in the Contention stage holdup; who killed "Old Man" Clanton and his companions and why; the reason Ike Clanton desperately wanted Doc Holliday dead; who and what initiated the Gunfight at the O.K. Corral; who pulled the trigger on the cowboys; who ordered paid assassins to kill the Earps, and who these bushwhackers were; who was involved, **sub rosa,** in Ike Clanton's death in 1887; detailed revelations by Doc Holliday, and much more. Here are the answers to the questions that have baffled and intrigued historians for over a hundred years.

During his life Wyatt Earp was a man who was frequently thrust into unusual and dangerous situations. However, he performed extremely well on each occasion, having the ability to make difficult decisions and to enforce their acceptance. His personality was such that many liked and respected him while others hated and feared him. There was no middle ground in these likes and dislikes.

The era of Wyatt Earp is gone and will never return. By his personality and actions he towered above other men in a land filled with tall men.

Boyer has taken this man of myth, legend and illusion, and transformed him into a human being who possessed valid explanations for his deeds.

Boyer, who thoroughly understands the Earps, their friends, and their time, has, in his masterful style, written the saga of these Tombstone immortals whose lives, deaths, and headlong rush to destiny radiate the violence, adventure, and romance that was the part of life in boomtown Tombstone that was most fascinating.

With this book, Glenn Boyer has ensured that Wyatt Earp and that time and place will be remembered as it was, and those people will live forever as genuine — yet special — humans.

Ben T. Traywick
Tombstone, Arizona, 1993

EDITOR'S FOREWORD

When I first attempted to straighten the picture of the Earps with my first book manuscript in 1964, it was generally accepted that all that would ever be known about Wyatt Earp and the Earp Saga was already between the covers of books. Principal among those books were *Wyatt Earp, Frontier Marshal* by Stuart N. Lake (1931), and *The Earp Brothers of Tombstone* by Frank Waters (1960). The former had made Wyatt famous, created, through movie and T.V. **spinoffs** a folk hero of the stature of Boone and Crockett. Waters' book is quite simply a debunking smear, based on personal malice toward Wyatt's widow.

Closed minds among Western editors made it impossible to market new insights, even though supported by Wyatt Earp's surviving relatives. Editors even refused to credit the possibility that Wyatt had living relatives and suspected I was attempting a hoax (while they continued to embrace their perennial Earp books that might as well have been hoaxes).

Finally, I subsidy-published *Suppressed Murder of Wyatt Earp* in 1967. The title is allegorical, referring to the "doing in" of the real man by fictional biographies, such as Stuart Lake's, and replacement of the man with a plaster saint (or devil, in the case of Waters' book). Whenever possible, both went to extreme lengths to **suppress** evidence of what they'd done, thus the allegorical title. Lake was embroiled till the day he died in fending off doubts and suspicions about his work, particularly those raised by Waters' book. (For example, Lake's torturous writhing under interrogation by Robert M. Mullin and the Cleveland Corral of Westerners about the alleged arrest of Ben Thompson in Ellsworth, Kansas on August 15, 1873.)

Suppressed Murder is a detailed diagram of how myths are made. It revealed the genesis of the Earp myth. It also told in detail the story of Wyatt's tragic second wife, Celia Ann "Mattie" Blaylock Earp, whom he deserted at Tombstone for a young beauty, Josephine Marcus, who later became his third wife. Mattie despondently committed suicide six years after Wyatt abandoned her.

By 1967 I had also obtained, from Earp relatives, both of Josephine Marcus's attempts at memoirs and spent several years of additional research verifying and amplifying them before finding a publisher for the final product (University of Arizona Press, 1976). As will be seen, my resources at that time were not adequate to entirely rein in her efforts to whitewash Wyatt's memory, yet the book was, and is, invaluable as the only detailed record yet to surface, of a woman privy to the causes of violence in that time and place, and her views of it all.

Gradually these books and a score of articles altered the public perception of the Earps and their lives. The perennial "truth-at-last" Earp novels, (written by "meticulous researchers," according to their dust jackets) started to "meticulously" reflect my research. Today, it is so well accepted that few know that my once-reluctantly-accepted books and articles are the basis of the now-well-entrenched new picture of the Earps. The revised view, ironically, is as firmly in place today as the one I found almost unalterable in 1964. Fortunately, it's a lot closer to the truth.

As I continued to do research on the Earps, I made other major discoveries, among them the autobiography of Wyatt Earp, prepared by his friend, John H. Flood, Jr., who had completed the manuscript by 1926, three years before Wyatt's death. This work was the basis of Stuart Lake's highly dramatized *Frontier Marshal*. All copies of it dropped from sight and Lake claimed later he'd never read it, a self-serving assertion contradicted by his own correspondence with the Earps. Evidence that such a work once existed was found in correspondence between Wyatt, Flood, William S. Hart (star of silent Western movies), various editors of publishing houses, and a few years later, Lake. Hart, at one time, planned to make a movie based on it, in which he would play Wyatt. The lost document was dubbed the Flood Ms. by collectors eagerly seeking to find it. In 1977 I found two bound copies of it in the possession of the heirs of Wyatt's widow and purchased them. I had the most legible typescript published in facsimile in a limited edition of ninety-nine copies, cased and leather bound. Such is the interest in Wyatt Earp that they sold out at $300.00 each within a year. (Despite Flood's turgid style, the document is important because it reveals how far Lake exceeded the modest statements that Wyatt himself **apparently** had made **for publication**.)

Regarding my further discoveries, the Appendix to this book contains a summary of that information listed under the names of numerous people who provided it, many of them Earp relatives. Persistent effort uncovered a mountain of previously unknown facts about Wyatt, his cohorts, and their sanguinary adventures. As referenced in that Appendix, many of my informants placed restraints on what I could say, and in some cases forbade quoting them by name. I have respected all such wishes. What can be told is fascinating enough and resolves the mystery about the Earps at Tombstone which has always lingered, despite each "meticulous researcher's" airy dust jacket claim to have uncovered "the truth at last."

I am now under few restraints. Therefore, what follows is a **very frank** account at last. The core of it is the *Ten Eyck papers*, as I call them. Theodore Sr. demanded never to have his true name made public, one of the major restraints under which this book must be presented. Naturally the same must apply to his son, who gave me this material, or it would be simple to identify the father.

The public may therefore conjecture that this approach to relating history is a literary device. Even if that were so, the facts presented here — the most intriguing of them for the first time — are incontrovertible, in that they are confirmed by other sources cited. (One must consider that it's entirely probable that Ten Eyck, in later years, wasn't proud of the things he'd been involved in at Tombstone, recorded by others than himself, under his true name.)

In any case, if I am to keep faith with my informants this is the only manner in which "the true story at last" is authorized to reach the public through the resources provided me.

Some editorial style-changing was necessary for consistency of voice, therefore the Ten Eyck papers are occasionally merged with other equally incontrovertible sources, enumerated in my Appendix. Chief among those are the recollections of Bill Miller, probably the man who, along with John Flood, **really** knew Wyatt best, each in a different sense. It is my view that Wyatt was more frank with Bill, since he considered him the son he'd always wanted.

Bill was like a father to me, just as his wife Estelle, daughter of Wyatt's sister, Adelia, was as dear to me as a mother. In the past, due to their wishes, I have had to portray Wyatt as a sphinx, even with his family. As Bill said, "If it got out that we spilled the beans, there'd be a lot of family squabbling. Give it twenty years after we both croak." It's been at least that.

Nonetheless, Wyatt Earp was a sphinx as far as most outsiders were concerned. He was far from frank in the Flood Ms., in which I suspect he had little part personally, and about as much interest.

This book illustrates the delightful circumstances of Wyatt's first unburdening to Bill. He obviously had a lot bottled up in him for years and had finally found a confidante he trusted. Rather than talking to satisfy Bill's curiosity, however, Wyatt's remarks were aimed at setting the picture straight before he went to the grave. He hoped Bill would someday pass on what he said, which he did.

Ted Ten Eyck is a blended voice in a few instances, since I have, where I thought it was desirable, merged what he wrote himself with what other Earp intimates contributed on the same subject. This was necessary in order to avoid a cumbersome delivery, like Greek drama, with character after character stepping front and center to declaim. (Nor did I want the work to be cluttered with footnotes, which no less an eminence than Herbert Bolton termed as akin to the debris left by sloppy workmen around a newly completed edifice.)

The sense of nothing was changed in adopting this approach. I have listened to many old people telling of events I did not witness, relating rumors, conversations, things **they** saw, or that Wyatt Earp and those of his time and place knew of and told of — so that I sometimes feel I have been present, even that I know, as they did, that the writings

18

they often scoffed at, especially old newspapers which are so carelessly accepted at face value, are not reliable because of the unrecorded motives behind them. Such self-serving contemporary accounts in competing media emphasize that words are often used to conceal meanings, rather than convey them.

I am a living link with the past because of these people (see Appendix). In this case it is a past in which thousands happen to be interested, therefore, I am quite conscious of a responsibility to tell as much as I can of what I know for the benefit of that audience. Moreover, I am fulfilling the desire of Estelle Miller, to have the picture set straight on her uncles, all of whom she loved and revered. (Even profane Uncle Jim; perhaps him most of all.) In that sense, this is a work of love and dedication. However, a word of caution is in order about her concerns that reveals something essential about her mythical uncle Wyatt, who is now a truly legendary American. (His name was used in the U.N. to illustrate a point.) Estelle laughingly confessed to me one day, "If I'd known my uncle Wyatt was **going to be** such a big, important man, I'd have paid more attention to him." (Which is to say, Lake made him famous **only after** he died.) As it was, she paid enough attention to contribute a great deal to the insights that underlie this book. About some things, Wyatt was more apt to confide in her than in Bill. **She was blood kin.**

One final subject. "Where did I get so much

material missed by earlier writers?" Answering obliquely, to better illustrate the point, when I obtained the letters of Morgan Earp's mysterious wife, or mistress, Louisa, I got them **from her family**, along with intimate photos never before published. A collector commented in envy, "Why always him?"

Because I am not skeptical of any possible avenue of information until it is proven a false lead. Louisa's letters were rejected by the *Tombstone Epitaph Journal* as improbable inventions. Her nephew, whom they practically ejected from their premises, bought a copy of *I Married Wyatt Earp* before he left the centennial celebration of the Gunfight at the O.K. Corral in Tombstone. He read it, was impressed and wrote to me, starting his letter with the words, "You do not seem like the sort to leave any stone unturned in your research." I was shortly hosting his sister on a trip by her to *Wyatt Earp Country*, and remain in touch with both of them as correspondent and friend. So some of my informants came out of the blue, hearing of me through my publications.

Through my several books and over a score of articles, I have become a magnet for those interested in the Earps. I got the inside story of Wyatt's secret second wife **from her family**; of Big Nose Kate (Doc Holliday's mistress) **from her family**; as soon as I discovered they were still living I strapped on an airplane and went to see them, taped interviews, was given photos (and friendship); I got Johnny Behan's life story plus photos, etc. **from his family**. In most cases, I looked for and found them where others hadn't even looked. (Recall the incredulity of editors at the notion that Wyatt Earp had still-living relatives.)

I spent years cultivating by phone the relatives of the McLaury boys and finally was invited to visit them. I now can boast of photos of me with their grand-nephew on the porch of his home, the ranch house of the mysterious Will McLaury, the brother who hired the attempted assassination of Virgil Earp and the murder of Morgan Earp. (They discovered that I was not a rabid pro-Earp advocate, as they might well have expected me to be, and that I was not bent on character assassination of the McLaury Boys, whom they knew as simply having got into bad company, i.e. the Clantons at Tombstone. I have a standing invitation to visit these people.)

I am a grass roots historian, not a paper shuffler, not a pallid bibliophile, chained to smelly public buildings, going blind grappling with secondary sources, though my gleanings from such often-rich material, are considerable and contributed greatly to the authenticity of this book.

Much of my collection is not in files and never was, but in my head or still walking around on two legs. Moreover, these latter informants became and remain my friends. The only exception was petulant little Hildreth Hallowell, grand niece of Allie Earp, who objected to my prior friendship with the Wyatt Earp branch of the family, but helped me anyhow, bless her.

21

In view of the number and generosity of those who assisted me, no one should be surprised at the remarkable resources I have uncovered.

In this book is what the Ten Eycks (and the others enumerated) had to relate. I have employed, as my literary approach, the well-accepted and effective device of the **nonfiction novel** as Capote did for *In Cold Blood*. But it is only a device — what it relates is biographical fact. Its advantage over a dry recital of annotated facts is that it is not dull, not an arid recording of events and dates but a highly-informed carrying of the reader into time and place, into the minds, hearts and heartland of the adventurers involved. And, as I said above, it is a better avenue to an otherwise obscure world. Otherwise, mood cannot exist, feelings do not come to life; in that world, we find a better avenue to the truth than a crumbling newspaper account by a hack with an ax to grind, a by line to earn, an editor's approbation to seek.

This work could not be source-annotated to any purpose, since footnotes would only relate to already well-known public documents, which are usually mentioned in the text, the rest being based on material solely in my collection, some only in my memory — as I have said — recollections of conversations with those who knew the story through participation, or from first-person recitals by participants. These sources are covered in my Appendix. I am profoundly conscious of a responsibility to tell what I know, rather than take it to the grave with me. This knowledge is committed to copy here for the first time.

I anticipate carping over the necessity to maintain the anonymity of informants, especially Ten Eyck. As a parallel, I once offered a newsman a juicy lead, provided he didn't tell where he'd got it.

He grumbled, "What good is that?"

I said, "Let's assume you got lost in the wilderness and I offered to show you the way out, provided you told no one who told you; would you consider such information useful?"

This book is Ten Eyck's map out of the wilderness of prior, conflicting claims about "what really happened" at Tombstone. In a sense this is Wyatt telling his own story **in full for the first time**, through Ted Ten Eyck and some others, who often quoted him directly to the best of their recollection, who knew and remembered him very well indeed, and told what he did or said, how he looked, what they felt he was thinking or feeling, as best they recalled it.

Through them, I think the reader will end up knowing Wyatt very well, too.

I have spent fifty-six years in preparing for this undertaking, since a November 1937 feature article on Tombstone in the *Chicago Tribune* aroused my youthful interest in Wyatt Earp. I was almost fourteen years old.

FOREWORD

THEODORE TEN EYCK, JR.

Wyatt Earp and his wife, Josephine, were my friends. Knowing them as intimately as I did, an effort is necessary to remind me that these two real people are now the stuff of myth, and even history.

I was born in 1900. Therefore, when I knew them they were growing old while I was still a kid. I was twenty-nine when Wyatt died; forty-four when Josephine passed on. My father, of course, knew them both much better than I. You might say he shared their greatest adventure. He was in Tombstone, Arizona as a newsman when they met. Arizona was still a Territory, and it was the time of the violent events that were later to make Wyatt an American legend.

Being a writer, father rather naturally wrote about them. He realized before he died that his modest, un-talkative old friend, Wyatt Earp, whom he'd always rather taken for granted, had by some magical process become famous. Recognizing the unusual circumstances, father tried to tell what he knew of the real man behind the myth, and how he'd become a myth. Unfortunately, so

25

far as getting that published, even if he had desired, which he didn't, he would have been thwarted during his own lifetime by his concern for the feelings of Josephine Earp. To tell the whole story would have offended her after she'd grown old and proper.

So he left their story behind unpublished when he died. This is it and probably comes as close as anyone ever will to the true story of Wyatt Earp at Tombstone. And, I might add, of his lifelong romance with Josephine Sarah Marcus Earp, his third and last wife — his one great love — who had been the Helen of Troy behind the Tombstone Vendetta that immortalized him.

I have no heirs and pass this information to Earp chronicler, my friend and Earp family friend of many years, Glenn G. Boyer, to pass along to the public whom I realize have a great interest in Wyatt Earp.

Theodore Ten Eyck, Jr.
Los Angeles, California
April 1979

Chapter 1

I Go West

I had never heard of Wyatt Earp before I met him early in the year 1881. Now that he is famous, that assertion undoubtedly will be hard for many to believe. Millions have seen him portrayed in movies or have read Mr. Stuart Lake's highly readable biography, *Wyatt Earp, Frontier Marshal.* Those who have done either, argue with me when I tell them that the man simply was not widely known in his own day — at least not when I first met him. Nonetheless, that is true. The pens of the myth-makers didn't touch his name until a few years before his death in 1929. When they did, the process of myth-making took solid hold.

Hollywood had discovered the gold in Western movies by then, and Wyatt Earp's story appealed to Hollywood — especially Mr. Lake's version. The name Wyatt Earp soon outstripped all the old heroes such as Wild Bill Hickok and Buffalo Bill. I know. I watched it happen and was amazed. I knew the real man. In many ways he wasn't much like the myth at all. But in the elements that make a real man he was. **No one knew him better the I.**

I first set foot on Wyatt Earp's stamping ground in what was then Arizona Territory in January, 1881. Not a very auspicious date for it — the thirteenth. However, it wasn't Friday but Thursday. At about noon the Westbound reached Benson, and I hopped off. Benson was a little burg, newly born, trans-shipping point to the boom town of Tombstone, my destination, and also for Camp Huachuca, an Army post. The Army presence reminded us that the Apaches still periodically went on the warpath, and Army uniforms were very much a part of the busy scene at Benson. The cavalrymen were there to escort freight shipments to the post, and their uniforms added color to a spectacle already colorful. How vivid that setting is in my memory even yet! Everything about it was thrilling to a greenhorn fresh from New York.

The most obvious commodity in sight was hay. As could be expected, a lot of horse traffic was also in evidence. It was a horse economy. There was no railroad to Tombstone or to the Army camp, and all that hay was hauled by wagons. It supported the tremendous number of horses and mules, and sometimes oxen, used to move whatever needed moving to maintain a substantial population.

All the silver ore from the Tombstone mines was hauled by horsepower to the stamp mills along the San Pedro River, the only place with enough water to operate the mills.

Benson was located about half way up a long sloping hill on the west side of the San Pedro River. In those days it sprawled along both sides of the Southern Pacific tracks. The village was less than a year old in 1881, and as disorganized as could be expected. Nothing resembling a street met the eye; just two long, beat-down, rutted and dusty trails about a hundred feet wide on both sides of the tracks, with traffic going where it pleased. The small passenger depot sat like an outhouse on the north edge of the tracks, lacking the refinement, by comparison, of even a single hollyhock.

I must have looked as lost and bewildered as I was in all that strangeness, standing on the small platform, holding my valise and looking around for a clue to the location of the stagecoach office. My stomach was also telling me that it hadn't been attended to since the day before. I hoped there would be time to eat before the stage left for Tombstone. Probably because he guessed my problem, a stranger I judged to be a cowboy got up from where he'd been lounging on a bench and approached me.

"You look a little lost, pard. Can I help you?" he asked.

I'd heard of the famous western hospitality — also of the famous bunco men who infested all railroad stops on the transcontinental lines. He didn't look like a bunco man to me, but they seldom do. He grinned, undoubtedly because he'd figured what I was thinking, and I decided to risk him, though he was a hard looking article.

"I need to get a stage to Tombstone," I said. "Also a bite to eat if there's time before the stage pulls out."

"Happens I'm waitin' for the stage up to town myself," he said. "It doesn't pull out till three so there's plenty of time for chuck."

I wasn't sure what chuck might be, but I rightly guessed it meant something to eat. Later I found out the word was adopted from the Indian habit of referring to food or eating as chuck-a-way, no doubt picked up by them from hearing whites referring to eating as "chucking it away."

"Where do I go?" I asked, looking around.

"I'll show you," he said.

I noticed he didn't hesitate to leave his baggage lying on the station platform. It was my first revealing acquaintance with Western habits. People were trusting and had a right to be. There were few petty thieves in those days, and what few there were generally got their desserts quickly enough. Besides, although I had no way of knowing it, stealing from my new friend was apt to be like committing suicide, and almost everyone knew it.

So, because I think it makes the story better if I tell who my good samaritan was, I'm going to let the cat out of the bag. The man who amiably escorted me to the stage station was the arch-bad-man, Curly Bill, a central figure in the Earp saga.

Wallace Beery played a Curly Bill part not long ago in a movie, as I recall, and I remember reading in George Parsons' Tombstone journal the words,

"Curly Bill is our chief outlaw around here right now."

This, however, didn't prevent him from being human. Nonetheless, what I was doing amounted to the same thing as walking down the street with John Dillinger.

If I'd known who he was, my walk to the stage office would have been a nervous business. I wasn't accustomed to rubbing elbows with outlaws, but looking back over a long life I'm safe in saying that our Western variety beat bankers for company. Curly Bill sure did. As the saying went in those days — well, maybe we'd better stick to the way it's come down to us today — "Curly was a **good old boy**." And he didn't even mind if you said it the way they used to, provided you were his friend and grinned when you said it.

The ticket office was in the hotel, and so was the restaurant. We threaded our way through a throng of freight wagons, travellers on horseback, one burro train probably up from Mexico, assorted pedestrians including chickens and dogs, and even a few women in respectable dress, suggesting they were not dance hall girls.

I remember a great deal of eloquent profanity from freighters reasoning with their teams, and considerable dust. A brisk breeze out of the southwest had been whipping dust through the air ever since my arrival, but it wasn't cold, and the dusty, smokey air had an exhilarating edge to it, typical of the Western high desert.

The whole thing was exciting. Until a few days

31

before, all I'd known of the West was gleaned from books which turned out to be none too factual. Now I was surrounded by stark mountains and seemingly limitless desert, under a vivid blue sky, and rubbing elbows with a crowd of pistol-packing frontiersmen in high heeled riding boots. You can bet it thrilled this impressionable young fellow to the core. It may be trite to say so, but that was the first time I really felt fully alive.

The old Virginia Hotel (still standing in 1940) housed, as I said, both my immediate needs; the Kinnear stage line's ticket office and a small eatery.

Knowing almost nothing about Western etiquette, I wasn't sure whether I should thank my new acquaintance by inviting him to eat with me or not. Later I discovered that simple good manners would get you by in the West as well as anywhere else. I'd have sense enough to say, "Say, pard, how about tying on the feed bag with me?" But then, feeling a little awkward and I'm sure sounding like a dolt, I said, "I don't know your name, sir, but I'd be pleased to buy you a snack for your kindness."

He looked startled. I can't say I blame him.

"Name's Bill," he said, "and I'd be mighty obleeged, pard. I don't believe I got yore handle."

Somehow I had sense enough to know he meant my name.

"I'm Ted Ten Eyck," I told him.

He was all steel. He never batted an eye over that "handle." He grabbed my hand and pumped it. "Glad-a-know-ya, Ted," was all he said.

Silently he steered us to our destination, probably ruminating over such a queer name.*

I noticed that Benson had a great number of wooden buildings, probably because it was on the railroad where it was easy to get dressed lumber, but there were also a number of adobes and nondescript hodge podges. Almost every place had a corral or horse shed, with fences made of the native Ocotillo. The long, willowy, spined branches made enclosures few creatures would care to break out of.

The whole town, and everyone in it, was hustling. That, as I recall, formed my first impression of the place and is still my principal recollection — how busy it all appeared.

The only exceptions were Mexicans and Indians. The former had sense enough to take life easy, and the latter were not in the economic mainstream and had nothing to do, which was probably just the way they liked it. Mostly they squatted around looking picturesque and panhandling. Some Mexicans were hauling long bundles of Mesquite wood packed on burros. They kept the Benson home fires burning. The whole town had an enticing smell of wood smoke from heating and cooking fires. In this the whole West was much the same. There wasn't much coal in use.

I suspect that some may think I sound like a Baedeker, but it was all new to me, and the memory is fresh after almost sixty years. There was

* Not Ten Eyck, but equally unusual — **GB**

simply no place like the frontier West, and I wish that I was back again setting foot in Benson for the first time.

I've refrained from mentioning my business because it makes a better story told the way Curly Bill fished that out of me like the typical, shrewd Westerner that he was.

Because of my calling, the world renown of my employer, and nature of my mission, I had some youthful notions about keeping my identity and business a secret until the proper dramatic moment. It didn't quite work out like that.

I'm afraid I've never learned proper discretion, even at my age. Just the other day I was over to take Mrs. Earp out to dinner and managed to put my foot in my mouth.

Since so many of Wyatt's old enemies, over the years, almost psychopathically (certainly speciously) have maintained that Wyatt never did kill Curly Bill, that killing had been on my mind. I am satisfied that it happened substantially the way the story came down to us in Lake's book.

"Josie," I asked, "did Wyatt ever tell you how he killed Curly Bill?"

It got awfully quiet on her side of the cab. I glanced her way and was startled to find myself getting the famous Josephine Sarah Marcus Earp look. She has never lost the facial appearance of a great beauty. From my earliest recollection, her way of looking at men — inferior beings that God undoubtedly made simply for her to manipulate — was a faintly imperious stare down her nose, a delicately modelled instrument but nonetheless a devastating weapon when employed as part of Josie's "putting-someone-in-his-place" arsenal. I battened down for the coming storm, relighting my cigar which was still lit.

"Theodore," she said, and I knew I was in for it. She normally calls me "Ted." The voice was her iciest. "You know as well as I do that my dear, dead husband was not a killer. And," she added, "he never talked of such things."

The word dear came out like "deah," a charming little affectation she assumed when remembering Wyatt in one of her sacred moods. Sometimes, as I well knew, she also remembered him when among friends who'd known them both, as "that exasperating man I married."

"Now, Josie . . ." I started but was promptly cut off.

"Don't 'now Josie' me, Theodore," she snapped. My name also came out as Theodoah, since she hadn't shifted gears out of her "deah" mood. There was no choice but to let her go on. She plowed along with a thought that had obviously come to her mind in response to my innocent question. She said, "Just last month I was catching the Lark to San Francisco. A conductor saw the 'Mrs. Wyatt Earp' on my grip and asked if I were related to **Two Gun Wyatt.** I gave him a piece of my mind."

"I'll bet," I thought. Pity him. I wondered why she didn't leave her name off her bags if she wanted to avoid such situations. But it didn't take a great mind to figure out why. She enjoys basking in reflected glory.

After awhile she calmed down and said quietly, "If he did kill Curly Bill, it was because he had to do it. It was kill or be killed. That gang had just killed his brother, Morg, which you know as well as I do."

That conversation is what began the recollections that led to my putting the story I know so well down on paper. Before the last of us are gone, the intrigue, violence, and great passions of that fascinating place and time should be recorded. Whatever the entitlements of Wyatt Earp may be to lasting fame, there was a Homeric quality to the events of his years in Tombstone.

I, of course, suspected none of this when Curly Bill and I walked over to board the stage together, that afternoon in January, 1881. However, even green as I was, I noticed a certain tensing in both men when the coach's shotgun guard, a tall, cold-eyed blond fellow, almost bumped into Curly. They reminded me of a couple of dogs that scrapped whenever they met. They both stopped and eyed each other, but finally Curly grinned and said, "Howdy, Morg?" It broke the tension.

"Howdy, Curly?" the other responded and went on to mount the seat next to the driver.

Not quite satisfied with a truce, my companion yelled up at the driver, "Hey, Bud, better keep yore hand on yore wallet." He was careful to grin, though, and Morg, at whom the sly dig had been directed, grinned also.

With the prospect of war called off, we crawled inside. Bud popped his whip a few sharp cracks, and the horses lurched into the lope that was the accustomed stagecoach pace wherever the road permitted. In those days there was a lot of competition among the companies. Speed was a necessity. The feelings and safety of passengers and horses were, however, completely overlooked. The horses were usually half-broken broncs, cheap and easily replaced. So were some of the passengers in the eyes of the community.

Soon after reaching Tombstone I learned what had occasioned the tension between the shotgun guard, who was Wyatt Earp's brother, Morgan, and Curly Bill. A couple of months before, Curly and a bunch of his gang had been terrorizing Tombstone, shooting at the moon and yelling in typical cowboy fashion. The Marshal, Fred White, came on the run to break up the party. While disarming Curly Bill, the latter's pistol had discharged in a manner that could have been accidental.

Marshal White took the shot in his groin. Wyatt Earp, then a deputy sheriff, had reached the scene shortly before and grabbed Curly from behind. White then jerked at Curly's pistol to take it from him. When White fell, Wyatt knocked Curly out cold with the barrel of his pistol. (In the West this was known as "buffaloing" a man. Wyatt, like most professional Western lawmen, was an expert at it.) A lot of those others, probably most of them, would have shot Curly, but that wasn't the Earp style. In the half hour or so after that, Wyatt, his brothers Morgan and Virgil, and their hardcase friend, Doc Holliday, rounded up the rest of Curly's gang and gave them a dose of the same medicine. The crowd was in the calaboose with sore heads the next morning.

Curly Bill, when I met him, was coming back from the county seat at Tucson where he'd been in jail awaiting a hearing for killing White. As it happened, Wyatt Earp's testimony on Curly's behalf substantiated the accidental nature of the shooting. His testimony was the key factor in getting Curly discharged.

EDITORIAL COMMENT:
This is perhaps a slip of memory since George Parsons' journal has Curly out of jail earlier.

In any event, knowing the strict concept of personal honor of gunmen as I now do, the Earps were justified in expecting a man like Curly Bill to be more inclined to remember the blow to the head (and ego) rather than the good turn.

I was unaware of all this; a fortunate circumstance, since I would have been unprepared to cope with any part of it. The name Wyatt Earp meant absolutely nothing to me. If I'd known that someone of that name was destined to kill my newfound friend, I'd have been prepared to hate him mercilessly. After all, Curly was a "good old boy" to my then untutored mind. And my opinion hasn't changed over the years. Curly may have been naively homicidal at times, but he was "a good old boy." It's a pity Wyatt had to kill him.

I'm sure that's about what Josie was thinking after I asked her my indiscreet question in the cab. As for Wyatt, few ever guessed his thoughts. Maybe eventually he regretted it, too.

Chapter 2

My First Two Gun Man

Everyone on that stage must have known who Curly Bill was except me. A little experience soon taught me that a man like him, wearing two pistols, wasn't an ordinary cowboy. At the time, I only thought it was exciting.

Even I had a little Smith and Wesson .32 in my coat pocket, but I couldn't have hit the proverbial side of a barn with it. I imagine there was some idea in my mind that it would protect me from bad men and hostile Indians. Maybe it would have — at least in the case of the bad men, if I got "the drop" on them first.

The first few minutes on the road we were all trying to settle down and find a comfortable position to fend off the bone-jarring jolts inescapable in an unsprung coach rolling on anything but a billiard table. Cochise County's roads were far from being a billiard table. Of course there wasn't a Cochise County yet, and that, too, is an important part of my story.

I was riding to meet the piratical crew that even then were scheming to make (then effectively steal) Cochise County. Twenty four hours repaired my ignorance, but it took a lot longer for me to recognize that the others were all a lot worse than Curly Bill. (Wyatt didn't tell Lake that part of the story, the mystery that everyone senses is there, unexplained and demanding an explanation because without it nothing makes sense.)

We rolled over the iron-hard caliche, the steel wheel rims making a racket like they were running on cobblestones. You could nearly always hear a stage coach coming a mile away in that country from the combination clatter of those tires, the jingling trace chains, the rapid churning of two dozen scrambling hooves, and the frequent yelling, cussing and whip cracking of the drivers. The latter were a picturesque lot, heroes in that day to little boys, somewhat like Mark Twain's riverboat pilots in *Life on the Mississippi.* Our driver, Bud Philpot, a veteran of the business, had a little over two months to go before he would be killed in a holdup.

Our action and the whipping wind kept an almost constant stream of grit blowing through one set of windows and out the other — that is, the part that didn't settle on us to stay. My ears and mouth were soon full of fine dirt. A stage coach looks quite romantic in its Hollywood setting on the screen; riding in a real one was something else. I'm surprised that more people didn't break their ribs in them. Plenty bruised them. It was a hell

41

of an inconvenient way to travel, but a necessity.

By the standard of the day, our coach was practically empty. I was sitting next to Curly Bill on the rear seat. He had an old blue Army overcoat thrown around his shoulders. (For the record, I didn't notice that he smelled particularly bad, either.) There were two miners facing us on the front seat about whom I couldn't say as much, and ditto for a cowboy on the middle seat with his back to us.

I can't imagine why the stage wasn't packed since most of the time as many as fifteen people were crowded on board, passengers even riding on top. It wasn't safe, but the companies didn't care, and the passengers wanted to get to their destination and get rich if they were newcomers.

Only Curly wore two pistols in sight, though the rest probably had at least one. Since it wasn't cold in spite of the wind, I thought it strange that they all carried or wore some kind of heavy coat. When the westering sun dipped behind the Whetstone Range later, I found out why. In only my suit coat, I damn near froze to death. The high desert is usually a frosty place after sunset, sometimes up until late May.

No one spoke for the first mile or so. Then Curly felt around in a side pocket of his overcoat and produced a bottle of whiskey. He uncorked it and took a healthy pull. "Ahhh," he sighed, wiping his mouth and mustache with the back of his hand. Then he offered me the bottle. "Here, kid. It cuts the grit outen yore throat."

At the time I'd not had much acquaintance with whiskey, only enough to know I'd rather not take any. But some sage soul had warned me before I headed out that it was a mortal offense among Westerners not to accept a drink when invited.

I couldn't see a polite way out, so I grabbed the bottle and took a short pull at it. I knew enough to expect a bite, but nothing about the cheap variety of whiskey known as "Old popskull." It came in a lot a brands but only a single variety — poisonous.

Curly kept a straight face when I coughed as soon as it went down. He probably suspected I had a hard time to keep it from coming back up.

"Great stuff," he allowed, as he offered the bottle around. Everyone else had a big pull without batting an eye.

"The best money can buy," he observed when he got the bottle back. Then he grinned and added, "Wal, the best four bits can buy anyhow."

After a short while he turned to me and said, "I guess you English fellers ain't used to good American whiskey."

"I'm not English," I told him. Boy, was I innocent. And what a lawyer he'd have made.

He did a professional job of looking surprised. "I'd o' swore you was English from the way you talk. You ain't pullin' my leg are you?"

"No," I was quick to assure him, remembering those two pistols. "I'm from New York City."

"You had me fooled," he said. "We got a lot of New Yorkers around. Doin' right well, too.

You'll like settlin' here most likely."

"Oh, I'm not planning to settle."

He looked right at me with it written plain on his face that an explanation was in order as to what the hell an Englishman masquerading as a New Yorker was doing out there. All he said, however, was, "The only New Yorkers I've seed out here that went back was beer salesmen."

"I'm a writer," I told him. So far he hadn't missed a thing he wanted to find out, softening up the witness with an injection of alcohol.

He gave me another sharp look. "A writer? I ain't never met a writer. Waddya write about?"

I'd invited the question and could hardly dodge it. "I write for the newspapers," I said.

He took another pull at the bottle. I hoped he was planning to hoard the rest, but was out of luck. My second shot went down a little better than the first. The bottle went the rounds again and came back with about one slug left. Curly squinted at it, tossed it off, and threw the bottle out the window. Inwardly I heaved a sigh of relief.

"Newspapers," he said after a minute. "I never read 'em. All bullshit!"

"Not *The Herald*," I protested.

"Never heered of it," he said.

Of course he was leading me on, and I was too green to know it.

"Oh surely," I countered, "you've heard of James Gordon Bennett's famous *Herald*."

"Nope. *Lesley's* and the *Police Gazette*, but not any *Herald*."

44

"Didn't you ever hear about how Bennett sent Stanley to find Dr. Livingstone?" I asked.

"I didn't know the sonofabitch was lost. If he's that sawbones over to Silver City, they shoulda left him lost." He held a crooked finger up in front of my face. "See that damn crooked finger? That old bastard Livingstone set it like that." He paused again like a true story teller to see if he had everyone's attention. He sure as hell did. They were all getting ready to bust as soon as I wised up.

Curly went on. "Why I asked old Curly Bill hisself for a job road agentin', an' he seed that crooked finger and turned me down cold. Can you imagine that?"

I couldn't. In fact, I couldn't believe my ears.

"Dr. Livingstone was a famous missionary who was lost in Africa," I explained like the nincompoop I was. "My boss, Mr. James Gordon Bennett, sent the well-known explorer, Stanley, to find him."

Curly speared me with a black-eyed stare and shook his head. I was hoping he wasn't reaching in his other pocket for another bottle, but was out of luck again.

"Well, I'll be damned," he said. "I learn somethin' new almost every day. They shoulda sent old Doc Livingstone out here if he was a missionary. We got Injuns that ain't ever got the good Word."

He offered me the bottle. I needed it, especially after he calmly observed, "Course them red varmints most likely woulda cooked the sonofabitch's

45

brains upside down on a wagon wheel over a fire 'fore he got the Word across." He shook his head as though deeply perplexed by missionary societies. "Who'd Bennett sent you out here lookin' for? The long lost Charlie Ross?"

I was surprised he'd heard of the famous, un-solved Pennsylvania kidnapping. Also, I was stuck with answering his question about why I'd been sent to Tombstone.

"Mr. Bennett personally assigned me to do a story on Tombstone's new mayor, John Clum. He used to be my neighbor up in New York."

That seemed to amuse Curly. "Wal, do tell? Any friend of ole John's a friend of mine. He's one of the best liars in the Territory. Why he prac-tically made me and the boys famous single-handed."

There was a general laugh over this that I didn't get since I didn't know who Curly was, or that Clum's paper, *The Epitaph*, had labelled Curly and his followers, "The Cowboy Curse." The term "cowboy," was locally synonymous with rustler or road agent, thanks to Clum's paper. Curly was the co-leader, along with Old Man Clanton, of the so-called "Cowboy Gang."

"Clum's an awful good liar. Come to think of it, that's how he made me famous, so I got no kick." Curly laughed at his own words and took another pull of the fresh bottle. He wiped his mouth and passed it to me as a matter of course.

I was beginning to feel the liquor and getting a don't-give-a-damn attitude. Bravely, I decided to do a little probing of my own.

"I never did get your full name," I said.

"Brocius," he said. "Curly Bill Brocius they calls me." He laughed again, long and loud. All the others joined him.

"I thought you said Curly Bill turned you down for a job," I said like a knucklehead after the laugh was over.

Curly chuckled. "He wouldn't dare."

Then he threw back his head and roared, the rest with him, and I had sense enough to join in. I'd finally got the idea that I was expected to recognize and appreciate the honor of having my leg pulled by a notorious character who, moreover, was likely an outlaw. But the whiskey had done its work, and I simply didn't give a damn. Besides, I could see that he had decided I was a new, special friend.

"Don't mind me, kid," he said finally. "I'm a helluva joker."

He was that all right and a lot more. I have it on good authority from an old friend of Curly's that his rough exterior was an act to keep from offending his outlaw pals. Putting on airs wasn't exactly a shooting offense, but he'd never have gained the loyalty of his rough following if he'd done it. I even heard that he'd studied for the ministry, but don't believe that. At any rate, there was a good, sharp mind carefully concealed for whatever reason, under that rough exterior, an enigmatic circumstance in view of the life he led.

About sundown we slowed sharply and pulled

through a wide, sandy wash with steep banks near what was known as Drew's Station, about a mile short of the small town of Contention. The site sticks in my mind because at that site a couple of months later, our driver, Bud Philpot, was killed in a famous stage holdup.

That event was the real start of the Earp-Cowboy feud that is the main theme of my story. There was friction before then, but that holdup was the genuine start of **killing** bad blood. It left many corpses around that part of the country during the next year, most of them unpublicized.

That wash was a lonesome spot, especially just before dark, sunken in deep shadows and surrounded by clusters of black-branched mesquite. A lone coyote slunk from the brush, looked at us briefly, then trotted away down the wash. Curly pointed it out to me and said, "Coyote," rightly suspecting I'd never seen one. It added the final wild touch to the scene.

We pulled into Contention through a steep, narrow notch in the Chop Hills just as the first stars were coming out in a luminous sky. Most of Contention was then on a gentle slope on the east side of the San Pedro River. Ore reduction mills were its chief business. A year later, when the railroad arrived across the river, the town spread to the other side.

We picked up a passenger and changed teams. When I reboarded the stage, the Western sky still held the faint, brassy luminosity characteristic of the early dark in that country. The East never

48

had sunsets that matched the West's. And that evening I began to form my resolve to move to the wildly beautiful West for good.

When we reached Tombstone, it was full dark. The sky was an explosion of bright stars. Curly and I had been dozing, leaning against each other and sleeping off the whiskey. I remember looking at my watch as I left the coach at the Post Office at Fourth and Fremont. Several gas lamps were lit. It was 7:32.

The wind had almost died, but I was chilled to the bone and looking forward to a hot meal and a warm bed. I didn't know fate had decreed I would have that meal with some of the most star-crossed and fascinating characters in Arizona. That's saying a lot, considering those times.

It should have meant something to me, but it didn't, that Curly jumped down and greeted the first fellow he met with a hand shake and a "Howdy, Johnny."

Johnny was wearing a star on his vest under an open coat. All that occurred to me was that Curly had been kidding when he implied that he might be an outlaw. How wrong I was!

Johnny said, "Howdy, Curly. Glad to see you back. We were all pullin' for you." He was referring, of course, to the outcome of Curly's trial for killing Marshal White.

Morg Earp jumped down, looked at the two men briefly and noncommittally, then disappeared into the Post Office with a couple of mail sacks.

I was standing there waiting to get my grip and

planning to ask Curly where to put up for the night, but he'd forgotten me for the moment. It gave me a chance to study him. He was a lithe, powerful six-footer with a swarthy complexion and coal black hair that matched his eyes. His countenance was hawk-like with a Roman nose, actually somewhat sinister until he smiled or laughed. He wore a handlebar mustache that added to that appearance.

Right now he was grinning about something Johnny had said. Also, he'd put the touch on him, which may have explained why he had been willing to accept my offer of a free meal. Conceivably, he was broke. Then he remembered me and turned my way.

"Johnny," he said. "I wancha ta meet my young buddy, Ted something-or-other."

"Ten Eyck," I said.

"Yah," he said but didn't try to repeat it. "Anyhow, Johnny, how about lookin' after him?"

We shook hands. Johnny had a likeable smile heightened by sparkling brown eyes. Very soon I learned he was an Irishman, and a very typical specimen of the breed "Irish politician." He wore the popular Western mustache, though more neatly trimmed than was the style, and was of medium build and height. His handshake was not firm, and his hand was soft and uncalloused, unusual in that part of the world.

"Ted has come to make us famous," Curly announced, "or at least to make the new mayor famous."

50

Johnny laughed. "Hell, he's already famous. Or at least infamous."

The latter word pegged Johnny as a man of tolerable learning, since he even pronounced it right.

Curly joined in the laugh, and I did to be polite. In those days I wouldn't have thought of injuring anyone's feelings even if they needed it.

"Damned if he ain't," Curly admitted. "Anyhow, Ted works for some Eastern newspaper in Noo Yawk," as he pronounced it, "and they rescue missionaries and the like. So I reckon he's out here to rescue old John for us."

"The Herald," Johnny said.

I suspected that at least one denizen of this backwater had the rudiments of learning. Obviously he'd heard of Stanley and Livingstone.

I nodded. "That's right. I work for James Gordon Bennett's *Herald.*" Somehow in those days I never seemed able to simply say *The Herald* without attaching the name of its famous owner. He was indeed impressive, especially to a young reporter to whom he sometimes deigned to speak. I suspect he did so due to family connections. I'd gotten my job through a wealthy uncle who knew Bennett well enough to play billiards with him.

Curly retrieved his war bag from the stagecoach and paused a moment before leaving us.

"Don't take any wooden nickels, kid," he said, "unless you need some kindling." He laughed at his own joke and disappeared into the night, his high heels sending back hollow clomps on the board walk.

"We still got your saddle somewhere," Johnny yelled after him. "Dunbar'll see you get any nag you want."

Then he turned to me.

"If you want to meet Clum, he's probably in the Post Office sorting mail right now. He's also our postmaster. Pulls at as many public teats as he can grab."

The problem was that I didn't know if Clum was aware that I was coming. I had planned to keep my purpose a secret until I dawned on him with the glowing importance of an emissary of the mighty *Herald*. But the time wasn't propitious. Besides, it was obvious that Johnny was no friend of Clum's, and it seemed better to wait and see him under other circumstances.

"Right now," I said, "I'd rather catch something to eat and turn in. I'd rather see him tomorrow."

Johnny nodded. "Suits me. Why don't I take you up to the Cosmopolitan and get you a room, then you can join some of us for supper? We could take a hack, but it's just around the corner."

How naive I was, not realizing that Behan's invitation to eat was his way of working himself into a position to worm my real business with Clum out of me if it differed from what I'd told him. But this smiling Irishman simply oozed charm. His whole manner made it impossible not to warm to him on first acquaintance. Even Wyatt Earp later admitted that he could never exactly hate Johnny after their fatal split.

At first they were close associates and political

allies despite party differences. As I discovered that evening, the falling out hadn't yet occurred, and Wyatt still figured prominently in Johnny's political ambitions.

"I didn't catch your last name," I told him as we started down the walk.

"Behan," he said, pronouncing it Bee-un.

At the next corner we turned left, and I got my first glimpse of Tombstone's famous Allen Street, the block where almost everything that's now history except the famous Clanton-Earp street fight, took place; the block between Fourth and Fifth — Whiskey Row as it was called.

We rounded Hafford's corner named for Colonel Roderick Ferdinand Hafford who owned the saloon on the northeast corner. In less than a year, the Earp brothers and Doc Holliday embarked from there to go down and kill three of their mortal enemies and put several others to flight in the West's most famous gunfight. My companion tonight would claim to be a witness to that fight and was certainly at least contingently responsible for its occurrence.

I still get a vivid picture of that turn to the left into Allen Street proceeding eastward. Although I couldn't identify them at the time, here were located the places now famous in the well-publicized vendetta — the Occidental Saloon; the Grand Hotel where the Cowboy Gang hung out; the Alhambra Saloon, later to be Earp headquarters; the Cosmopolitan Hotel almost across from the Grand; Hatch's saloon where Morgan

Earp would be assassinated; Vogan's Bowling Alley, a name that would gain fame the very next day; the Eagle Brewery saloon across from the Oriental, which was at that time the Earp's principal hangout. Allen Street was comparatively well-lit by gas burners in front of almost every establishment, although they gave only a non-penetrating illumination.

I noticed that my companion spoke to almost everyone by name, and everyone seemed to know smiling Johnny. It struck me as just dandy to be acquainted with one so prominent. As a newsman I'd learned the importance of having an 'in' no matter how slight.

As Bennett said, "It don't matter what the hell they know you for, just so your name pops in their mind when they see you." In my long life I've found that true. Even known felons get the glad hand from the police when they're not wanted at the moment. Looking back, I think that explains Johnny's lifelong success as a political appointee. He made sure everybody knew him.

As he ushered me into the lobby of the Cosmopolitan, I was on the brink of receiving a degree in practical politics from some masters of the trade who didn't realize that their pursuit of wealth and power was about to blow up the whole district. But then, if they had known, they wouldn't have cared.

Chapter 3

The County Ring

Johnny Behan piloted me inside and introduced me to several people loafing around the lobby. After I'd registered he suggested, "Why don't you get your possibles up to the room then come back and join me. As we say in Missouri, 'I'll pizen ya with suthin.'"

Seeing my puzzlement he explained, "That's the Pike County way of saying I'll buy you a drink. And believe me, what they drink in Pike County'll come close to pizenin' ya."

"I could use something good," I admitted, thinking of Curly's concoction. "And something to eat."

"This place can handle it," Johnny assured me.

Before I was halfway up the stairs, I noted that he was already in friendly conversation with some of the bystanders who had snooped over my shoulder when I registered.

For its day and place, the Cosmopolitan was some hotel. Heavily carpeted throughout, original oils and water colors hung on the walls and good

55

statuary stood here and there. The woodwork and panelling were hand carved. The place was lit almost like an opera house, with gas fixtures in the rooms, halls, stairwells and even out back. Such substantial edifices, and the town even then had several, was one reason Tombstone was compared to towns like Virginia City rather than being considered just another wild camp like Deadwood or Bodie where the 'badman' hailed from.

Nonetheless, plenty of bad men hailed from Tombstone, not all bearing the ear marks. They weren't six foot four, two hundred and twenty pounders with dirks and revolvers in their belts. They were distinguished citizens, and it was to a company of this type that I made an unexpected addition that first night.

When I got back to the lobby, Johnny had been joined by a small group, one I'd never have gotten close to if he hadn't found out I represented *The Herald*. This wary group suspected that the Eastern papers had somehow gotten wind of their plans, and at that key moment, they didn't want the wrong kind of publicity.

Johnny bounced over to meet me, literally leading me by the hand toward his cronies. "This is John Dunbar," he introduced the first man. "My partner in the Dexter Livery Stable."

I shook hands with a broad bear of a man with a moon face in which were set alert blue eyes. Like almost everyone, he wore a large handlebar — black in his case. I judged him to be about thirty.

"Howdy," he said, gripping my hand in a large paw and giving a friendly shake — totally unlike Johnny's limp-rag grasp. "Glad to meet you, Ted." I was surprised to detect a Down-East accent. Later I learned he was from Maine, a fact of considerable portent.

Johnny introduced the other three, and we shook hands all around. Harry Woods was the editor of Clum's competition, *The Nugget*. He was a smooth, foxy-appearing blond with a Southern drawl. He reminded me of a wiry terrier ready to yap at everything. My first impression wasn't far wrong. He wielded a pen that was in every way mightier than the sword. It eventually drove the Earps from Southeastern Arizona where even assassins' bullets had failed to daunt them.

Woods eyed me speculatively, but said only, "Glad to have you in Tombstone, Ted. We'll arrange for you to see the elephant and hear the owl," a remark that elicited a general laugh.

Art Fay, the third man, was at least nominally Woods' boss at the time. By way of introduction Johnny said, "This is Art Fay who owns *The Nugget*."

Later, Clum told me that Fay was a front for the real owner, Hugo Richards, a power in Arizona politics, who planned to use the paper to back his aspirations to become governor. I can only describe Fay as a nondescript redhead. Although I spent a good deal of time with him in the months that followed, he had what you might call a forgettable face.

The fourth man, a scowling, heavy-jowled individual bordering on fat, looked the part of the classic bartender, with spit curl, handlebar and fancy vest. I wasn't surprised to hear him introduced as "Milt Joyce, owner of the Oriental saloon."

"Well," Johnny said, "Let's go tie on the feed bag."

He led the way to the Maison Doree restaurant located at the rear of the Cosmopolitan. I was surprised to find a tastefully decorated dining room with immaculate linen, sparkling crystal and very respectable silver service.

When we were seated, Johnny, the obvious mainspring of the group, said, "First of all, I promised to 'pizen' Ted here with 'suthin' Pike County style. How about you geezers?"

Teetotaling wasn't one of the West's vices. We were all oiled up before we got around to the menu. I was too green to suspect that part of the conviviality was designed to loosen my tongue just in case I hadn't stated my whole mission.

They softened me up with a few stories to prove what a bunch of shakers and movers I was with. Somehow the conversation got around to the current Territorial Governor, General John C. Fremont.

Johnny said, "The first time I ever saw him he was just back from one of his exploring tours. I was just a kid. He met his wife, old Senator Benton's daughter, Jessie, at my gramp's hotel, the Harris House in Kansas City."

His eyes sparkled in anticipation of his own story. "Well, here came the famous explorer who hadn't seen his little, loving wife for a year and a half, clumping into our front parlor in a big set of jack boots expecting a kiss and a hug. It had been raining all week, and Jessie spotted his muddy boots first off. 'Get those damn boots off Mrs. Harris's nice rug, John,' was the first thing she said to him. Well, he trotted outside like a little boy and came back in his socks and got his kiss. Then she introduced him to me. I was sort of a favorite with her, being just the right age for her to mother me."

There was a general chuckle. Then Johnny went on. "She ain't changed much, either. She's still got a ring in his nose. He doesn't dare fart for fear she'll hear about it and scold him. You'd have to kick Jessie in the head to knock his brains out. I wonder how the hell he made it on all those explorations without her. Maybe old Kit Carson wiped his nose for him. She still tries to mother me whenever she gets a chance."

"Some motherin' job, I'd say," Woods commented.

"Amen," Dunbar added.

Johnny ignored their remarks and turned to Art Fay. "What's happening with Galey's metropolis these days?"

Galeyville, east of the Chiricahua range, was already outlaw headquarters for such leading lights as Curly Bill, John Ringo and their fifty or so minions in free-bootery.

A Pennsylvanian, John Galey,* was developing the Texas Mine that was the town's bread and butter. He'd purchased the claim from Fay. Curly Bill's crowd liked the climate high in the hills, and the isolation. Galeyville was more than a hundred miles from the Pima County Seat and the sheriff at Tucson.

"Old Galey told me the last time I saw him he was expecting to get some of the Mellon money into the place. He's back East now working on it." Then Art added, jokingly, "He'd better get at least a hundred of it before he gets back. That's what he owes Ringo. Old John said he aims to plug him if he hems and haws. John'll do it, too. Said, 'A damn capitalist shouldn't have to borrow money from the likes of me.' I'd hate to owe Ringo money."

Ringo, it developed, was another "good old boy." The problem with the West's good old boys was that so many of them had itchy trigger fingers. Ringo was no exception. Even his own gang avoided him when he was drunk and unpredictable.

"I've got an attempted murder warrant on old John right now," Johnny said. "But it's a helluva ride over to Galeyville. It'll keep."

That got another general laugh.

"Why don't you get Shibell to deputize Earp again and go after him?" Woods suggested. "He'd as soon knock Ringo on his ass as look at him.

* He later brought in the Spindletop oil field, a cornerstone of the Mellon fortune — **GB**

None of those fellows want to tangle with the Earps."

Johnny shook his head. "Wait till we get our own County. I'm planning to make Wyatt my under-sheriff. There's no hurry. Anyhow, that crowd over there doesn't bother us. They might even be useful."

"We ain't got the County yet," Joyce said, speaking for the first time. "How's that stand, Harry?"

"Well, it looks pretty good. I'm going back up to Tucson Monday. Tom and I got it pretty well ironed out with the Tucson crowd. The only snag was apportioning the county debt, and I think we'll get off light with about ten thousand, and," Woods winked, "a little sugar under the table, of course."

There was another general chuckle. Behan turned to me. "I guess this is all Greek to you," he said. "We're talking about the new county we plan to have with Tombstone as County seat. It's all greased. Harry, here, and Dunbar's brother, Tom, are in the legislature. Everything's already rigged. Tom is going to introduce the bill next week. It'll go through slick as a whistle. We know that Fremont'll sign it, too." He winked. "My old Ma, Jessie, took care of that for me. Besides, I've done the old fart a few favors and know where a couple of skeletons are lying around in closets."

I nodded. "I see." Indeed I was beginning to. In New York I'd never got to sit in a council of practical politicians such as this, but I knew what took place in them.

61

We were eating by this time, and Johnny paused over his steak. "We've even got the jobs figured out," he said. "I'd just as soon you didn't mention that to Clum. A newspaperman doesn't want to shut off his sources by being too gabby." His statement was half request and half threat.

"I know when to keep my lip buttoned," I assured him.

"Good." He gave me a speculative look. The others were watching him. He seemed to be debating whether to say more.

"Go ahead," Woods urged. "It's all rigged so damn tight no one's going to upset our apple cart now. The Republican sons of bitches running this town aren't even going to get a smell of it. Only the bill to pay afterwards." He snorted over the thought.

"Well," Johnny said, "as you may know, Ted, in a Territory the governor appoints the first set of officers in a new county. You're looking at the new sheriff. Dunbar'll be treasurer. Milt, there will be head cheese of the county board of supervisors. Harry and Art get the printing and will transcribe the records from Pima County for a fair piece of change. By the time the first election comes up in the fall of '82, we'll have the place sewed up. It's worth a fortune, and all honest."

I was amazed at how sure of themselves they were, and was calculating the value of this information as a newsman. "How about my doing a feature story on all this?" I asked.

That was, of course, what they all had in mind

— the first solid brick in the public relations edifice that would plant their political dynasty firmly in the saddle and make their fortunes. They knew that the real fortunes, just as in the days of '49 or in Virginia City, weren't made grubbing underground. They were planning to repeat the feats of Stanford, Huntington, Crocker and Hopkins only in Arizona. And they might have done it if it hadn't been for Wyatt Earp whose name was about to enter the discussion.

Joyce said, "How the hell did you get around Wyatt Earp on the sheriff angle? He wanted the job, and he's a Republican. So's Fremont."

Johnny looked smug. I wish I'd noticed Dunbar's expression, but I didn't. The reason I say that is something I learned years later about how Democrat Behan was appointed sheriff by a Republican.

Johnny said all they were letting out for public knowledge. "I made a deal with Wyatt. That's why I said he'd be under-sheriff. I agreed to split the fees with him if he'd handle the criminal end of the business. I have no intention of getting my ass shot off, and Earp doesn't care for politicking. He **does** like money. And he isn't scared of the devil himself."

"Suppose Earp gets **his** ass shot off, and you end up holding the sack?" Woods speculated.

"Fat chance," Johnny answered. "The hardest crowd in the West had their try at him in Wichita and Dodge City and got their bellies full. And he'll bring in his brothers as deputies. Nobody wants to tangle with them."

"Curly's crowd made old Morg do a dance to the tune of some six-shooter music last year, I heard," Joyce observed, obviously relishing the thought.

"Morg didn't have a gun on him," Johnny said. "Besides, he knew they were joshing him. There weren't hard feelings until the Earps took in Curly and his crowd when Curly shot White."

This was the first I'd heard of that incident.

"You think that was really an accident?" Woods asked.

"The court did. Curly just got off the stage not more'n an hour ago. I loaned him a ten. He was flat broke." Johnny turned to Dunbar. "Did he pick up his saddle and get a horse from you?"

Dunbar nodded. "Sure did. Saddled up and lit a shuck like he had business somewhere."

I was stunned. Even as green as I was it was obvious to me that these people were not kidding me and that the amiable Curly Bill had killed someone.

Reading my mind Johnny said, "Your pal Curly is famous around here. White was the town Marshal till Curly did him up."

My mouth was wide open over that revelation.

"Ted came in on the same stage as Curly and made a hit," Johnny revealed. "Curly asked me to look out for him."

"Is he really an outlaw?" I asked.

Johnny's reply covered the case. "He'll sure as hell do till one comes along. I've never had a warrant on him, but folks around here don't consider it too healthy to complain about Curly and his pals. It ain't habit forming."

I got the point.

"He seemed like a real pleasant fellow."

"He is if he doesn't have anything against you," Johnny said. "I consider him a friend. But don't cross him."

"Which brings up an interesting point," Woods said. "Do you think Curly'll try to even the score with the Earps?"

"Not from the front, they all know better," Johnny said. "Hell, Curly still had his gun in his hand when Wyatt dropped him. Curly told me Earp didn't even have a gun in sight, snaked one out from somewhere and pasted Curly over the head so fast he never knew what hit him." He laughed, then continued. "The way Curly put it was 'The sonofabitch is pure lightning,' and coming from Curly that's saying something. Wyatt didn't survive five years in Kansas without learning how to take care of himself. If he was a killer like Wild Bill he'd need a pool cue to get all the notches on it. Most anyone woulda shot Curly instead of taking the chance of knocking him down."

"All the same," Joyce said, "I for one don't like the poker-faced bastard, and the Earps have a lot of enemies around."

"Who said I was in love with him?" Johnny retorted, stung into saying more than he'd intended. In a lower voice he added, "Wyatt's going to be plenty damn useful."

Little did he suspect how wrong he was.

On that note the party broke up.

"Stick around, Ted," Johnny invited. "Tombstone hasn't come to life yet. I'll stake you to a damn good cigar and trim you at pool. Do you play?"

It sounded good to me. Pool and cigars have been two of my lifetime vices.

By inviting me to dinner and then to play pool, Johnny had set the stage to pump me dry of information. I'd received the "sincere confession" treatment used by politicians the world over. That is, I'd been told what was already common knowledge to everyone but me and was expected to feel so flattered that, in turn, I would reveal my own secrets. Happily, I hadn't any to tell.

At the pool table Johnny started out with a final dose of confession. He said, "I don't know what brought you West but to be frank I left Missouri during the war because I was just the right age to join one army or the other or explain why not. If you know anything about politics back in Missouri, you can see the problem." He paused for a minute, selecting a cue. "Besides," he went on, "Ma's folks were strong Southerners and my Pa leaned the other way. He'd been in the army after he came over from Ireland in the '30's. As for me, I didn't favor getting a minie ball up my ass for either side, so I did what plenty of others did. Went West. If I hadn't I might be in the same boat as the Younger boys and the Jameses. I headed out to live with some relations in San Francisco.

66

Then I heard the Arizona country was opening up around Prescott so I had a look and decided to stay. I was up around northern Arizona fifteen years till I came down here last year."

I knew enough to realize it wasn't considered good protocol to pry into a man's background, but he'd been so forthright that I hazarded a question. "What'd you do for a living up there?"

He didn't seem to mind my prying. "Oh," he said, chalking his cue deliberately, "a little of everything. I was sheriff one term, under-sheriff, deputy sheriff, clerk of the court. Even went to the legislature twice, though there's no living in that. I was sort of jack of all trades. That's the short history of my life. How about you?"

With that apparent candidness on his part, I thought I could hardly keep my full mission from him without being rude. As I've said, I had a lot to learn. I didn't stop to consider that he'd told me very little. Among other things he didn't mention was the fact that he'd been divorced by his wife in Prescott. She was the former Victoria Zaff. Her principal grounds had been his keeping flagrant company with a prostitute named Sada Mansfield as Harry Woods told me later. (There was no love lost there.)

"Well," I told him, "I'm not out here to stay although I like the country better than any place I've ever been. Bennett sent me out to do that story on Clum, but I suspect I'm supposed to puff the mining prospects so his big shot friends can make a killing on their mining stock in the district."

"Who might the big shots be?" he inquired, lining up a shot, appearing to have his attention focused on the game.

"The only ones I know of are Corbin and Disston. They're pretty thick with Safford." The latter was a power in Arizona politics and had been governor of the Territory, also the organizer who had found financial angels to develop Tombstone's early prospects.

"The little Gov., eh?" Johnny said. "He's got his finger in a lot of pies." He was quiet a minute, turning that over in his mind. Then he said, "It'll do us a lot of good if you give us a puff. Help keep big money behind the place."

He sounded like a modern booster. What he really meant was what it would do for Johnny. He knew if he played his cards right, Tombstone would be his making. He might end up a rich man. In addition, he could have used Tombstone as a springboard to the governor's chair, and might well have been its first senator instead of Marc Smith or Ashurst.

It's hard to see how someone as shrewd, calculating, and at the same time as charming as Johnny Behan could have missed the boat. I know how. I saw it happen. The big problem was then known as Mrs. Behan. She's known today as Mrs. Earp.

We made a few more shots without significant conversation, then he said, "Is that all there is to the Clum story? I can hardly see Bennett sending someone all the way out here to do a local boy makes good story on small potatoes like Clum."

My caution was overcome by his adroit charm. Why shouldn't I tell a good friend like smiling Johnny the other side of my assignment? After all, what would it hurt?

I confessed. "There's a little more to it besides that. Bennett got a tip there's a big land grab going on in Tombstone. Something called the Townlot Company set to take over. You probably know more about that than I do."

He feigned an innocent look. "It's news to me if they are," he said. That was an out and out lie. His associates were involved, and he was in it up to his ears. In fact, the killing of Marshal White was probably traceable to that affair.

"I think he's barking up the wrong tree," Johnny said. "There's been a squabble over titles, but the Townlot Company is all on the up and up. Clum and his bunch are the ones causing all the trouble. He wouldn't have been the little bird that told Bennett about that business, would he?"

"I don't know."

There was a faint, unmistakable suggestion in the tone of his next remark. I took it as a hint to be on guard against Clum. He said, "What do you **really** know about Clum?" He followed that up with, "Have you ever met him?" His expression mirrored a world of concern for my possible gullibility. He was a consummate actor.

"Only when I was a kid," I admitted. "We're both from the same town." I couldn't help but add, defensively, "I've read nothing but good about him." Then I asked the inevitable question based on his innuendo. "Why, what's wrong with him?"

"Oh, nothing," he said lightly and made a deliberate bank shot.

With a few pointed words he'd undermined my previous unquestioning faith in the integrity of the man I'd come to interview. Johnny and I parted with the agreement that I join him and his wife at some later date for dinner.

I felt a warm glow of friendship toward my influential new acquaintance. And a dawning distrust of John Clum. It tarnished the glow of anticipation I'd had at again meeting my noted townsman.

But I was paid to do a job, like it or not. It hadn't occurred to me before I wrote this, but I wonder if Johnny had known of my impending arrival and been on hand to meet me.

In any event, I'd spent my first evening in Tombstone with the king pins of what John Clum's *Epitaph* would shortly make known to the world as the County Ten Per Cent Ring.

They were a rare breed of schemers, likeable but ruthless. It took me quite awhile to find them all out, but in the process I got to know them as well as anyone who ever lived.

Chapter 4

My First Western Lynch Mob

The next morning the mirror by which I shaved reflected a sober, thoughtful face with perhaps the advent of a dawning new maturity.

In a head where hardly a serious thought had ever dwelt, there were now several serious ones corralled and milling around waiting to be sorted and branded.

It wasn't a bad looking face in spite of my inexperience. I sported the customary mustache of the day, and mine was the thin, patrician nose apparent even in paintings of the patroon Ten Eycks of the 1600's. Brown eyes and curly brown hair were also a family trait. My only individuality was a set of thick, quizzical eyebrows that enabled me to assume a supercilious look when needed, not a bad trait for a newsman, but not much armament for a fellow who was overly fond of squiring the young ladies.

Still, my short time in Tombstone had made obvious changes. Meeting a badman such as Curly

71

Bill was alone enough to occupy my thoughts. He'd even seemed to like me. Why? The notion never occurred to me that badmen were human.

Perhaps that's the most profound knowledge garnered from my experiences in the West. Humans are far more alike than different. Experience may have made us different superficially, but millions of years of common evolution has decreed that in the fundamentals we are all the same.

Man, whatever else may be said of him, is a superb adapter, hence, survivor, and that was important in an environment such as Tombstone's.

As someone observed, "The cowards never left home, and the weak died on the way West." Tombstone had few weaklings, and that included the women as I was to discover.

Josephine Behan, as she was then known, was one of the strongest-willed women who ever lived. The world wouldn't be a day older before I would meet her for the first time.

Just then, however, I was concerned with my impending interview with John Clum, owner and editor of *The Epitaph* and first elected mayor of Tombstone. It was not the pleasurable anticipation it had been before hobnobbing with Behan and his urbane associates. Johnny, by no specific word or action but with precise effect, had made me wary of Clum. I also recalled Harry Woods' remark about "The Republican sons of bitches running the town."

Familiarity with Boss Tweed's New York political shenanigans was all that was needed to alert me to the possibility of skulduggery. Of course he was a Democrat, but who could say to what lengths political underhandness might be carried in a wild land such as this where amiable jokers killed the City Marshal yet remained on good terms with the law?

"After all," I asked myself, "just what the hell do I know about old hometown boy John Clum?" The answer was an emphatic, "Nothing!"

True, the papers had reported his effectiveness as an Apache Indian agent. He'd captured the renegade Geronimo with the assistance of a band of Apache police he, himself, had organized and made national headlines. But who knew what brutalizing sights and deeds that association with the murderous Apaches had conditioned him to accept?

It was in this frame of mind that I walked over to *The Epitaph* office after breakfast to look up my boyhood acquaintance.

Clum was five years my senior.★ My recollection of what he looked like was hazy. That was probably just as well, or meeting him would have been a shock. Not over thirty, Clum was as bald as a cue ball. I didn't suspect that the affable, erect figure in shirt sleeves and a compositor's green eye shade who greeted me as I entered the building was Clum, himself.

"What can I do for you, sir?" he asked.
I told him.

★ Clum was born September 1, 1851 — **GB**

73

"I'm John Clum. We've been expecting you," he said.

That was the first of several shocks that day. Clum must have read my surprise because he explained, "Bennett sent us a wire telling us you were coming."

That blew my big scene for sure, and I was more than a little put out. Recovering as best I could, my next thought was that John certainly didn't look the part of a political schemer, the spider lurking at the center of the web of intrigue, yet that's what I suspected. My notes made shortly after that interview confirm that. I wrote:

"Clum **appears** forthright and candid. Greeted me as an old friend. Imagine my surprise when he told me I'd been expected. That made me feel foolish somehow, though why is hard to tell. Perhaps I'm too sensitive."

(In those days I was long on self-analysis; like most youth I'd set myself an early time table to become perfect. I've observed in most cases that this boils down to becoming immune to embarrassment through perfecting the delusion that **we** are always right. Sadly, I must reflect that I am still behind schedule.)

After the preliminaries, Clum got down to serious business. "I'm really glad you're here," he said. "A few days poking around will show you how we stand. Maybe a little national news coverage on the rotten situation will get us some action out of Washington. What we need is an investigation of the whole business."

He didn't sound to me like a man with a deep secret, a fact which took me by surprise. I blurted, "What situation?" then regretted the question. Reporters are supposed to radiate an air of omniscience.

It was Clum's turn to be surprised. He said, "Why, the Town Lot Company situation."

What followed was a detailed explanation of the scheme Johnny had glossed over the night before. While I was listening to Clum, my mind was darting around trying to detect the deception that had to be concealed in his logical presentation. Johnny's personal magnetism had cast its spell, and I was blind to the truth for a long while.

"My predecessor as Mayor, Alder Randall, was up to his crooked eyebrows in a lot-jumping conspiracy. He's skipped town since he smelled a little new hemp coming his way if he didn't. Things had come to such a pass they were definitely planning to hang him."

"Who?" I asked.

"The Citizens Safety Committee."

"What's that?"

For the first time he hesitated as though debating whether to tell me or to dissimulate.

"The Vigilantes," he said finally, which was perfectly true. "Nobody knows much about them."

That wasn't true. He, himself, was the nominal head of the organization. I must say, he didn't look the part.

"At any rate," he continued, "Randall acted on a technicality in the city charter. It provides for

75

the mayor to appoint an agent as intermediary to convey to an initial owner the deeds to land formerly in the public domain. The idea is to allow the mayor to obtain the assistance of qualified real estate men or lawyers to handle the details of establishing titles. Randall deliberately misinterpreted that provision of the charter to convey title to the Town Lot Company. The slippery devil at the head of the company is Colonel James Clark. His partner is Mike Gray, one of our JP's. There are two other fellows in the background, Rouse and Anderson."

While I was scribbling notes and trying to digest all this, he continued as if giving a lecture.

"The situation at the time a legal townsite was approved was that most of the businesses here today were already located right where they are. The owners were just waiting for the legal steps to be taken to formalize their earlier occupancy. When Randall deeded the townsite in bulk to Clark and Gray, everything changed. They acted like they were dealing with unoccupied pieces of real estate and advertized sale to the highest bidder." He looked at me from beneath his green eyeshade, assessing my reaction.

"Everybody knows that this is blackmail. The owners have to pay Clark and Gray for what they already legally own. But instead of a ten or twenty dollar filing fee, Clark and Gray are after anywhere from three hundred dollars up on business lots and fifty or so on lots on the outskirts. It's plain highway robbery."

It's amazing to me now that I didn't agree immediately. But I didn't. In those days of the robber barons when men like Rockefeller and Carnegie were secretly envied by those who reviled them loudest, there was a 'get rich quick' attitude that appealed even to the victims. Few wouldn't have altered their own ethics if they'd been on the inside.

Even Clum finally paid Clark and Gray for a clear title to *The Epitaph* lot when he sold and left town a year later. Furthermore, he urged others to do the same. I might add that he skipped just a jump ahead of a $50,000 damage suit by Clark and Gray that stemmed from a prior suit he'd initiated against the Company. He told me about that next.

"Some of us got out an injunction to trim Clark and Gray's sails. I got so hot about it I got on the ticket for mayor at the last minute. Eccleston, the original candidate, didn't want it anyhow. He has his hands full with the hardware store, and he isn't too well on top of that. Anyhow, George Parsons did a bang-up job as my campaign manager. You'll have to meet George. He got me in by a landslide by Tombstone standards. I got 532 votes to Marc Shaffer's 165."

While Clum had been talking, I'd been aware of a distracting noise in the distance. John also seemed to be speculating on it even while he talked. It dawned on both of us that an angry mob had formed and was shouting. John headed for the door, and I was close behind.

77

"Come on!" he said. "It's over on Allen Street."

We went at a trot, and when we got to the corner of Fourth and Allen we saw that Whiskey Row was packed from sidewalk to sidewalk with a howling, milling mob from about the middle of the block down.

Showing the quick presence of mind that was one of his characteristics, John pulled me inside the Cosmo. "Follow me," he directed, taking the steps to the second floor two at a time and then running down the hall to the balcony.

We had a box seat there, almost to ourselves except for a couple of lady guests attracted by the hullabaloo. Pistols were visible on almost everyone, and some rifles and shotguns were in evidence. The center of excitement seemed to be on the South side of Allen Street and to the East near the corner of Fifth.

A small clear space surrounded a group of armed men who were standing off the mob in the doorway of Vogan's Bowling Alley. In view of the tinderbox potential of the situation, John ushered the ladies back inside and then returned to watch.

I later learned that much of the excitement was over by the time we reached the scene. Shortly a light wagon pulled up in front of the bowling alley. It was driven by deputy sheriff, Johnny Behan. The crowd gave way at his approach, but only because several of the other officers herded them back at gunpoint.

"Those are the Earp brothers with the guns," Clum told me. "They're hard as nails."

I could believe that, remembering Morg's cold-eyed confrontation with Curly and Johnny's remarks about Wyatt.

"Wyatt was our deputy sheriff before Behan. His brother Virgil is a U.S. Deputy Marshal. There's another pair of Earps with guns up there, too. Morgan and Jim."

I made a mental note to meet this Earp clan before I left town.

By this time the leading edge of the mob started to trickle away, those further back dodging after them when they came directly under the threatening guns. When all that remained was a crowd of grousing observers, a runty fellow, obviously a prisoner, was brought out of the bowling alley under armed guard.

Clum said, "I don't think I know the guy under arrest, but the ones with him are Doc Holliday, Fred Dodge, and Jack Johnson. Get a good look at them for local color. They've all got reputations for having got their man, and they're all friends of the Earp boys."

Soon I would hear the Earps and their friends less politely referred to as "The Earp Gang," a loose confederation of gamblers with nominal loyalty to Wyatt Earp. But let me clear the air on this right now. This gang, if it were a gang, was loyal to Wyatt Earp purely through friendship. I was to learn that he was one of those rare people who extract strong loyalty purely through force of character. Equally, and for the same reason, his character engendered deep lasting animosity in those who feared or envied him — deep enough to lead to bloodshed, as happened in Tombstone. I should also add that gambling then was both legal and respectable.

But I'm getting ahead of my story. I had yet to meet Wyatt Earp, and when I did I didn't like or trust him for what I still regard as ample reasons.

Now I watched him mount a big bay horse and lead the cavalcade of lawmen down the street, a double barreled shotgun at the ready in his hand. Behan followed driving the wagon with the prisoner, accompanied by several guards also in the wagon, among them Virgil Earp.

Regarding what I'd observed, I'll let the clipping I still have of *The Epitaph*'s news article tell the story for me. John Clum wrote on January 17, 1881:

"Dismounting in front of Vogan's Saloon John ('Johnny-Behind-the-Deuce' O'Rourke) asked for protection, acknowledging that he had killed his man. In a few minutes Allen Street was jammed with an excited crowd, rapidly augmented by scores from all directions. By this time Marshal Sippy, realizing the situation at once, in the light of the repeated murders that have been committed and the ultimate liberty of the offenders, had secured a well-armed posse of over a score of men to prevent any attempt on the part of the crowd to lynch the prisoner, but feeling that no guard would be strong enough to resist a justly enraged public long, procured a light wagon in which the prisoner was placed, guarded by himself, Virgil Earp and Deputy Sheriff Behan, assisted by a strong posse well-armed. Moving down the street, closely followed by the throng, a halt was made and rifles levelled on the advancing citizens, several of whom were armed with rifles and shotguns. At this juncture, a well-known individual with more avoirdupois than brains, called to the officers to turn loose and fired in the crowd. But Marshal Sippy's sound judgement prevented any such outbreak as would have been the certain result, and cool as an iceberg he held the crowd in check. No one who was a witness of yesterday's proceedngs can doubt that but for his presence blood would have flown freely. The posse following would not have been considered; but bowing to the majesty of the law, the crowd subsided and the wagon proceeded on its way to Benson with the prisoner, who by daylight this morning was lodged in the Tucson jail."

I must explain this completely misleading account by *The Epitaph*. The town Marshal, Ben Sippy, had recently been John Clum's running mate on the law and order ticket. In keeping with journalistic ethics of the day, John's article was a face-saver for Sippy who had arrived late to the affair. In fact, I can't remember seeing him there. John knew the Earps had saved the day as well as I did. If he'd substituted Wyatt Earp's name for Sippy's in the article, it would have been perfectly accurate.

Later in the year it became apparent even to

Clum and his supporters that Sippy simply wouldn't do, and they got rid of him, replacing him with Virgil Earp as Chief of Police. (Marshals had to be elected and couldn't be appointed under the city charter.)

I see by my notes that John turned me over to his friend George Parsons while he went back to *The Epitaph* to write his article. This was my first meeting with George, who in those days was an earnest and religiously inclined young man. He was earnest until the day he died, but as an old man I heard him get off a cuss word or two, especially when he told about how he tried to help Mrs. Earp write her life story.

Which brings to mind that I first met that strong-willed character who today is Wyatt Earp's widow the same day I met Parsons.

As it happened, after introductions, Clum turned me over to George with the remark, "George is as qualified a man as there is in camp to show you the mining end of the thing."

He was, indeed. The rest of the day we tramped over the nearby hills, accompanied by a Mr. Stanley with whom Parsons had a deal going for an investment in the Crown Point Mine.

There was a lot of incidental talk between us about the big excitement and the mob. Although Parsons was a staunch law and order advocate, he didn't sound like a friend of the Earps.

He said, "That little gutter snipe they were trying to lynch is known as Johnny-Behind-the-Deuce. He's a gambler. Killed an engineer named

Schneider over at Charleston. He ought to be shot like a dog. Those were some more of his kind that rescued him."

He didn't mention any names, but he knew who the Earps were. As Milt Joyce said, the Earps had a lot of enemies. Like me, George Parsons was, at the time, no drum beater for Wyatt Earp. But the Earps were hard to know. They weren't glad-handers like Johnny Behan. And they kept their own council.

Chapter 5

Our Own Helen Of Troy

Later that day we came dragging back in; at least I was dragging. The only thought in my mind was a hot bath and bed.

As I entered the Cosmo I ran into Johnny Behan. I confess it wasn't his reminder of our projected dinner engagement that altered my plans. It was the young lady he presented as his wife, Josephine. I'm sure I stood, mouth agape, at the sight of her devastating beauty. I swept off my hat, and figuratively did so as well to jovial Johnny for having captured this vision.

She acknowledged our introduction in a soft voice. "How do you do?" Hers was an educated manner of speech, unexpected in one so young and in such a place.

What hypnotized me were her eyes — deep and secretive and fringed with long, dark lashes. She seemed to regard me from their recesses with half-concealed amusement. Later I discovered that she treated all men to the same enigmatic, slightly haughty gaze. Her heavy hair was brown, almost black, her mouth expressive as well as sensuous. Her faultless complexion was faintly olive with a natural pink glow.

What I am laboring to convey is that Josephine Behan was a sensationally beautiful young woman — and I was a young man most susceptible to young women, beautiful or not.

Her softly spoken, "Please join us," demolished my former resolve. I was back with bells on after a hasty bath and shave.

The dinner was delightful. During the animated conversation, stimulated by some surprisingly excellent wine, we talked of how it was universally expected that Tombstone would become the seat of a new County to be named after the Apache Chief Cochise.

"Johnny expects the governor to appoint him sheriff," Josephine told me.

"I already let him in on it," Johnny said.

This brought the discussion around to the law business, which brought up the Johnny-Behind-the-Deuce mob.

"I don't like the idea of you mixed up in such dangerous affairs, dear," Josephine objected. "Your stable pays a good enough living."

Johnny laughed. "The danger was all over by the time your precious treasure got there. The remarkable Mr. Earp and his brothers had everything under control. That's one reason I intend to make sure he's my under-sheriff."

At this point he lowered his voice to a confidential tone and continued, probably for my benefit since Josephine must have heard it before. "And another is what Joyce brought up last night. The governor is a Republican, and so is Wyatt Earp. You can't be too careful. Politics, as I have reason to know, are fickle. Besides, splitting fees with Wyatt won't be half so expensive with Dunbar in as treasurer."

He laughed again, undoubtedly at his own cleverness. "Earp's a good man, but what he doesn't know won't hurt me."

Personal relations between Johnny and Wyatt were, at that time, cordial, though Johnny wouldn't hesitate to hedge on financial dealings. He had a great deal of respect for Wyatt's prior record as a lawman in those two tough spots spawned by the Texas cattle trade, Wichita and Dodge City.

On that subject he said, "Cops in those two dens of iniquity weren't blue suit, tin hat bulls walking a beat with a night stick. Their lives were on the line every minute because some drunk Texan with a grudge over the Lost Cause could try to even the score in a Damnyankee town. Or some kid could try to start his reputation as a tough by getting himself a cowtown cop. It wasn't the kind of job I'd have on a bet."

The subject switched to Johnny-Behind-the-Deuce, and Behan told us that Wyatt had held off the mob with a shotgun while the law got organized. I expressed a desire to meet Mr. Earp, and Johnny, glancing over my shoulder said, "No sooner said than done. He just walked in."

For some reason I noted that Josephine turned her head in that direction a little too quickly. Her expression had altered in a way I couldn't place. Then I realized that her dark pupils had dilated, turning her eyes almost black.

I made little of it then. Recalled later, it seemed quite significant. I remember that she assumed an expression of nonchalance which would have been convincing if she hadn't first turned so quickly toward the object of our discussion. I'm surprised that Johnny didn't notice, especially after a lifetime during which I've learned so much of the suspicious, calculating side of the man. Fortunately for Josephine, he did not yet realize what was happening.

Instead he called, "Oh, Wyatt. Someone wants to meet you."

I turned my chair to observe a young man perhaps thirty years of age approaching. He projected the same cat-like grace I'd seen earlier when he mounted the horse and led the lawmen with their prisoner through the crowd. He was a tall man, not heavy, but his body suggested great strength. I noted the florid, self-contained face, the deep set blue eyes beneath craggy blond brows. He was almost a carbon copy of his brother, Morg. They both had cold, forbidding eyes. I'm sure women considered him extremely handsome. I know Josephine did.

I rose to shake hands as Johnny introduced us. There was a springy strength in the grip of his long fingers, though his was not the bone-crushing hand shake I detest. Those steady eyes bored into mine, and as they did I felt a strange chill. In fact the hair tingled on the back of my neck.

It is positively impossible that this was due to anything I'd been told regarding Wyatt's reputation. The man, himself, possessed a strange, animal presence, a self assurance visible in his posture, in his imperturbable countenance.

"How do you do?" he said formally, in a deep voice in which I caught a touch of the South.

Then he shifted his gaze to Josephine and made a slight, courtly bow. "Good evening, ma'am," he murmured.

She inclined her head, smiling slightly and flushing. Again I noticed sparks between the two, and Johnny also seemed to sense something, acknowledging it with a puzzled frown.

"Can you join us, Wyatt?" he asked.

The unsmiling eyes shifted back to him. "Can't do it," Wyatt said. "Business."

With that curt explanation he again inclined slightly toward Josephine, nodded to me, and walked toward the rear of the restaurant where he was joined by some others. I recognized Morg and judged from the resemblance that the other man was also a brother.

"Morgan and Jim Earp," Johnny explained. "Virgil took our prisoner to Tucson. He's a deputy U.S. Marshal."

Perhaps forgetting herself, Josephine turned to me and asked, "Don't you think they're all strikingly handsome?"

Johnny frowned distinctly. Before I could answer he said, "Don't forget, pet, they're all two-gun men. They're useful associates, **not friends.**"

She didn't seem to notice his pique. I did. I was positive that something interesting impended here.

By the time I was next to see these three, the trouble had surfaced. Before then, James Gordon Bennett arranged a quick sea voyage for me — to the Sandwich Islands. Mr. Bennett, a noted advocate of Manifest Destiny, mentally had the islands safe in Uncle Sam's ditty bag when the hostile King Kalakaua came to power and upset his hopes. Bennett routed me from Tombstone to sound out the situation, why I can't imagine, since the hostile Hawaiian Excellency had already been on the throne for years.

Chapter 6

The Portentous Kinnear Stage Holdup

When I next passed through Tombstone it was March, 1881. I made the side junket there at my own expense to renew friendships.

"Why not?" I asked myself. "Since I'll pass so close on my way back to New York."

I had already fallen under the spell of the place, but if I hadn't made that detour at that time, I'd have kicked myself. As it was, I had a box seat at the opening act of what was to become Wyatt Earp's Tombstone Vendetta.

During my absence, the attraction between Josephine and Wyatt had assumed substantial proportions. At first, of course, I was unaware of the problem. Nor did I know that the arrangement between Johnny and Josephine had never been embarrassed by a marriage ceremony. This was, undoubtedly, Johnny's choice. He never remarried after his first experience, although he was constantly embroiled with women and often with several at once.

90

Note by Theodore Ten Eyck, Jr.

"Josephine played all of this down in her memoirs. It is my view that she protested too much. I think that she was a significant cause of the continuing rift between Wyatt Earp and Johnny Behan. As my father pointed out, there were other reasons why Johnny couldn't appoint Wyatt Earp under-sheriff, but the hostility needn't have existed, to the extent it did, over that alone. If that rift hadn't occurred, the early history of Tombstone would have been far less lawless and bloody.

I've inserted these observations as a damper on Josephine's deprecatory remarks in later life regarding her part in what my father referred to as "The opening act of what was to become Wyatt Earp's Tombstone Vendetta."

Continuation of My Father's Account

I reached Tombstone about noon on the 15th of March, and immediately hunted up Johnny. He was "delighted" to see me, as I was to see him, and he extended an invitation to dinner that evening with him and the beautiful Mrs. Behan. It is possible that I had some very un-Victorian hopes in that direction, myself. All I could see was her beauty.

The weather was ideal that evening. A light snow had fallen in the afternoon, then cleared up. The moon shone through scattered clouds and accented a night graced by crisp, bracing air.

Before dinner, to which I looked forward with relish, I idled on the boardwalk in front of the hotel smoking a cigar and watching the passing crowd, some afoot, some on horseback, a number in buggies. Occasional drays and wagons were still working. The subdued light contributed a charm that is lacking in today's well-lit downtown glare. Everything seemed mellow. Objects resolved into recognizable shapes as they entered the patches of light, then dissolved as if by magic into the shadows. Even a single figure formed little moving patterns of warm light and dark, like a quilt.

I always associate that scene with the pungent smell of woodsmoke, a pervasive odor in those days. So much has altered in only a little over half a century of so-called progress. I would love to relive the Tombstone of that time, if only for an hour, and that hour would be the one just after dusk on a crisp, moonlit night.

Unbeknownst to me, however, as I savored that good life at its zestful best, less than twenty miles to the northwest two innocent men were shot to death near Drew's Station in the gully where Curly had pointed out my first coyote. It was one of the West's more violent and dramatic stagecoach holdups, but before the news hit town I enjoyed an evening memorable for other reasons.

Josephine Behan was a vision of loveliness when Johnny escorted her to dinner. She wore her hair long and flowing, a daring way for a woman to be seen in public, but at that time of her life public opinion meant absolutely nothing to her. She was almost, but not quite, wanton.

"Good evening, Theodore," she said in response to my greeting bow.

I would have kissed her hand but lacked the courage. She pronounced my name for the first time as though it might be Theodoah, an emphasis she used for a purpose. I thought it charming. In fact, I thought everything about her charming. I had a terrible crush on Josephine Behan, was prepared to become her slave. Perhaps I did over the years, but not as blindly as I would have then. I love her dearly for what I know she is, defects included — perhaps even more because of them.

To start the evening I ordered wine and offered a belated toast to Behan's good fortune at having been appointed sheriff. "To your well deserved good fortune," I said, and we three touched glasses, our eyes meeting in companionable amiability. I, for one, was happy to be alive in such good company and in such an adventurous place.

No doubt if I'd had to exchange places with a typical miner my enthusiasm would have soured soon enough. As it was I was shortly to be treated to another glimpse of the dark side of Tombstone, and again the Earp brothers were at the heart of the turbulence.

Before the storm broke, however, we three finished a leisurely meal interspersed with small talk.

Innocently, since I didn't know the facts, I asked if Johnny had appointed Wyatt Earp under-sheriff. My question ruffled his equanimity. He shot a brief glance at Josephine before he answered, while she seemed occupied with her plate. Perhaps she actually was unaware of the problem between Wyatt and Johnny, though I fail to see how. In any event, if it was an act, her nonchalance was superbly feigned.

"I had to defer it for the sake of politics," he explained smoothly. "Wyatt understands. I'll probably put him in before the year is out. Right now Harry Woods is under-sheriff."

Knowing Woods' part in the creation of Cochise County, it was obvious even to me that his appointment smelled of a political pay off. At any rate, I recognized a touchy subject and dropped it. Johnny, however, dwelt a little longer on County politics.

"All the rest of the appointments we mentioned went through," he said.

"Good for you," I responded. "You and your friends pretty well have the County sewed up then."

He nodded, smiling complacently.

Of course, John Dunbar's appointment also smacked of political rigging. It would have been considered too open if his brother, Tom, who introduced the bill creating Cochise County, had accepted a political plum himself, but it was still "all in the family."

Another factor to be considered was mirrored in the strange fact that Republican Governor Fremont had appointed Democrat Behan as sheriff. This was why I regretted missing a reading of John Dunbar's face when the subject had first come up.

The Dunbars, from Maine, were well connected with their fellow Mainer, that power in national Republican politics, James G. Blaine. Undoubt-

Blaine missed the Republican nomination for president twice, first in 1876 to Hayes, then in 1880 to his friend Garfield, who appointed him Secretary of State.

Dunbar's friendship with Blaine explains a great deal of the questionable shenanigans that Washington officially ignored in Cochise County politics during the next couple of years. It is certainly adequate to explain the fact that a Dunbar associate and crony like Behan obtained a political appointment assuming Blaine gave the word. The Secretary of State could dictate territorial affairs to whatever extent he wished; moreover, even without office, a power in the party such as Blaine could secure appointments almost anywhere.

Just as we had finished dessert and were sipping our coffee, the lobby door opened letting in a flurry of excited conversation. My back faced that way, but the expression on Johnny's face caused me to turn. I was surprised to see Wyatt Earp carrying a shotgun, closely following an excited, shorter man who was obviously looking for the sheriff.

I learned shortly that he was Marshall Williams, the Wells Fargo and Company agent for Tombstone. "There's trouble!" he called as soon as he saw Johnny. "Stage holdup! Bob Paul just called from Benson.* Two men killed." By this time

* There was telephone service in operation between Benson and Tombstone — one of the earliest long distance services (March, 1881) — **GB.**

95

Johnny was on his feet, although he appeared uncertain what to say or do. Wyatt relieved him of his uncertainty, although his presence was probably the cause of Behan's embarrassment in the first place.

Wyatt said, "Virg has a U.S. posse getting together. They're after some horses now. The holdup was at Drew's Station. They shot Bud Philpot and a passenger."

Johnny was obviously irritated by this turn of events, although Virgil Earp had a perfect right as deputy U.S. Marshal to get together his own posse without conceding the sheriff the courtesy of a 'by your leave.' This does show one important fact. At this time, the Earps harbored no ill feeling for Johnny despite the under-sheriff appointment. But their complacency was not mutual.

"Who's coming?" Johnny asked abruptly, referring to the possemen.

"My brothers, Bat Masterson, Marsh here," Wyatt said.

"I'll get some of my deputies," Johnny stated, a significant nuance.

Turning to me he said, "Would you see Josephine home? Take your time, finish your coffee. There's no telling when I'll be back." He headed for the door with the other two.

Recalling his remark about two-gun men made to Josephine during our previous dinner, I noted that Wyatt was wearing two pistols visible under an unbuttoned heavy knitted sweater that hung to his hips. He was also wearing spurs.

The look Josephine cast after them as they left I interpreted as concern for Johnny. "Be careful," she called, more to herself than to them, and too softly for them to hear.

Employing hindsight, we may guess with whom her heart might have ridden on that wild moonlight night.

"Terrible," she said after a moment. "Two innocent men killed. Their poor wives!"

There was no haste in my approach to seeing her home. If there had been, I'd have missed a fascinating encounter. Our coffee cups were just being refilled when a strange man came to our table.

Politely he addressed me first. "Pardon me, sir. The lady is an acquaintance. I just stopped to pay my respects." At this he bowed to Josephine.

She inclined her head in acknowledgement, then smiled. To me she said, "Theodore, this is Mr. Holliday." To him, "I'd like you to meet Mr. Ten Eyck, John." The "John" was no surprise to me at the time, since I had absolutely no knowledge of the situation. But it has always given me pause that Josephine was that intimately acquainted with the notorious Doc Holliday. I wonder if she'd have called him "John" if Behan had been present. In fact, I wonder if Holliday would have paid his respects at all in such a case.

I invited him to join us, hoping he wouldn't. To my disgust, he did. Perhaps this occasioned his grin in my direction as he seated himself. Now that I knew Tombstone a little better, I wasn't dismayed at catching a glimpse of a pistol slung under his left armpit. I simply wondered if its twin was on the other side. However, the sight of even one pistol suggested to me the advisability of being pleasant. If I'd known more about our guest I'm sure I'd have been very pleasant, indeed.

Here it's essential to jump ahead of my story to mention that within a few days Doc Holliday would be accused of having been a participant in the robbery attempt and murders that had just taken place at Drew's Station.

I have two observations to make on this subject. One is that if he did, he was the most nonchalant new-born culprit imaginable, and the other is that he must have ridden away from the scene of the crime on a horse with wings. I say this since he later established by witnesses the same thing he told us that evening. That he'd been gambling at the Oriental for the preceding two hours and that he'd had a good run of luck. For this reason he insisted that we join him in a bottle of Hock.

The reader today (1940) who has heard of Doc Holliday (and who hasn't?) might be interested in his appearance at that time. In person he had none of the signs of emaciation visible in the most common picture of him which was taken by C.S. Fly in Tombstone. He was quite robust. I should judge his weight at perhaps 150 pounds on a frame of about five foot ten; not husky, but not as lean as some have pictured him, and with a distinct wiry strength.

His eyes, light blue and piercing, were his most

striking feature. His hair was blond with only a touch of gray. Oddly, he was lightly freckled, even the backs of his hands, but overall he was a handsome man with a straight nose, strong chin, and broad forehead. He wore a neatly trimmed mustache curled at the ends. And contrary to popular stories, I found him amiable and entertaining, both on first acquaintance and at all times afterward. He had a low pitched, drawling Southern voice, the words interspersed with a pleasant chuckle when the subject was droll, which it often was if he had chosen it.

That evening we talked of the stage robbery and killings. More to Josephine than to me Doc said, "Wyatt wanted me to chase around with his posse, but I put him off. I had a hot streak going bucking the tiger." He chuckled. "I'll bet they're out there going in circles and freezing. You can't track in this rocky country at night, moon or no moon."

That last was directed at me. I must say again, if he had a hand in the affair he was the coolest one at hiding his guilt I can imagine. But as events showed, he certainly did not have a hand in it. Doc's problem was that he'd been in and out of so much trouble it was easy to suspect him of almost anything. This was bad for him, but he bore it lightly. It was worse for Wyatt Earp. For him the consequences were disastrous. Yet in all the years I knew him he never uttered a single complaint regarding the trouble his friendship with Doc caused him.

But I'm sure that my readers are more anxious

to hear the details of the stage robbery attempt and the subsequent chase than to hear about the warts on Doc Holliday.

Here is the story as it was reported in *The Epitaph* of March 16, 1881. Later I will include many observations about the story, almost none of which have ever been made public.

HOLD!
Eight Road Agents Attempt to Stop Kinnear's Stage

At about 11 o'clock last night, Marshal Williams received a telegram from Benson stating that Kinnear and Company's coach, carrying Wells Fargo and Company's treasure, had been stopped near Contention and "Budd" Philpot, the driver killed and one passenger mortally wounded. Almost immediately afterwards A.C. Cowan, Wells Fargo and Company's agent at Contention City, rode into this city bringing a portion of the details of the affair. In a few minutes after his arrival, Williams, the Earp brothers, and several other brave, determined men were in the saddle, well armed, enroute to the scene of the murderous affray. From telegrams received from Benson at *The Epitaph* office, the following particulars of the affair were gathered:

As the stage was going up a small incline about two hundred yards this side of Drew's Station and about a mile the other side of

Contention City, a man stepped into the road from the east side and called out "Hold!" At the same moment a number of men — believed to have been eight — made their appearance and a shot was fired from the same side of the road instantly followed by another. One of those shots struck "Budd" Philpot, the driver, who fell heavily forward between the wheelers carrying the reins with him. The horses immediately sprang into a dead run. Meanwhile Bob Paul, Wells Fargo and Company's messenger, one of the bravest and coolest men who ever sat on a box-seat, was ready with his gun and answered back shot for shot before the frightened horses had whirled the coach out of range. It was fully a mile before the team could be brought to a stand, where it was discovered that one of the shots had mortally wounded a passenger on the coach named Peter Roering. As soon as the coach could be stopped, Paul secured the reins and drove rapidly to Benson, and immediately started back for the scene of the murder. At Benson a telegram was sent to *The Epitaph* office stating that Roering could not possibly live. There were eight passengers on the coach and they all unite in praise of Mr. Paul's bravery and presence of mind.

At Drew's Station the firing and rapid whirling by of the coach sent men to the scene of the tragedy where they found "Budd" lying dead in the road, and by the bright moonlight saw the murderers fleeing rapidly from the place. A messenger was at once dispatched to inform agent Cowan of the circumstances, and within 20 minutes after the news arrived Mr. Cowan had dispatched nearly thirty well-armed volunteers after the scoundrels. He then rode rapidly into Tombstone, when the party mentioned above started out to aid in the pursuit. This, with Mr. Paul's party, makes three bodies of determined men who are in hot chase and Mr. Cowan stated to an *Epitaph* reporter that it is almost impossible for the murderous gang to escape, and the pursuers are close at their heels and have the moonlight in their favor. Should the road agents be caught, they will meet with the short shift which they deserve.

"Budd," the murdered driver, whole real name is Eli Philpot, was one of the most widely known stage drivers on the coast. For years he had borne a high reputation as a skillful handler of the "ribbons," won on the principal stage lines in California, and during a year's residence in Arizona most of the time in the employ of Kinnear's (formerly Walker & Co.) line. He will be sincerely mourned, not only by hosts of personal friends, but by thousands of passengers who have ridden on the box seat with him and been captivated by his simple manners and frank, manly ways. It was a rare treat "to make the trip" with him, for his memory was rich in reminiscences of the "old stage days" in California, and when he so willed he could keep a companion's attention riveted by his quaint, droll conversation. He has a wife and a young family at Halistoga*, California, who had the tenderest place in his heart. And now there is another little home in the world which has been desolated and despoiled by the ruthless bullet. There is something inexpressibly sad in the sudden death of such outwardly rough, and inwardly brave, true hearted men and no better representation of this class could be found than the man whom the murderers last night sent unwarned to his last home. He was as proud and fond of his team and the big new coach on which he met his death as if they were human, and the horses always seemed to know when "Budd" was at the other end of the lines. — (March 16, 1881).

It is a typical, saccharine news story of that time, but beyond that is worthy of comment. **Eight** robbers are mentioned. When one of them was captured, he mentioned only **three** accomplices. Everyone seemed to accept his story as gospel. I did at the time, and even had the questionable honor of meeting and talking to the captive. His name was Luther King, **he said.**

Everyone conveniently assumed that in the darkness and excitement observers had seen more

* Actually Calistoga; this was a misprint — **GB**

robbers than there were. But when it became convenient, another was added to that number — Doc Holliday. A great segment of the public believed this.

It is my opinion that the original count was correct, not including Doc Holliday. My candidates for the missing bunch are Curly Bill and three of his associates: Ike Clanton, Frank Stilwell, and Pete Spencer.

Chapter 7

The Earp Boys

In view of what was taking place, I dearly wanted to interview the Earp brothers. Unfortunately this was impossible since they were out on the trail of the stage robbers. However, I wired Bennett at *The Herald*, related what was transpiring, and as expected received his O.K. to stay and cover whatever sequel took place. While I waited the return of the posse, good fortune put me in the way of George Parsons to whom I complained regarding the lack of news, particularly with respect to the Earp boys.

"There are two other brothers," he told me. "Jim and Warren. Jim's the oldest and probably still in town. He was crippled in the war and doesn't ride any more than he has to. I think I heard the young one, Warren, is back in California visiting his parents, though."

George thought for a minute, then said, "Jim's the one who could give you background on the family. They're just local business men with some experience as lawmen, especially Wyatt. They're all gamblers, too, but they keep pretty much to themselves and mind their own business. But they're always at the service of the community. You saw them in that Johnny-Behind-the-Deuce thing, and it was the same when Fred White got killed. I wish they'd thrown Johnny-Behind-the-Deuce to the wolves, but who are we to judge?"

With this preamble, George took me down to where Jim Earp was tending bar and introduced me. I told Jim who I was and what I was after. He looked me over thoroughly in a somewhat owly fashion as if weighing the wisdom of talking to me at all.

Jim had the typical light blue Earp eyes and a strong facial resemblance to the others, in addition to having the same shade of blond hair and a fair complexion. He was much shorter than the rest, about five feet eight, altogether a dapper little man with quick movements despite his game shoulder.

He seemed to reach a decision in my favor, based on what rationale I can't imagine. "Come on down to the house about seven," he invited. "We can talk there. George will show you where it is."

With that he dismissed us both by looking down at the beer mugs he was washing. George gave me a knowing look and motioned with his head. Outside he informed me, "It doesn't pay to push any of the Earps. They all go their own ways. I've been here more than a year, and they're just thawing out with me. If I hadn't been with you, Jim probably wouldn't have spoken to you except as a customer."

When I didn't answer, he said, "Don't mistake me. They're good boys, but clannish. Morg's the exception. He's easy to get to know, but they all hang together. If one likes you, the rest do. If you cross one — look out! I imagine they've all got their man before now, maybe half a dozen or more. No one knows too much about them except for Wyatt's reputation as a lawman in Kansas. And they don't talk about themselves."

This gave me something to look forward to that evening. By way of preparing the reader, I found Jim a most remarkable man in one respect. He was the most profane person I've ever known. In addition, contrary to Parson's observation, he was comparatively open in discussing his family, probably due to their already well laid plans to achieve local political power. Undoubtedly he felt that publicity from *The Herald* would further Wyatt's ambitions to be sheriff the first time the office became elective in November, 1882.

As far as talkativeness goes, the beer also helped. Josephine once commented in later years, "Jim's limit was none," and I also heard Virg kid him about a whiff of the cork putting him under. But at the time it was no concern to me when he sent his stepson, Frank, out for a growler of beer shortly after my arrival.

With apologies to the sensitive, I report Jim's conversation as I recall it. He was so profane he almost approached poetry. His wife, Bessie, a remarkably handsome blond, started to remonstrate at one point, but she didn't get far.

"Goddamit!" he cut her off. "Don't 'now, Jim' me, Precious."

His words didn't ruffle her in the least, although they startled me, since profanity in front of ladies* was a mortal sin in my background. Bessie, however, only smiled indulgently, shrugged, and left us to ourselves in the small front room.

A big nickel-skirted German heater provided welcome relief from the outdoor chill as well as the fragrance of wood smoke. Jim's was a well furnished middle class home, filled with the usual Victorian clutter. There was even an organ, though I never found out who played it. Most likely Jim had won it in a poker game.

To break the ice in what I discovered was a typical fashion for him, he looked me in the eye and announced, "I never knew a newspaperman yet that didn't turn out to be a no good lying son of a bitch, barring John Clum."

I had sense enough to grin. Besides, on reflection, I had to agree that he came pretty close to the truth. Actually, I wasn't too sure about John Clum, either, though he proved to be a staunch, lifelong friend.

Apparently my grin was the right response. Jim had been watching me with those sharp eyes, but suddenly he grinned, too. "You ought to know better'n me, eh boy?"

---

* This **lady** was madam of a whore house in Wichita at one time — **GB**

He laughed at his own remark, and I joined in. Somehow he'd known exactly what I was thinking, a trait I was to find in all of the older three Earp brothers. They were good psychologists. Jim, at forty, had seen a lot and was a wise old bird, indeed.

"Now what kind of bull shit are you looking for to blow up way to hell out of reason?" were his next words.

I couldn't see any point in doing anything but levelling with him. "I guess I'm most interested in your brother Wyatt since I've heard he was a gunfighting marshal in the cowtowns."

Jim guffawed, but didn't interrupt, and I stumbled on as best I could. "Actually I came out here to get a story on John Clum. We were neighbors back in Claverack, New York. *The Herald* wanted a feature article on him, but while I was interviewing him that Johnny-Behind-the-Deuce mob cut loose."

I was congratulating myself on having learned and used some Western jargon, but Jim didn't seem to notice. "Anyway," I went on, "Clum pointed you fellows out to me then, and I wanted to do a story, but never got the chance. I'd like all the background on you I can get, and I'm going to stay around long enough to interview your brothers and Bat Masterson when they get back. I understand Mr. Masterson was a famous sheriff himself at Dodge City."

Jim guffawed again at that, but this time he had something to say. "Hell's fire. Old Bat is the biggest load of bull shit in the West, and he'd sit here and laugh till he shit his pants to hear me say that. He floated those stories about himself to dumb shits like you that ate them up. But he's one of the best goddamn guys you ever want to meet. Him and Wyatt were both star toters back in Dodge, but Wyatt was a cop in Wichita before that."

He took a drink of beer and wiped his mouth. "Neither one of 'em's a fuckin' gunfighter. Virg's the one has got his man. Had to kill two bastards up at Prescott because the sheriff was too fuckin' weak kneed to do the job himself. Then like an asshole, Virg was sorry he did it. Soft hearted son of a bitch. So's Wyatt. But when there's a job to do us Earps were raised so we'd do it. That's how Ma and Pa taught us."

"How about some background on your parents?" I suggested, staggered by the barrage of profanity.

"Weeel. . . ." he began, calling up long unused information. "Let's see. Pa's from North Carolina. His family lived in Maryland during the Revolution, then Virginia, then they'd moseyed on to Carolina by the time Pa was born. That was 1813. Then they moved to Tennessee then Kentucky. Pa got married there, and I was born there. Pa's first wife died. I've got a half-brother, Newt back in Kansas from that marriage. There was a girl from the first wife that died as a baby, too. Pa's first wife was Abigail Storm. My uncles Lorenzo and Josiah are married to two of her sisters."

The family history seemed to be coming back to him in a steady flow. I noticed he didn't use profanity on this subject, only on his roistering friends and brothers.

"Our Ma was Virginia Cooksey before she married. I'm the oldest kid of that marriage. Me and Virg were both born in Kentucky. The rest in Illinois or Iowa. Two girls died, so there's me, Virg, Wyatt, Morg, Warren, and Adelia. She lives out by the folks near San Bernardino. Married Bill Edwards."

"Where did you live in Kentucky, Iowa and Illinois?" I asked for the record.

"At Hartford, Kentucky, then Monmouth, Illinois and Pella in Iowa. We must've moved to Monmouth in '44 or '45. We went to Iowa in 1850, and the folks left there for California in 1864 because Pa was a Southerner and didn't cotton to keeping his trap shut up in Yankeeland. But Newt, and me, and Virg were all in the Union Army. Pa never said anything against it, figured it was our damn business. He just couldn't stand a bunch of mealy-mouthed son of a bitchin' Dutchmen at Pella spouting patriotism and then dodging the draft. So he pulled his freight for San Bernardino. I was invalided out of the fuckin' army and went with them. Then cut to Austin, Nevada." He grinned and shook his head, remembering. "What a Jesus-Christly crooked fuckin' shebang Austin was. The son of a bitchin' place made Tombstone look like a goddamn church."

It was Jim's detour to Austin that fated the Earp

111

boys to become gamblers. Jim had picked up the know-how from a professional in the army, and perfected it at Austin and other camps. He indoctrinated the younger boys as they grew up.

He leaned back in his chair and went on. "The old man moved back East again in '68, then over to Lamar, Missouri. Pa farmed there a few years, and Wyatt got his first law job. Town constable. Then they all got itchy feet again. Pa went back to San Berdoo, Virg went to Prescott, and Wyatt, Morg and I roamed around the cattle and buffalo country awhile."

I wondered if he was being a little vague on specifics, but figured it wasn't a good idea to pin him down on details, even though by this time the beer had loosened him up and slurred his speech. Besides, it had occurred to me that he might take a six-shooter to a smart alec newsman, so I was being polite, giving him his head.

"Wyatt and I were in Dodge planning to start a cattle spread in the Texas Panhandle when Virg talked us into tryin' our hands in this goddamned oasis, so here we all are. We're doin' our best to buy up the place. She's bound to last. We got mining claims, a lot of water and timber rights, and own most of this end of town. I've got a saloon, Wyatt's got a piece of a couple and his gambling layouts."

He took a deep breath, exhaled, and broke wind. "Par' me, ladies," he said to no one in particular, grinning. "Anyhow, Virg and Morg gamble when Virg ain't lawin', and Wyatt and Morg work on

112

the side for Wells Fargo. Wyatt was deputy sheriff, but he resigned in November, and now that little ass kisser Behan's got the job. And that about covers us. We're just a bunch of goddamned business men tryin' to make a buck in a lousy hell-hole out here on the desert. You got any more questions, come back. I'm goin' out and piss, then I'm hittin' the hay."

He was unsteady as we went out. "I gotta stumble around here and find the shit house," he said in farewell.

The last I heard, he was breaking wind thunderously, and if my eyes didn't deceive me he was relieving himself in the side yard. I was thoroughly shocked,* but then I hadn't seen much of the world, the West, or the Earps.

* The ladies in San Bernardino kept their kids inside when Jim, as an old man, was sitting on his porch in fine conversational form with one visitor or another — **GB**

113

Chapter 8

Doc Holliday — Accused Stage Robber

The first fruits of the manhunt for the stage robbers materialized in the person of one Luther King. Johnny Behan and Marshall Williams brought him in under arrest. No one, then or ever, openly admitted to knowing very much about him. Some said he'd been a cowboy working for Len Redfield down the San Pedro. At least that's where the Earp posse overtook and captured him under very strange and incriminating circumstances. On the other hand, I think I know a lot about him. I'm inclined to believe his real name was Woods.

I'll let Wyatt's own words describe King's capture, but to lay the proper background, I must relate that King escaped from custody almost as soon as he reached Tombstone.

The **alleged** circumstances were covered in a story in Harry Woods' *Nugget.* I say "alleged," since I happened to be present, not by anyone's intent, when King escaped.

This was the news story.

"Luther King, the man arrested at Redfield's ranch charged with being implicated in the Budd Philpot murder, escaped from the sheriff's office by quietly stepping out the back door while Harry Jones, Esq., was drawing up a bill of sale for a horse the prisoner was selling to John Dunbar. Under-sheriff Harry Woods and Dunbar were present. He had been absent but a few seconds before he was missed. A confederate on the outside had a horse in readiness for him. It was a well planned job by outsiders to get him away. He was an important witness against Holliday. He it was that gave the names of the **three that were being followed** at the time he was arrested. Their names were Bill Leonard, Jim Crane and Harry Head."

The story doesn't specify exactly where King was when he escaped. He was in the sheriff's office which consisted of two rooms and a small, barred holding tank which was not, regularly speaking, a jail. King, however, hadn't been kept in the tank or at the jail at all. During his short period of detention he'd been more like a personal guest of Harry Woods.

That should have been enough to start a smart young fellow, like I thought I was, thinking. It started some others; George Parsons, for example. On Monday, March 28, 1881 George wrote in his

115

now well-known journal:

"King the stage robber escaped tonight early from H. Woods who had been previously notified of an attempt at release to be made. Some of our officials should be hanged. They're a bad lot."

The way I happened on the scene was that I strolled over to the sheriff's office after dinner* that day to see if I could pick up any news about how the chase was going. Behan, I knew, had two deputies still in the field who supposedly were sent to join the Earp posse because they were excellent trailers. Their names were Billy Breakenridge and Buckskin Frank Leslie, both destined to become well known local fixtures. Leslie, in fact, already was. He'd killed a man named Killeen the summer before and promptly married the widow.

When I reached the sheriff's office no one was in the front room which served as a reception area for visitors. I heard voices in the rear but thought it best not to interrupt. Instead I sat down on a bench and picked up a back copy of *The Police Gazette* that was lying there. My browsing was arrested by the urgent argument in progress in the back room. I recognized Harry Woods' voice; he obviously had no idea anyone had come in the front door.

"Goddamit, Lute," I heard him say, "this is the

* As the noon meal was commonly called in those days — **GB.**

116

last son of a bitchin' time your big brother is going to stick his neck out and bail your ass out of trouble. You're going to slope the hell out and never come back. Hear me?"

I couldn't make out the reply, but thought it was an excellent time to leave and make a loud re-entry, which I did. That broke up the quarrel. Shortly after, Woods came out looking sour and said, "Oh, it's you. What do you want?"

Before I could say anything, John Dunbar barged in followed by a man I'd never seen.

"Howdy, Ted," Dunbar greeted me pleasantly. "This is Harry Jones." Turning to Woods he said, "Is King here? Johnny said he wants to sell his horse to the stable."

"In the back room." Woods motioned with his thumb. Then he yelled, "Hey, King! Come on out here!"

It was the first time I saw Luther King close up; also the last. He came out looking sullen, still angry over the recent argument with Woods. Since it was obvious that no one else was back there, and since there was an unmistakable resemblance between Woods and King, the startling impact of what had been said dawned on me. I hoped my face didn't give me away.

Dunbar explained why they were there, and Woods produced a bottle and set it on the desk. "To seal the deal," he explained. Then he turned to King. "You got that bill of sale on you?" I can't be sure but I think he tipped King an obvious wink.

"In my coat in the back room," King said nervously and went to get it.

Woods passed the bottle, and we all had the ritual Western pull at it. That took up a crucial minute at least. Only Harry Jones and I were ignorant of what was really going on.

Harry pulled some papers out of his inside coat pocket and sat down at the desk and began writing. Dunbar flopped his heavy frame down on the bench next to me and let out a sigh. "What a helluva day," he said. It wasn't over yet.

"What the hell's taking you so goddamn long, King?" Woods yelled. When there was no answer, he stuck his head in the back room. "I'll be goddamned," he exclaimed. "The son of a bitch is gone!"

We all went into the room with Woods. There was a side door opening into the hallway I'd entered by. Woods went over and tried it. It was unlocked. "I'll be go to hell!" he shouted. "That damn door is never supposed to be unlocked. I'll have some one's son of a bitchin' head for this!"

It was a consummate performance for our benefit, and it wasn't over. Woods rushed back to the outer office and sagged into the chair Harry Jones had vacated.

"Behan'll have my ass," he moaned. He was so good that none of us thought to suggest we get on the trail of the fugitive. After providing King at least another minute lead time, Woods jumped up and led the way down the hall to the rear door of the building. It opened into an empty lot cluttered with tin cans and litter. A burro was out

118

there, maybe eating the tin cans for all I knew. A small Mexican boy was camped on the animal's haunches. He looked up when we rushed out the back door.

"Hey, kid!" Harry yelled. "Did you see anyone come out of here just now?"

The boy looked him over, wondering from the tone of voice if he were somehow in trouble. "Si, Senor," he said. "One hombre. He jumped on the horse and vamoosed."

"What horse?" Woods asked.

"The horse that was tied near the door," the boy said.

"Did you see who tied the horse there?"

The boy shrugged. "No, Senor."

Hind sight prompts me to believe the look on Harry's face at that news was one of sheer relief.

I heard him say, "It was Holliday. It had to be. King would have squealed on him."

That didn't make sense to me yet.

I didn't know that Dunbar and Woods had an earlier conversation that led to Doc Holliday's candidacy not only as King's accomplice but as stage robber as well. Doc was unfortunate enough to have rented a horse from Dunbar and Behan's stables on the day of the holdup. He was seen leaving town on that horse, heavily armed.

EDITORIAL COMMENT:
That casual bit of information was all the clever Woods needed to embroider the only real substance, tenuous as it was, into what has become

an elaborate tapestry, illustrating the nefarious adventures of the Earp Gang of stage robbers. The initial work was improved on by Woods, repeated by the "Tombstone Nugget's" echo, the "Arizona Star", and later by Ike Clanton in court. This specious canard has been elaborated upon to this day by an absurd, sensation-mongering group of writers, who have deceived an ignorant public.

So clever was Woods at all this that I didn't suspect the truth, even with all that happened under my nose.

I left after that to file a news dispatch. Surprisingly, there was no major effort started on a search at the time of my departure. In fact, Harry Jones told me they all sat down and had another pull at the bottle.

Jones had a motive for swapping allegiance from the Behan to the Earp faction, and what he told me was only after the swap. The problem was that Jones had a vivacious wife, Kitty, who often found Tombstone boring. Johnny Behan was Tombstone's expert at alleviating feminine boredom. But I'm getting ahead of my story. It's interesting to note, however, that Kitty was initially Josephine's best friend in Tombstone and had, in fact, accompanied her when she first came there to live.

Jim Hume, Wells Fargo's chief detective, had arrived in Tombstone as a result of the stage holdup. Even though the treasure had not been stolen, Wells Fargo had a warm interest in putting any and all highwaymen out of business, and they were never too particular about how that happened. Hume was burned up over King's escape. He personally joined the Earp posse, carrying the bad news. As a result, it was decided that Wyatt and Hume would leave the rest on the track of Leonard, Head, and Crane and would return to Tombstone to try to pick up King's cold trail.

I, for one, was completely roped in by Woods' propaganda blast at Holliday. Of all people, I should have known better, and in fact could have alibied Doc by merely telling the truth. Nor did I suspect that Woods' real purpose was to diminish Earp's political chances by using his notorious friend, Doc, as an Achilles' Heel. I rather liked the idea of Holliday getting in trouble. He was altogether too friendly with Josephine.

Another one of those paradoxes that, due to my ignorance, puzzled me so often during my early days in the West was just about to beset me. I hadn't yet got the hang of the idea that in the West it was considered good business to put your thumbs in your enemy's eyes.

Chapter 9

A Close Up Of Wyatt Earp

As a result of my acquaintance with Jim Earp, I was one of the first to see Wyatt upon his return from the chase. Jim Hume was with him. I'd never seen Hume before. He wasn't young then, having been a lawman since the days of '49. They reached Jim's house well after dark one evening about a week after my first visit there.

I didn't know how close Wyatt had come to his quarry, but he hadn't been close to a razor for some time and was a very hard looking specimen under a ten day growth of beard. Why he stopped first at Jim's instead of his own house was a mystery to me.

"Get Clum and the others," he said to Jim.

Trying to be covert, Jim indicated me with a surreptitious thumb.

Wyatt gave me a poker-faced stare. "You're the man from the New York paper, right?" he asked.

"Bennett's *Herald*," I told him, hoping that Bennett's name would do some good.

Wyatt shrugged. "Let him stay," he said to Jim. "He'll learn more than he bargained for, and it might do us some good." He was right in the long run.

Jim sent his stepson, Frank, out to fetch the proper people. Clum arrived after what was, for me, an uncomfortable interval during which Wyatt, Jim, and Hume ignored me and drank coffee, conversing in tones too low for me to hear.

I was surprised to see George Parsons come in with Clum. The two others who accompanied them were introduced to me as Mr. Gage and Mr. Gird. I knew them by reputation as community leaders, but wasn't savvy enough to figure out until much later that I had been in plenary session with the high moguls of the Tombstone Vigilantes.

Without preliminaries, except to settle the wisdom of my continued presence, Wyatt launched into a description of the chase. The notion that he was laconic to the point of incoherence is a modern misconception. When he had something to say, he talked very well, indeed.

Here is what he told us as close as I could remember when I set it on paper afterward. To save space I have eliminated the interruptions of minor questions put to him.

"We got tired of waiting around town for Behan to get ready and went down to Drew's Station ahead of him — me, Morg, Virg, Marsh, and Bat. It was too dark to tell much, about two in the A.M., but lots of people had been there milling around. Cowan's posse, I guess. We never saw

123

them, but their tracks showed they'd been there and churned up the ground so it was hard to read sign when it got light enough. God knows what trail they followed. We built a little fire and cooked some coffee to kill time till it got light. By that time Behan and Breakenridge showed up.

"We'd already found where the robbers waited by the road, where somebody had held the horses, and we found seventeen empty rifle cases in the road where they'd pumped those shots and killed the passenger. We also found some rag masks that they sewed frayed rope onto to look like whiskers.

"About that time Bob Paul got back from Benson and told us right where the holdup men had stood when they yelled for the stage to stop, only he thought there were a lot more than four. There could have been for all we could tell with the ground churned up. If that's the case, the others sneaked out right on the road, because we circled around and only found where four horses had headed East.

"By that time Behan thought he was in charge like a rooster bragging about laying an egg. He said the killers had too big a head start to catch them and we should forget about following them, but when he saw we were going ahead without him, he tagged along.

"We tracked them past Helm's ranch in the Dragoons, then they cut back to the San Pedro. We camped on their trail and followed it up again at daybreak. I don't think they thought anybody was still on their trail since they'd done a pretty good job of covering their tracks at the beginning. Anyhow, it was easy to follow them to Len Redfield's where we caught up with King.

"Before we got that far we found one of their played-out nags in the barn on that ranch that used to belong to a fellow named Wheaton. By then the trail was plenty warm. It led to Hank Redfield's first, and he swore nobody had been there, but he'd probably let them have at least one fresh horse. We weren't on to the Redfields yet. If we had been, we'd have taken Hank along with us for safe keeping.

"From his place the trail led right down to Len Redfield's ranch, and King made a break from the corral just as we rode up. Morg and I rode him down. He tried to tell us he worked there and was milking, but he was wearing two six-shooters and had about twenty boxes of cartridges inside his shirt. It was pretty clear he was getting milk and cartridges for his crowd and that they were probably still holed up close by unless they'd heard the commotion and lit out.

"We asked King what he ran for if he wasn't on the dodge, and he said he thought we were outlaws. I forgot to mention he grabbed a rifle when he headed for the brush, but he never offered to shoot Morg or me. He was pretty scared. Bob Paul and I got him alone long enough to throw the fear of God into him. Up till then we hadn't said what we were after him for. Behan said he was against arresting him merely on suspicion and went into Redfield's with Breakenridge for breakfast.

"I had an idea that I thought would get King to talk, and I told it to Bob Paul. He thought so, too. So we told King Doc Holliday's woman, Kate, was on that stage coach and was killed when they did all that shooting after it in the dark. King looked white around the gills after that."

Wyatt chuckled grimly at this point, then continued. "King wanted to know if Doc was with us. He knew Doc's reputation well enough to know he'd settle personally with anybody who'd had a hand in killing Kate. We let him fidget awhile, and pretty soon he said, 'Will you guys tell Doc I was the one that held the horses if I tell you who the others were?'

"That's what we were after so we said yes and let him sing. That's the first we were sure that Leonard, Head, and Crane were our fish. Bob Paul thought that left at least four more unaccounted for, so we sweated King on that, but if there were more he was afraid to squeal on them. My bet is that some of Curly Bill's crowd and maybe the Clantons were the others, and he was sure they'd kill him if he squealed. If it was them, they probably headed back to Charleston, and their trail got covered up by that mob Cowan had out there chowsing around in the dark.

"About then Behan and Breakenridge came out. Johnny was curious to know what all the palaver was about, so we had King repeat his story. Then he let the cat out of the bag by saying, 'I didn't know there was any woman on that stage, and I wasn't the one that killed her.'

"Johnny saw the light right away. He said, real quick, 'There wasn't any woman killed on that stage, that's for sure.' The look on King's face was worth a million when he found out we'd suckered him. He cussed a good bit over it. About then Hank Redfield rode in. King was just finished calling us a bunch of such and so's and saying he'd be damned if we got another word out of **him.**

"If Behan had kept his trap shut, we'd have got King to tell us where the other three were hiding out. We were beginning to wonder about Johnny, and our mistake was leaving him with King and the Redfields while we circled for sign. I told Johnny not to let King talk with them, but he must have because later on we backtracked and saw where Hank Redfield's tracks led straight to where Leonard, Head and Crane had camped.

"If Hank had known where their camp was, he'd have gone straight there and tipped them off. As it was, I figure Johnny let him talk to King, so Johnny's the cause of their getting away. Hell, there was still a fire burning when we found their camp."

Gird interrupted at this point. "What do you make of Behan's attitude?"

Wyatt reflected before answering. "Well, at the time I thought he didn't want us Earps to be in on the capture because he knows I aim to run against him for sheriff and that would help me out at the polls. But since he practically let King walk out of jail, it's hard to say what to think."

Clum, who was never one to mince words, put in a couple that didn't please me. "It's plain as the nose on your face that the conniving little fourflusher is hand in glove with the holdup men. It won't be the first time something like that happened. Look at Plummer up in Montana back in '64."

We were all familiar with how Sheriff Plummer had been the leader of organized outlawry at Bannack, Alder Gulch and Virginia City during the Montana gold rush. I saw nods of thoughtful agreement with Clum's conclusion, but I thought they were all foolish.

However, the first small doubt about Johnny crept into my mind that night. The Earps and Clum were his political enemies, so their views could be discounted, but Gird and Gage were something else. They were the recognized leaders of the community; Gird as one of the co-founders of the district with the Schieffelins, and Gage as their general manager at the Tombstone Mining and Milling Company.

What Wyatt had said was the significant part of the story of the chase. The balance of the posse followed Leonard, Head, and Crane all over the Southeastern part of the Territory, finally losing the trail in Southwestern New Mexico.

There was an additional piece of conversation worth mentioning. Clum asked Wyatt, "What about the rumors Doc Holliday was mixed up in the holdup?"

Wyatt shook his head. "Jim Hume here told me

about that, and all I have to say is if Doc was there he must have had wings to get back to Tombstone by the time I saw him. That was about eight P.M. or so, just after the holdup as near as I can figure. I will say that Billy Leonard's been a friend of Doc's for years, but that's about as much connection Doc had with the affair." He shook his head again as another thought occurred to him. "Anyway, if Doc had been in on it, our story about Kate being killed would have fallen flat with King. As it was, we scared him half to death."

"Well, *The Nugget* is playing it up big that Doc was in on it anyhow," Gage put in. "Maybe they figure that part of it won't come out now that King's gone."

Wyatt agreed. Then he said, "We've got to figure the source. Woods is probably in this as deep as Behan, **if they were** in on it. But a story like that throws suspicion off them for letting King get away."

That was the substance of the part of the meeting I was permitted to overhear. I must say that Wyatt had been a fair prophet. I "learned more than I bargained for." But as I left I was wondering how much I should tell Johnny about what I'd heard. Like a ninny, I still trusted him, so decided to tell him everything.

I was, however, capable of learning. As I write this fifty years later, another thought occurs regarding the suspicions people have held against Wyatt.

It is that Jim Hume was Wells Fargo's ace chief of detectives and remained so for many years, during which Wyatt retained his trust and friendship. Hume would have been out of a job if Wyatt, his brothers, and Doc had, indeed, been accomplices of stage robbers or had been stage robbers themselves, as some have accused them of being.

Two important things happened relative to that meeting with Wyatt Earp.

The first was that I had a positive conviction that I would never like the man. I considered his story about the chase not entirely above question. Rumors were already afloat about the real robbers chasing themselves, which accounted for someone planting a horse for King's escape. I was inventing rationalizations to explain away the conversation I'd heard between Woods and his brother. After all, King had left through that side office door. Why couldn't a brother I didn't see have done the same?

Harry Woods' concern had been all too convincing. Suppose a ne'er do well brother really had got Harry into that pickle by unlocking the side door so that King escaped behind him? For that matter, blood was thicker than water. I wasn't sure but what I'd have done the same under similar circumstances, if I had a brother.

The second thing happened because I reported Wyatt's description to Behan and Woods. It was the following added news item in *The Nugget*.

"Evidence in the hands of the authorities

implicates four robbers and five accomplices and arrests will follow as soon as everything is ready. Meanwhile it is certain that several men around Tombstone, among them one who was a participant in the preliminary pursuit, are under surveillance."

The latter reference was to Wyatt Earp.

The Ring was beginning to play hard ball. It wasn't the Cowboys' guns that ran the Earps out of the country. It was Harry Woods' pen. Goebbels could have learned his trade from Woods.* A substantial number of the descendants of early ranchers still living around Tombstone believe the Earps were outlaws. But that figures. Their grandpappies laid the cornerstones of the family fortunes, such as they are, with cheap brood cattle rustled by Curly Bill and Company out of Mexico.

The standing joke in Tombstone at dinner in those days was that the steaks were already half-cooked when the chef got them, heated up by Curly Bill and the Clantons running them out of Mexico. It was another common laugh that much of the stock around mooed with a Spanish accent.

At this point I was thinking of asking Harry Woods for a job on *The Nugget*. It never occurred to me to ask Clum for a job. Behan and Company had done too good a propaganda job on me.

* Referring to Hitler's propaganda minister, Goebbels; therefore this sentence was inserted sometime after the original manuscript was started in the early 1930's — **GB.**

Besides, my parents were lifelong Democrats. I never did more than think about the prospect, however, because I received a wire calling me home. My father was dying. When he did, I was in line for a tidy sum of money which was not, of course, uppermost in my mind. Seeing my father before he passed on was. I caught the three A.M. stage to connect with the Eastbound train.

Johnny was there to see me off. "I hope everything turns out O.K," he said, shaking my hand. "And come back to see us."

He waved as the stage pulled out. What a great friend! He owed me a hundred dollars, but I wasn't worried about it. He died owing it to me — and a lot more besides.

Chapter 10

Wyatt Earp Talks

1910

It will be natural enough to wonder why I am jumping from my temporary absence from Tombstone, when my father died in 1881, to 1910, so I'd better explain. It wasn't until that year that I had the full story of Wyatt Earp's Tombstone Vendetta (except for one small piece of the puzzle, which I picked up later, from Jim Earp, as I will relate). I learned a great deal about those days myself after I returned to Tombstone in the fall of 1881, and will go back and cover that part when necessary. But my authority for the inside story is so exquisite that I see no better way to tell that inside story than this. And who was my informant? Wyatt Earp himself. The Sphinx talked at last. The place was up at his Happy Day Mine.

To bridge the years 1881 — 1910, Wyatt left Tombstone in March 1882, one jump ahead of Johnny Behan's posse of killers. He never returned. Even Josie sneaked out of town. She joined him later and they roamed the West, from one boom camp to another, even to San Diego, during a real estate rather than a mining boom, and finally to Alaska during the Gold Rush days at Nome. They left there for the last time in 1902 and returned to California. I will quote Josie's memoir directly to explain how they ended up at the Happy Day mine which is located across the Colorado River from Parker, Arizona in the Whipple Mountains. (By the way, Parker wasn't there when they reached that country, only a ferry across the Colorado, operated by Indians.)

They had just returned from Alaska to Los Angeles and decided to head for the current mining boom at Tonopah and Goldfield, Nevada. They had a nest egg of $85,000.00, made in Alaska, a true fortune then, and could live as they pleased.

Josie wrote:

"At last everything was arranged so that all we had to do was to follow where inclination should lead. We had sufficient money for the future so that we did not find it necessary to engage in anything that was not wholly to our enjoyment.

"It was not a hard thing for us to agree to WHERE we both wanted to go. We would go into the desert, that was certain.

*****

"We would sometimes sit and plan like a couple of children where we would go, what sort of equipment should be taken along and, when we struck it rich (which we undoubtedly would) what fun we would have with all that money. We were, in reality, having our fun right then and for the years that followed. We had already "struck it rich" when we found ourselves able to cut loose from the grind of wresting a living from a reluctant world."

They really did "strike it rich" in a modest fashion and filed on their Happy Day mine. Josie wrote:

"It showed something like six per cent copper and twenty-five dollars per ton in gold. Now we had found it. Our days of wandering were at an end. If only the ledge would not pinch out. We made plans for the future, great plans full of hope and bright expectation. We would keep our mine in our own control and work it for our own profit.

"The desert would be our home henceforth, the desert that we both loved so well, and it would yield us wealth instead of only taking from us as heretofore. We would spend all our remaining years upon it."

That was in 1905. I took to spending a week or so up at their mine with them from time to time, because like them I'd "struck it rich," only in real estate in my case. I generally timed my trips to find some time alone with Wyatt, usually when Josie would visit her relatives in the

Bay Area; not that I didn't enjoy her sometimes prickly company till the day she died, but because Wyatt preferred not to be alone. Strange, this "loner" loved company — so long as it didn't run off at the mouth too much — and really hated to be entirely by himself.

To reach their mine, the Earps sometimes went by train to Needles and "teamed" in by a real covered wagon from there. Other times they went to Yuma by train, then up the Colorado River by small boat, on the line run by Mellon and Polhamus. Their third route, and their favorite if they were in no hurry, was by wagon from Los Angeles, either through Banning or Cajon Pass, camping from water hole to water hole. In time they knew them all, as well as the roads which were usually no more than sandy, and often rocky, trails that changed every year due to rain storms.

Oh yes, it rains in the desert. In July and August, usually, and sometimes June and September. Denizens of that country call it the Monsoon season. It rains like the devil in cloudbursts. Cumulo nimbus clouds build up when blazing sun blasts the desert floor, causing convection currents that rise for miles, lifting wet air with them until condensation occurs. After that clouds build all by themselves, as high as forty thousand feet. By two or three o'clock in the afternoon the sky may be dense with thunderheads from horizon to horizon. That's the time to batten down your tent if you're camped out there. The sky is going to open, accompanied by strong, gusty winds and blowing sand ahead of the storm. Sometimes it rains all night on and off, thunder growling and lightning flickering in every direction. As soon as the water comes down everything cools off. This phenomenon is what makes for blanket weather at night across what is called the High Desert, from California's Mojave to the place where New Mexico's mountains drop off into the Llano Estacado.

Nonetheless, the Earps generally left for the Coast before the really hot weather set in. They preferred to winter up on the High Desert. It also rains there in the winter, but not every year. When the winter rains are good, the desert comes to life the following Spring. Seeds that have lain dormant for years, spring up and the valleys and hills are carpeted with flowers.

The Earps were not peculiar in picking the desert for their home. They wanted solitude for one thing, and in those years there was no more isolated place in the U.S. than the Mojave. It was also strikingly beautiful, and even hospitable to those who learned how to live with it.

The desert, unlike popular perception of it, is not a desolate, uninhabited place, though its vastness and rugged appearance move many to refer to it as desolate. Yet, it teems with interesting plant and animal life, though it has rightly been said that everything there either has fangs, claws or thorns. Most dread the presence of the fearsome rattlesnake. It is, in truth, a shy creature that avoids man, or anything else that is not its natural prey, if at all possible. If one is struck by a rattlesnake it is truly an accident.

The desert's secrets were known to few before the days of good highways and autos which gave birth to widespread tourism. The Earps learned to read the desert like a book. They lived like the few people who were there when they arrived. Indians, prospectors, hermits. There was hermit in both of them. I have known them to sit for hours, not speaking, watching their desert, wrapped in their own thoughts, not wishing to be disturbed with talk while they enjoyed an inner existence. It was probably this mutual trait that kept their turbulent natures united. It led them to far places together before then, seeking adventure — and equally, solitude — as much as their fortunes. By the time of my 1910 visit, they had found both.

I took the train up to Needles where Wyatt's nephew, Bill Miller, met me with their light wagon and team of mules. He had brought Josie up to the catch train on her way to Oakland to visit her sister, Henrietta. The three of us had a meal at Harvey's El Garces while she waited for the Westbound. After we got her on the train we headed south, planning to camp as far down the trail as we could get before dark.

A word here about Bill Miller. He was a jolly young fellow in his mid-twenties then, sang, played a banjo, ukelele, guitar, harmonica; he was always in prime shape — an acrobat, in fact, almost professional caliber — and he'd dance all night when he got the chance and never get tired. He was an all around good companion. There was a remarkable affinity between him and Wyatt Earp, not entirely based on their mutual love of bird shooting together out on the Mojave. It was more a father and son relationship. Bill was the son that Wyatt never had. Josie liked Bill too, everyone did, maybe she even felt like a mother to him, but their bond was never the close tie that existed between him and Wyatt.

I'd been out with those two before this particular trip and knew how splendidly they got along. I'd also observed something else that has a direct impact on my story — the way Wyatt Earp handled a shotgun. He was a great wing shot. How he did it tells a lot about his methods and why he survived where others turned up their toes. He was quick but deliberate. I took to watching him shoot a shotgun after it occurred to me that I *never* saw him miss a dove or quail. Of course, he sometimes didn't get one because he simply didn't shoot when there was no chance of bringing down the bird. He never wasted time, energy or resources. When he did shoot, he swung his whole body, raising the gun as he did, trailed the bird's trajectory, passed it, still swinging and BANG! . . . . another bird in the bag. It was all so quick and smooth it looked easy, and not really fast. But, several times I counted "a thousand-one, a thousand-two, etc." to figure how many seconds he was taking. I was always surprised how often I never finished saying "a thousand-one." Bill was a good wing shot too, but not in Wyatt's class.

So it's no wonder Wyatt bagged Curly Bill with a shotgun, even though Curly had the jump on him and was trying to get him. Curly got in a hurry and missed, but Wyatt filled him with buckshot from his old .10 gauge double barrel. In those days when I went out with him and Bill, Wyatt used an old Winchester lever action .12 gauge, and later he had a .12 gauge pump gun. I carried a gun when we went out so no one would think I was simple, but my sympathies were all with the birds. I never shot a thing, not even rattlesnakes if they weren't close to our camp, and neither of those two ever said a word to me about it. They understood, and figured it was my business.

I remember it was coming on to a full moon when Bill and I headed out from Needles for the Earps' mine, and we didn't make camp till after the sun went down. Bill knew where water was out in that country as well as the Earps did, and we stopped at a well. Someone had put in a big prospect hole there and worked on it a long time, from the looks of it. There was even the remains of a floor and framework where they'd put up a semi-permanent tent, that surprisingly hadn't been carted off or used for kindling.

Bill set up camp and did the cooking, with what little help I could give him. I'm not a camp cook. I did the pot walloping afterward.

"Uncle Wyatt hates washing dishes," Bill said. "I handle all the camp chores and he handles the team and wagon when we're out."

We were sitting around the fire after eating, and I figured he might be leading up to a story and waited for the rest.

He rummaged around in the wagon and came back with two cigars. He handed me one, knowing I smoked a cigar occasionally. I'd just been wishing I'd thought to buy some before we left Needles. Nothing is better after a meal when you're sitting around the fire and maybe have a cup of good, strong camp coffee made the way we did before percolators and fancy stuff came out.

Bill said, "Uncle Wyatt likes a good cigar."

"I know," I told him.

I could have told him I'd seen Wyatt go into Hafford's in Tombstone, right after he'd pasted Tom McLaury over the head with a pistol barrel and left him lying in the street and come out in a minute and light up a cigar, cool as a cucumber, then rock on his heels a little, looking unconcerned as could be, while he glanced up and down the street for signs of more trouble. I was close enough to hear what he said, too, right after he knocked Tom down, which was, "I should have killed the son of a bitch!" I knew quite a bit about Wyatt Earp. He was no angel. Neither were his brothers. But they were the medicine Tombstone needed.

We got our cigars going, and Bill said, "It was one of these cigars that got Uncle Wyatt so he'd talk to me. We musta gone out two or three years in a row, and he'd let me fix camp and do the cooking, then we'd sit around and he'd never say a word till we turned in. He smoked his pipe and every once in awhile I thought he had something on his mind and was about to let it out, but he never did. Then, one year I brought along a box of good cigars, just like these, and handed him one. We both lit up, just like now, and he leaned back and blew a big cloud of smoke up in the air.

" 'Good cigar,' he said. I figured he'd sit there and smoke the cigar down and go to bed without saying another word, but in a little while he said, 'You know. . . . .' and he started talking about the old days. I couldn't believe my ears. The best any of us ever got out of him before then was, 'I've lived a long while and I'd think we could find something more cheerful to talk about than killing,' although I know he talked to my dad, who'd done his share of killing himself, mostly Indians. But, maybe he had to get it off his chest and tell us why the Earp boys did what they did in Tombstone. Did he ever talk about it with you?"

"A little. Of course, I was there and we naturally talk about the old days. He knows he doesn't have anything to hide from me." Little did I know. And I was about to find out on this particular trip.

We pulled in about sundown the next day, and Wyatt and his dog were out to meet us, since the pup had been barking a good five minutes before we pulled in. Wyatt always kept a dog or two in camp. I think I know why too, aside from the fact that he liked dogs and cats. He'd have been a big fool if he didn't know someone might be looking for revenge right up to the day he died.

EDITORIAL COMMENT:

Estelle Miller told me roughly the same thing that Bill said above, about Wyatt's usual reaction when questioned about killings and violence in general; obviously he didn't like to kill, but did it when he had to. He was certainly not the cold blooded killer that some think he was.

Chapter 11

The Happy Day

The little town of Vidal was coming to life, but the Earps preferred it out at their mine "where it was quieter," which is worth thinking about, since there were few quieter villages in the world than Vidal at its busiest. Their camp always had a wall tent over a wood floor, a substantial wood door, because it kept the inside warmer on those cold desert nights, as well as keeping varmints out, and a good cooking stove inside, both for warmth and cooking. Outside there was a ramada where they ate when it wasn't too cold and the sand wasn't blowing. Water was a premium item, as it always is on the desert, and at first they hauled it in barrels from the river, then later from Vidal after Judge Brownell put in the first well there. They kept one barrel of water for the mules and horses and a big metal drum with a faucet on the bottom for themselves. There were few trees to offer shade, but their camp was under one of them; a fair sized mesquite. When they had company, which was surprisingly often, they would put up a separate wall tent that wasn't floored. Bill and I were sleeping in that one. Wyatt's older brother Jim occasionally spent months with them and batched in his own tent.

Wyatt kept a heavy work team sometimes, but water was always a problem until they moved into Vidal. Later, he and "Dude," his Indian pal, ran a freight outfit out of Parker, with Dude doing most of the running which included a light dray service in town.

On this particular trip, which I always think of as "the time the Sphinx finally talked," I spent the first couple of days around camp reading, while Wyatt and Bill hunted, or fiddled around cleaning their guns or the mules' harness, and once I went in with Bill to Brownell's and got several barrels of water. Dude had the heavy team across the river, freighting some stuff into a mine prospect for a couple of hopeful souls.★

The weather was ideal. We'd been eating outside and sitting around the campfire evenings, mostly wrapped in our own thoughts, like you do staring into a fire. The moon was full and the coyotes were giving it hell out in the brush. Wyatt's dog, the first one he had called "Earpie," or as Bill called him, "the Earp purp," charged out barking if he thought they were getting too close.

★ By that time there was little mining in progress, since the Happy Day was a bust, though Wyatt used to hire old friends in need of a job to do exploration work on it — **GB.**

I confess to trying to figure a good way to bring up Tombstone without being too obvious. We both still had friends all over Arizona from those days, but very few in Tombstone. The substantial element that had supported the Earps and law and order pulled out when the mines collapsed, except for a few like E.B. Gage who kept trying to bring the mines back into production. A couple of times he came close. Finally, I got a bright idea and said, "Did you know Phin Clanton died a few years back?"

Wyatt said, "So I heard," but nothing more for a long while and I figured that ploy had played out. A little later he said, "Phin was the last of the Mohicans, I guess . . . . . crooked like all the rest, but not a bad sort." He seemed to be thinking about something, maybe debating whether to mention it or not. Finally he said, "We knew the Clantons over at San Bernardino when we first went there in '64. The Old Man was the best of the bunch. I was sorta sorry to see him go."

To me, that was a puzzler. Everyone knew that Old Man Clanton was a leading light among the outlaws at Tombstone. Right up there with Curly Bill. I must have looked my question, because I was afraid to ask why he said that for fear of drying him up.

He said, "Ike got his Old Man killed, you know."

I wanted to ask "how come?" but figured that wasn't the thing to do. As Bill Miller had advised me, "Just wait him out. If he wants to talk, he will."

146

Wyatt finally said, "Why don't you stoke up the fire a little, Bill?"

I want to describe the way Wyatt looked in those days on the desert. He'd changed quite a bit from Tombstone, lost most of his hair on top, and always wore a hat during the day to keep from getting sunburned, not because he was self-conscious about his bald head. But, sitting there in the moonlight, bareheaded, with the fire lighting up his face from the other side, he looked like a bird of prey, his prominent nose etched strongly by the shadows, his eyes — piercing light-blue — like lanterns in the dark.

He knocked the dottle out of his pipe and refilled it carefully, got it going to suit him, probably grinning inside because he knew he had us on his hook. Don't think he didn't have a sense of humor just because he was notorious for never laughing. He did his laughing inside; sometimes he grinned, and rarely chuckled, usually over something his dog or cat did, or a horse.

Finally he said, "And I reckon I got Ike killed, indirectly." He added after awhile, "I can't say that I shed any tears over Ike when it happened."

I thought, "I'll bet!" If Ike had stumbled into Wyatt's posse when he was making his final cleanup of Tombstone's hinterlands, he'd have been left for the buzzards like a lot of others were. He was probably number one on Wyatt's list after Behan.

Since I was so close to it, it took a long while to see that what happened at Tombstone was more than an exceptionally bloody local incident. It provided a classic example of every aspect of frontier existence that caused violence; and **violence** is the aspect of those times that has perennially fascinated later generations. Cowboy movies make that case: you might see the hero without mountains behind him, without his horse, with no cows in sight, but never without his six-shooter, and maybe two of them and a Winchester to boot.

Tombstone and the Earp Saga were the Trojan War of the pioneer West. Wyatt was cast in the dual role of Paris and Achilles; Behan was the outraged Agamemnon; Josie, the temptress stolen by Wyatt, was Helen of Troy; and Stuart Lake, author of the epic *Wyatt Earp, Frontier Marshal* was the Homer who made it all unforgettable. (If she hadn't decided to be stuffy about it, Josie probably would have laughed at the idea of being the face that launched, not a thousand ships, but a hundred gunfighters; no mean accomplishment.)

In 1910 none of this had **fully** dawned on me, but I knew enough to keep notes on everything Wyatt said and on what I myself had witnessed that had a bearing on that great drama. Bill Miller, who was not a sophisticated person, sensed what I'm trying to express here, and kept a diary on his Uncle Wyatt. Even Wyatt Earp himself, and the few others like him — and there were precious few of them — sensed that they had been chosen by God for a special destiny, that they had been latter day knights of the Roundtable. Maybe he talked at last because he wished to be vindicated

148

by the lasting verdict of history. He likely chose me as confidante for three reasons: because he knew I was a writer of more than average ability, because I had experienced much of his great adventure with him and, most importantly, because I was a trusted friend.

With respect to having witnessed part of his adventure, I confess that because of my allegiance to the Behan faction in the beginning there was much I couldn't tell Wyatt. If I had, he may not have continued to view me as a trusted friend. Life is like that. Yet, I had done no more than Josie; I had simply been on one side first, then came to my senses and joined the other. (With a small, significant difference, of course: there had been no vendetta till she changed sides; the vendetta was in its final stages when I did.)

In any case, I thought I knew the whole story even before I heard Wyatt out on the subject. (As I'll tell later, Doc had told me a lot of what Wyatt confirmed, but I was still in for a surprise, since even Doc wasn't privy to the full story of Wyatt's backers, though he suspected the truth.)

Wyatt had to trust me implicitly, and Bill as well, to reveal what he did, because there is no statute of limitations on murder. Much of what he did could be considered criminal by later, softer generations who may think they know what the Code of the West meant, but really don't. It's remarkably simple; the Code at it most elemental meant: "The bullet holes were in the front of the late, unlamented sons of bitches!" No more, no less. That was the only way the Earps killed. Their enemies preferred the other way and only fought fair once, when forced to it, which explains the showdown between the Earps and Doc Holliday on one side and the McLaury and Clanton brothers on the other, in the street fight that Stuart Lake immortalized as The Gunfight at the O.K Corral.

What follows could well be made into a rousing book, perhaps with the title, *Wyatt Earp Remembers*. It is as much in his own words as I could remember when I wrote them down after the fact. I vouch that the sense of nothing he said is changed.

There, around the campfire, with the two sources of light painting the scene in a most haunting fashion, and coyote music in the background, Wyatt began:

"The trouble started at Las Vegas (New Mexico) before I was even sure I wanted to go to Tombstone. I quit 'lawing' in Dodge earlier that year (Sept. 1879) with my belly full. Never wanted to go back to it."

He puffed on his pipe to keep it lit and shifted in his chair, looking into the fire as though he was back there in Las Vegas some thirty years earlier. I hoped he wasn't going to stop there and looked across at Bill. He gave a warning shake of his head.

I don't think Wyatt even knew we were there any longer. He seemed to be talking to himself. He shook his head impatiently.

"I should have stuck with that. I went to Vegas

because Doc Holliday was there and said there were a lot of good business prospects. On the other hand, my brother Virg was wheedling me and Jim to go to Tombstone with him. Jim kind of thought we ought to stake out a place in the Texas Panhandle and start a cattle ranch, and I had the taste in my mouth for that. Looking back, I wish we had.

"Anyhow I met Jim Hume the first time in Las Vegas. I had a bum run of luck at the tables and was glad to take him up on it when he got me a couple jobs as shotgun guard on the railroad. Jim was chief of detectives for Wells Fargo, had been for years, was till the day he died a few years back. (1904.) I mentioned to Hume that we might go to Tombstone and he jumped on that and said, 'Be sure to let me know if you do.' That should have warned me I might be drawing cards in a rigged game.

"I didn't know it yet then, but Wells Fargo made a business of putting their own men into law jobs wherever they could in boom camps that didn't have any real law. They had Tombstone figured as such a spot. They sure as hell didn't miss their guess on that.

"Well, like a damn fool, I let Hume know when I decided it was going to be Tombstone for us Earps. He took me up on it so quick that I had a shotgun job on a stage taking a coin shipment in there while the rest of the family was following down with the wagons from Tucson. Charley Shibell offered me a job as deputy sheriff, but I didn't take him up on that till later, and then only because Jim Hume thought it would be a good idea. Wells Fargo had another fellow lined up for that part of the country too — Bob Paul. He'd worked for them on and off for years. He and Hume were friends going back to the Gold Rush days up in the Mother Lode country in California. Neither one of them were spring chickens anymore."

I assumed Wyatt was leading his story back to how Ike Clanton got his old man killed, which was how he'd started, and it did eventually, but before then I got a reading on a lot that happened at Tombstone before I got there in January 1881. By then the Earps had been there a little over a year. The seeds of bad blood had already been sown between them, as representatives of law and order on behalf of the principal business men of the community, and the Cowboy Gang and their local supporters such as Sheriff Behan and the McLaury Boys.

Wyatt went on, recalling how it had been:
"Wells Fargo had Bob Paul picked as their man to run for sheriff of Pima County against Charley Shibell. At that time Tombstone was still in Pima County, with the county seat at Tucson. Bob came in and worked like I did as shotgun guard and detective for Wells Fargo in 1880, waiting till the fall elections. He was a deputy U.S. marshal under Crawley Dake too, just like Virg. When I took the job as deputy sheriff under Shibell in July 1880,

I sent for my brother Morg to come over from California as shotgun guard on the regular runs."

This vividly recalled to my mind the handsome, blond young man who'd been riding shotgun on the very first stage that took me into Tombstone, tall, slender with the cold Earp eye, who'd almost bumped into Curly Bill as we were getting into the stage. Viewed in hindsight, I especially recalled the tense little scene when they eyed one another like two little feice dogs, then finally spoke. That young man, of course, had been Morg Earp. The tension between them related to the earlier, not necessarily gentle, arrest of Curly by Morg's brother, who was sitting here with us now and about to tell me more about the roots of that animosity than I'd ever known.

Wyatt, of course, had no way of knowing what his story had recalled for me, and continued: "The deputy job took a lot of time — I didn't know the half of it when I took it.* I was riding all over the country. That's when the trouble started that ended up in our street fight with the cowboys the next year.

"A Captain Hurst from Fort Rucker came to Tombstone shortly after I got the deputy job, hot under the collar over some mules that had been

---

* The case book of Judge James Riley is still informally on file with the Cochise County Recorder, and if Riley had been the only justice to whom Wyatt took cases, he would have been one of the busiest lawmen in creation, yet there were several other J.P.'s. — **GB.**

rustled from Fort Rucker. Going after them was Virg's job as Deputy U.S. Marshal since the mules were government property, but Morg and I went along as possemen. Hurst and a few soldiers came too. Long before I got the deputy's star, I built up ways to hear things by the grapevine. It's part of being an officer and I'd had a lot of experience by then. I had no trouble finding out who got the mules and where they were.

"We went down to the McLaury ranch about where the Babocamari runs into the San Pedro — this was before they moved over to Soldier Hole. I'd been told we'd find the mules there. The McLaury boys gave Hurst a song and dance about not knowing the mules were rustled. If they didn't they were pretty damn dense, since the U.S. brands had just been burned over into D.S. on the two they ran up out of the brush first. They said they'd get the rest in as soon as they could find them, and turn them over to Hurst if he'd camp there over night. He told us we could go on back to Tombstone because he wouldn't need us anymore. I said we'd better stick around till he got the mules, but he didn't think so. On the way back to Tombstone I told Virg Hurst would need several days' rations the way it looked to me if he aimed to stay around till he got his mules. Virg thought so too. We were dead right. Hurst never did get his mules and had a cussing match in the papers with Frank McLaury, who had a mean temper. Frank even came in and cussed Virg out for coming along with Hurst. Virg just laughed at him and told him if he was looking for a fuss he'd come to the right customer.

"From then on the McLaurys were our enemies, though we didn't know it yet. Virg wrote off Frank as a blow hard, though he set himself up to be a good shot. He had the reputation, and the next year I was over at their ranch and saw enough spent cartridges layin' around to believe they must practice a lot. Shooting it out takes more than that though, as Frank later found out to his sorrow."

That's as close as I ever heard Wyatt come to bragging. He obviously meant that Frank McLaury, who he really didn't like long before the shooting started, had been an innocent bunny rabbit against real fighting men.

Wyatt knocked the dottle out of his pipe and shoved it into his shirt pocket. Earpie came up about then from a cruise in the brush and asked for a pet. Wyatt scratched his ears and the dog lay down beside his chair and Wyatt put his hand affectionately on his head and idly continued to stroke the animal. I recalled Josie saying, "Wyatt likes animals better than people," but she didn't say it when he was around. I think maybe that was so, with the exception of her. At least animals hadn't double crossed him at every turn in his life.

He said, "Bill, how about puttin' on another pot of coffee?"

Bill got busy at that, but before he did he said,

"I brought you something I thought you'd like, Uncle Wyatt." (He never called him Wyatt, perhaps thinking it would be taking a liberty a young fellow wasn't entitled to. I'll vouch for the fact that Wyatt didn't look like the kind any kid off the street ought to try calling Wyatt.) Bill produced a cigar from an inside jacket pocket. He'd probably been keeping it there as his best bet to keep Wyatt talking, since it had worked like a charm the first time, as he'd told me. He gave one to Wyatt and passed a second over to me.

Wyatt looked the cigar over like it was a treasure and slipped it under his nose and sniffed it appreciatively. "Thank you kindly, Bill," he said, sniffing it. He wasn't used to people looking out for him very much and it always seemed to surprise him. Earpie got up to investigate the possibility that it was food and Wyatt let him smell it. "You don't smoke these," he told the dog, talking to him like he would a human. That seemed to satisfy Earpie who lay down again and put his head on his paws, watching Bill who looked like he might be getting ready to cook something.

"I believe I'll wait to light this up till I get a cup of coffee," Wyatt said. I knew how he felt. They seem to go together for a real cigar smoker.

It was awhile before we got settled with our coffee. Wyatt finished his and was puffing on his cigar before he took up his story again.

He said, "Bob Paul ran for sheriff that fall and since I supported him I resigned as Shibell's deputy. It was a relief to get rid of the job.

"About the last thing I did as deputy sheriff was run in Curly Bill for shooting Marshal Fred White at Tombstone. Fred went out to put a stop to what he thought was a bunch of drunk cowboys shooting at the moon. I was down at Vogan's where Jim worked a shift when the shooting started. I ran up the street to the fracas which was in an empty lot about where they built the Bird Cage Theater later. When I got there Fred was facing Curly Bill who had a pistol in his hand. I grabbed Curly from behind and pinned his arms. Like a damn fool White grabbed Curly's gun and it went off. It looked like an accident and might have been. Curly's pistol would go off on half cock, and he claimed Fred set it off when he jerked it out of his hand. In any case I didn't know that and turned Curly loose and pasted him over the head with my Colt. I gave him one hell of a whack. There was more shooting from the rest of his crowd. By then Morg and Fred Dodge got up there and I told them to take care of White and run in Curly while I rounded up the rest. I gave them the same treatment I gave Curly.

"It looked like some of Fred's friends might treat Curly to a necktie party so he waived examination right quick and I took him up to Tucson the next morning. We had Curly over a barrel, since my testimony could get him off, which worked out first rate."

I didn't follow Wyatt's line of reasoning there and almost asked him what he meant, but I didn't have to, since he realized he'd better explain it, and brought up something I really hadn't known about before.

"Just about then the election came off for sheriff and it looked like Paul lost. It also looked like that cowboy crowd stuffed the ballot box up in their bailiwick at San Simon. They turned in over 100 votes for Shibell in a precinct with half a dozen legal voters. To show you what kind of an election that was, the returns were turned over to Phin Clanton after the election. Paul came to me and said he'd been robbed. I figured I could get the crowd to squeal on Curly Bill's say-so. And I figured he'd give his say-so provided I got him off on the White shooting. I was right and it went to court where some of Curly's boys owned up and, after a lot of jawing Paul finally got the election.

"While he was waiting for the courts to decide the affair, Paul was still riding shotgun for Wells Fargo and generally working as a lawman. He was doing that when the stage was held up between Tombstone and Benson and Bud Philpot was killed."

Wyatt resumed his tale after a long pause with another new twist; at least new to me:

"You know what was behind that holdup? Paul had already been awarded the election as sheriff by Judge French at Tucson, but the case was on appeal. It looked like he was apt to win the appeal too. So when that crowd shot Philpot, it was plain as day they were trying to get rid of Paul and mistook the two of them since Paul was driving for Bud who was under the weather with a bowel gripe.

"That was paying off a political debt, since Shibell hadn't really bothered the outlaws too much. I had. But not on Shibell's say-so. Just the opposite. They wouldn't have liked Paul, but by then most of their dirty work didn't take place in his jurisdiction (Pima County) any more. Behan and Shibell had been pretty thick for years. They were both old Arizona democrats. Behan simply sicced his boys on Paul as a favor to his crony."

Wyatt took another breather. It was the longest speech I'd ever heard come out of him since the night he'd come in off the trail of the those stage robbers. His thoughts seemed to be running along the same lines as mine. He puffed on his cigar to keep it going good, staring into the fire with his mind obviously far away. Finally he said:

"That reminds me of something that we hushed up while we worked on the case. Paul knew there were eight robbers that jumped the stage, and the papers reported that, then let it drop. When we caught Luther King, he only mentioned three others: Harry Head, Billy Leonard, and Jim Crane. There was a good reason he didn't mention the others. He was scared to death of them. They were Curly Bill, Ike Clanton, Pete Spence and Frank Stilwell. All they had to do to get away was ride back up the road cut around Contention, then show up in Charleston and hang around the saloons, acting like they'd been there all evening. I checked up on that later and they'd all been seen

159

in Charleston that night.

"I'd stake my life on it today that Behan was in a helluva sweat about getting rid of King because he was afraid he'd cave in and squeal on *all* of them involved. It's a wonder they didn't kill him."

I could have told him why they didn't. Harry Woods wouldn't have stood still for having his brother put out of the way. But, of course, this was no time to tell Wyatt Earp how I knew that. I couldn't be certain that if I levelled with him for the first time after all those years it wouldn't have shattered his trust in me.

He rambled off a little on something else that it reminded him of:

"The democratic crowd had a lot of political pull. Behan and his cronies aimed to clean out the treasury in the new county by holding down all the good jobs. Johnny must have raked in a fortune in the two years he was sheriff, especially with his crony, Dunbar as treasurer. Wells Fargo had other ideas, at least about the sheriff's job, and tried to get the appointment for me. They didn't realize yet how slick those Arizona democrats were, though. Neither did I. Or how crooked Johnny Behan was either."

The desert night had turned chilly while Wyatt talked of the past, the fire had burned down again to coals, Earpie was sound asleep, and Wyatt still hadn't gotten back to his original point about Ike

160

getting his father killed. He hadn't forgotten though. As we got up to turn in, seeming to realize that he had us on the hook about that, he said, "About Ike — it'll keep."

I hoped it wouldn't have to keep this time as it had up till then, for almost thirty years.

Chapter 12

How Old Man Clanton Died

We didn't get back to Wyatt's story the next evening as I hoped we might because Dude came back shortly after sunup, shy one horse and riding the other, the wagon left down at the ferry. I heard Earpie barking long before he got to camp, but figured he was cutting loose at coyotes and rolled over and went back to sleep. A little later voices woke me up. They sounded urgent.

I heard Wyatt say, "What the hell happened?"

A strange voice said, "Some sonofabitch stole Tom, I think."

"He didn't just wander off?"

"Hell no. Two sets of tracks; his and whoever ran him off. I got in sight of 'em and the bastard dropped a round in front of me. Sounded like a .30-30. I only had the .22 with me."

Bill got dressed and went out before I did. I hated to leave the warm blankets because it was still plenty nippy that time of the year till the sun had been up awhile. When I poked my head out

I got my first sight of Dude. He was something to lay eyes on. I could see why Wyatt called him Dude. He **wasn't**. I remembered Wyatt's Second Class Saloon in Alaska — it **wasn't** either. It was the fanciest in town.

Dude was wearing an old overcoat, cut off just below the pockets and frayed out at the bottom, greasy corduroy pants that hadn't had a bath in a long while, three bandannas around his neck, two red, one blue, a very wide-brimmed hat that might have been white once but was now mostly green, beneath which his long hair streamed out on the sides and behind. He had an Indian face, but sure didn't talk like one, except for the peculiar rhythm that Indian voices have, no matter what tribe, a musical flow and intonation.

By this time Bill was busy with coffee and bacon. We even had eggs, since we'd brought down several dozen from Needles. Wyatt wasn't the kind to rush off on an empty stomach unless time was pressing.

While I was getting dressed I'd heard him ask Dude, "Which way did they go?"

Dude said, "Down the river. I hope I haven't lost us a horse."

"I don't think so," Wyatt said. Somehow, from the way he said it, I didn't think so either.

"Bring up the mules and saddle 'em while Bill's fixin' some grub."

After a quick breakfast, Wyatt went into his tent and came out wearing a six-shooter and carrying a rifle. Since a lot of people have asked me about

Wyatt's guns, for the record the six-shooter was an old .45 Army model he'd carried since Dodge City. (Except for the trail, he carried a .45 double action with a shorter barrel, usually stuck in his belt or in his back pocket.) The rifle was a modern .30-40 Krag bolt action like the Army'd used in Cuba. He handed that to Dude with a box of shells and went back in and came out with his lever action Winchester shotgun. I suspect that was loaded with double-aught buck. He carried it looped to the saddle horn. Dude had a saddle boot for the rifle.

Bill and I watched them mount up. Wyatt was mighty spry at getting aboard a horse for a man his age — sixty-two then. I needed a soap box or a rock to stand on and get my foot in a stirrup, I'm ashamed to say.

Wyatt circled his mule back to us and said to Bill, "How about a couple of those good cigars. I might be out awhile."

He shoved those in his pocket and took off after Dude. The sun was a couple of hours high.

To Bill, I said, "Can the Indian hit anything with a rifle?" recalling that gun sights were a mystery to most of them.

Bill said, "You'd be surprised."

I was. Later on I watched Dude powder a rock not much bigger than a man's head at three hundred yards, unloading a whole magazine into it, shooting offhand. I heard at the time that he'd been with the Army in Cuba, but never found out for sure. Also that he'd been in the pen afterward for a shooting. At any rate, he obviously wasn't your typical blanket Indian.

I was a trifle concerned when the two didn't get back by dark. I asked Bill, "You think something might have happened to them?"

He looked at me like I might be a little tetched. He said, "Not likely." Then after a little while, added, "I reckon something might have happened to somebody by now, but not those two."

I wished that I felt as confident as he did, but Wyatt wasn't as young as he used to be. I was slowing down and was younger than he. I didn't sleep too well that night, probably keeping an ear cocked in case they came back. Speculation about how we'd get some help for them occupied my mind for awhile before I went to sleep. It was something to ponder. The closest places to get help were Needles or Yuma, both a couple of days away, and neither with lawmen that had jurisdiction on our side of the river, not that they wouldn't have come out anyhow. Your hardware was your jurisdiction. We didn't stand on formality in those days. But, if Wyatt and Dude didn't come back and someone had to search for them, the likeliest candidates were me and Bill — with one big draft horse between us to ride. I couldn't see us doing a "ride and tie" jaunt out there in the Mojave with its scant roads and trails. I could have spared myself the worry. Wyatt and Dude returned about noon the next day with Tom in tow. He had a big reunion with his team mate, Jerry.

"I'm hungry," Wyatt said, even before he dismounted. I expected him to get down stiffly, but he hopped off as spry as Dude did.

Bill got a fire going in the outside grill where he preferred to cook and soon got potatoes in the pot and carved steaks off a beef quarter hung in the ramada. Wyatt sprawled in a camp chair and got his pipe going while Dude unsaddled, turned the mules loose and came over and squatted on the ground, rolling a wheat straw cigarette. I never saw him use a chair in all the years I knew him. He'd definitely gone back to the blanket in that sense — and many others, such as an aversion to soap and water. Neither he nor Wyatt said anything.

I finally risked a question. "What happened?"

Wyatt grinned and motioned with his thumb toward Tom. "We found him."

"So I see. Where?" I meant how, but was afraid to ask.

"Down almost to Charlie Welsh's ranch."

I'd heard of it; it was down near where Blythe was just about to hatch as a town that year. Anyhow, that was all I got out of either of them. Later, with Wyatt out of hearing, I overheard Dude tell Bill, "We kicked ass plenty on that bastard. I wanted to take his horse, but Wyatt said no."

I guess that meant they hadn't killed the horse thief. Somehow I was relieved to know that.

That night Wyatt seemed still primed to get the Tombstone story off his chest, as I'd prayed he would be. I was **really** eager to hear more after

I found out I didn't know as much about it as I thought I did.

Dude had gone down for the wagon and wasn't back yet, so it was just the three of us around the fire. Bill passed out cigars again, which may have been a charm. After we were lit up and comfortable, Wyatt opened up.

"I about got my voice back," he said.

"Good," I said, and wished I hadn't because he didn't say another word for a long while — I was afraid I'd sounded too eager and put him off. Finally he looked at me and said, "You knew Doc Holliday, didn't you, Ted?"

"Sure. Not too well, of course, but I had a talk or two with him."

EDITORIAL COMMENT:

Elsewhere, Ten Eyck mentions his playing down of his relations with Doc when talking to Wyatt, a newsman's instinct to cross check his informants. In his case it was a matter of concealing a great deal from Wyatt, probably wisely.

"Doc wasn't easy to know. I never figured out why he took a shine to me. I first met him down at Ft. Griffin in Texas. I sat in a few poker games with him. Later, in Dodge, he threw down on a drunk Texas cowboy that aimed to back shoot me. He didn't have any call to do that, but I wouldn't be here if he hadn't." He was quiet awhile, thinking about that. "Up till then I'd seen him around Dodge and had a speaking acquaintance, but we weren't pals. I think maybe Doc did that more because he didn't like Texans, than for me. He had no reason to like lawmen any more than he did Texans, but they tried to string him up down in Texas and he had to pull his freight damn quick. After that I had a talk or two with him, and we started to play poker together quite a bit. He stayed out of trouble in Dodge, which wasn't like him. In fact he had an office as a dentist, the last time I ever knew him to practice regularly, though he did it on and off."

"Doc was in trouble most of the time. He wasn't in Tombstone a week before he got into a fuss or two with somebody. He was usually tight when he did and mostly in the right, too. He just didn't let anyone step on his toes, and it got him a bad reputation. He'd killed a few men, but from what he told me, it was a groundhog case of kill or be killed."

I recalled Doc in his hey day. A good looking man when he was in Tombstone, well-dressed, always well-groomed, which made him stand out in a time and place not noted for either, in fact just the opposite. His eyes were unforgettable, light blue like Wyatt's, only with a ghostly look, as deep set as they were and wonderfully piercing. They looked right through you. He wasn't a mean looking man though, unless he was mad and, in fact, he was full of comic pranks, such as grabbing one of those little iron fire alarm triangles that were hung here and there on the sidewalks in Tombstone, and traipsing behind some dude with

168

a derby hat ringing it and pointing to the hat. No one ran him in for turning in a false alarm that I know of. Tombstone was the kind of place that thought it was pretty funny when he was like that. Doc's targets may not have thought it was funny, but after looking him in the eye, none of them felt like complaining. He had "the look." There's something about a killer that shows.

Doc wasn't the kind who would let some bruiser get close enough to manhandle him before he jerked a pistol. When he was drunk and mad only the Earp boys could get him under control. They were the only real friends he had and Doc had a code about friends, whether he was drunk or sober. They could do no wrong and his enemies no right. It was a credo that served the Earps nobly when the chips were down.

Wyatt continued his story, still thinking about Doc and the Kinnear stage holdup he'd discussed the night before.

"Doc's bad reputation set him up to take a fall over that stage holdup. Harry Woods made up the whole thing from what Harry Jones told me later."

How well I knew that. And a lot more. L.C. Hughes who ran the *Star* in Tucson picked up the *Nugget*'s lies and repeated them. Hughes, Shibell and Behan were old political cronies. I learned from friends in Arizona that there was a falling out later and Hughes branded Behan as the crook he was. Maybe Johnny played deadbeat on him like he did me. At any rate, I remembered how those lying newspaper stories about Doc being one of the stage robbers pulled the wool over a lot of eyes. Wyatt got to that next.

"The voters knew Doc and I were pretty thick. If he wasn't cleared of that robbery business it would sink my boat as a candidate for sheriff, which Wells Fargo had me set up for. I had to clear Doc to clear my own skirts. The best way to do it was pull in Leonard, Head and Crane and sweat them. Billy Leonard might have cleared Doc just because they were old friends from Las Vegas.

"I hadn't been able to get a lead on those three after they outran our posse. I'd bet a peck that Behan could have turned them up anytime he wanted to. He wasn't about to tell anyone where they were though, since he had more to worry about if they talked than anyone. I got thinking that there might be someone in his office that would spill the beans and Billy Breakenridge came to mind. Remember him?"

I laughed. "Who doesn't?"

"You knew he was a Queen, didn't you?"

Everyone did. He was Curly Bill's favorite, I discovered to my horror at the time. Of course, there was a lot of that among cowboys who weren't really that way — it was simply a case of not enough women, or none. Everyone on the frontier understood that. But the Queens were **that way** by preference. Billy was pretty popular, whatever the reason. In later years, after almost everyone who could contradict him was dead, he made himself out to be *Tombstone's Deputy*. Actually he was a janitor at the jail most of the time, and a sometime tax collector. They probably paid him as a deputy, so he had the title. Some of the old newspaper articles call him a deputy. I know of only three times he operated as a real one.

Wyatt continued, "Billy was a gossip. It's a wonder it didn't get him killed. Anyhow, I thought I'd butter him up and pump him a little, so I bought him a drink and mentioned what I had on my mind. I sort of dropped in word about the big Wells Fargo rewards on the robbers. Billy claimed he didn't know where they were, but a little while later Ike Clanton stopped me on the street and said he'd like to talk to me on the sly. I'd give eight to five that Billy put him up to it. Anyhow, I arranged a meeting where we could talk and Ike said he'd heard there were rewards on Jim Crane and his pals. To make a long story short, Ike said he could get those fellows to come in where they could be nabbed and was game to try provided he got the rewards without anyone finding out.

"Naturally I asked him how he aimed to do that. He said he'd tell them there was a big payroll due on a stage the same day every week and he wanted help to knock one off. That made sense, since I knew for sure by then that Ike had been one of the "eight" that Bob Paul had seen at the holdup site. He was plenty thick with all three of the ones I wanted, and they'd trust him. Breakenridge probably knew that, since Behan was bound to — he hired them for the job, and may have got

171

careless and dropped a word around the office and been overheard by Billy. Ike probably promised Billy a cut of the rewards for putting him onto a good thing, and to keep him quiet. Ike would have been in serious trouble with his own crowd if they knew what he aimed to do."

Here Wyatt was evading something he knew, that I later discovered — that Ike was actually playing him for a sucker, as I'll relate further along. Wyatt was sensitive to looking foolish. This may be why he told a similar story to both Flood and later to Lake, assuming that's where they got it.

Wyatt continued:

"Anyhow, Ike and I shook on the deal and he told me he'd need a couple of friends to help him; somebody he could trust. He said he'd get in touch with me and bring the others along. Sure enough, in a few days he met me out in that little court behind the Oriental and brought along Frank McLaury and Joe Hill."

Wyatt chuckled and said "I thought: 'Ike, you may trust these two, but I wouldn't trust them as far as I could throw a horse.' And, in their shoes, I'd have trusted Ike about that far too. None of them were fools and probably felt just about like I did. Anyhow, we cooked up a deal. Hill said he knew where he could find our birds, over in the Animas country, near Old Man Clanton's ranch. He would have them come over to the McLaury ranch, which by then was over around Soldier Hole, close enough to ride over to the road into Tombstone in a few hours. Ike would get word to me when they were in our net. Then he said, 'Say, does that reward go dead or alive?' I thought it did, but figured I'd better wire Jim Hume to be sure. I got a wire back and showed it to Ike. We shook on the deal again.

"Right after that the deal started to unravel on us. First of all, Leonard and Head tried to pull a stick up over at Hachita and got themselves filled with lead. I knew Crane was still alive though, since he got his crowd together and rubbed out the two that had killed his pals. Nevertheless, Crane was just as good a canary for my purposes as all three.

"I told Ike as much and I could see him practically licking his lips. He had good reason to hope we had to beef Crane so the last of that crowd that might squeal was pushing up daisies. After that Joe Hill came in with Ike and they said they'd located Crane. Hill would go over and offer him the bait. That talk was in Virg's office. After they left Virg and I talked it over. He wasn't for trusting Hill. I didn't blame him, though I thought in this case he'd probably do what he said. Hill was a shifty character with a bad reputation from over in the Lincoln County trouble in New Mexico a few years before — a Texas style killer."

If I understood that right he meant that Hill preferred to get them right where the suspenders cross.

"Virg had already asked Hill how we could be sure we'd ever see him again and he left his turnip watch and his bankroll with Virg as a sort of ransom. That's rich. He probably stole the watch somewhere. Hill told us he expected to find Crane over at Old Man Clanton's ranch which was right near the Mexican line near a place called Cloverdale. He promised to be back and tell us when the deal was set."

This looks like Ike and his pals were really planning to go for the reward at that time, and found reason to change their minds later, as I'll tell about.

Wyatt continued, "After Hill was gone Virg said, 'We can't trust him. Let's get some of the boys together and go get Crane ourselves. Maybe if we're quick about it we can follow Hill.' "

Wyatt stopped there as though he was seeing it all again in his mind. He said, "There was no way to get a posse together quick in a place like Tombstone without raising a stir. Someone would have been sure to start asking questions. In the first place most of the boys didn't have horses of their own and had to rent them from a livery stable. As it was they rented them from separate stables and it took till next day to line up outfits. Even at that there were probably people around apt to put two and two together. I told Virg, 'This is a damn fool stunt. We're gonna go on a wild goose chase. At least one of us ought to stay around town so some of the Cowboy crowd doesn't smell a rat and try to follow us and see what we're up to.'

"So Virg agreed to stay in town and manage to be seen. Even at that I led that posse against my better judgement. I was dead right in my hunch as it turned out."

Wyatt surprised me by grinning just then. He was obviously remembering something funny.

"Spill it," I couldn't help but say.

"We got together east of town before sunup, coming out separately to where the old powder house was. Doc brought along two of those big Mexican hats and gave me one. He said, 'Put it on. If we run into anyone, they'll think we're greaser bandits and give us plenty of room.' I told him I didn't want the damn thing, so Charlie Smith wore it.

"We spent the first night in the Swisshelms. Sherm McMasters was along because he knew all that country from working under cover for Jim Hume. Everyone thought he was a member of Curly Bill's gang till he came out from under cover. The next day we got over in the Animas country and in the afternoon almost ran smack into a herd of cattle being driven our way. Out there the odds were they were hot. We shagged out of the way in time not to be seen. We figured Crane might be with the crowd. Doc, who'd played poker with Crane, was the only one of us that knew what he looked like real well, so he took my field glasses and looked over the cowboys pushing that herd. When he came back he said, 'Guess who's along besides Crane, drivin' the wagon? Old Man Clanton himself.'

"We talked it over and decided to shadow them and throw down on them just as they were rolling out in the morning and nab Crane. The furthest thing from my mind was that they'd put up a fight. We worked up close by sunup, and I yelled for them to throw up their hands, and Sherm did the same in Spanish in case some of them were greasers. Between that and those two big hats they probably thought we were Mexicans after the herd, which they probably stole down there. Anyhow they put up a hell of a fight."

EDITORIAL COMMENT:

The newspapers of that day place the killing of Old Man Clanton and the others in Guadalupe Canyon, as does the memoir of John Pleasant Gray, whose brother Dixie Lee Gray was killed with that party. Billy Breakenridge, who was more conversant with the hinterlands of Cochise County and southwestern New Mexico than anyone except members of Curly Bill's gang, placed the killing in Skeleton Canyon. He had probably been told that by gang members, and may have had the spot pointed out to him by one or another of them at some time, even Curly Bill, himself. My personal familiarity with that country and the descendants of old-timers who lived there causes me to favor Billy Breakenridge. The Clanton Ranch was located about three miles south of the eastern entrance of Skeleton Canyon, and there was a good road through it at that time, of which traces are still visible on the east side, and a good road still remains on the west side of the divide. On the other hand, Guadalupe Canyon is far more difficult of negotiation. Couple this with the rec-ollections of the people living there that they were always told the site of the killing was Skeleton Canyon. There is no logical reason why a herd of cattle, unless just stolen from Mexico, which those being driven had not been, would have been headed through Guadalupe Canyon.

Ten Eyck continues his narrative, with Wyatt still talking:

Wyatt looked at me then and said, "You read about it in the papers. It turned out bringing those big hats along had a bright side. The one that got away reported that we were probably Mexican militia. Those fellows knew what'd happen to them if they ever fell into their hands, which was why they put up a fight. Doc got pinked in the leg and Warren took a bad flesh wound in the shoulder muscle. We had to smuggle them out of the country through Deming where we put them on the train. Morg took Warren home to Ma and Pa to heal up and Doc said he had a hankering to go back to Georgia for a visit."

Here was another complete surprise for me. It explained why Doc was getting around with a cane at the time of the street fight with the Cowboys and why Warren wasn't in town where he'd have been sure to join his brothers in that fracas.

I recalled rumors in Tombstone right after I got back in September that the Earps were suspected by some of having a hand in doing in Old Man Clanton. And, as the saying goes, "Murder will out!" Those suspicions deepened the animosity between the Clanton boys and the Earps and weren't the least of the reasons that Ike finally went on the warpath after them. By then he had another more pressing reason. The story of his attempted double cross of his associates came out, and he blamed Wyatt Earp for spilling the beans.

Actually though, there was a surprise angle even to that, which I learned from Jim Earp after I first wrote the above years ago.

When Wyatt wound up his story, he eyed me and asked, "Did that surprise you, Ted?"

Actually I'd heard a version of that story from Virg Earp up at Vandenberg. He and I and Allie had an old time get together when I was up there looking over the prospects. It is obvious to me that the Earps made two forays after Crane, maybe more, and Wyatt was a trifle mixed up or careless regarding which one he was telling us about. After all, it had been almost thirty years before. The one he told about would have been the first time if they went out right after Hill left. When they ran across the outlaws and killed Crane and Old Man Clanton would have been the last one. I think that after Hill came back with the news that Leonard and Head were killed, the Earps waited awhile for Ike to come up with Crane's whereabouts, then went out on their own to scour the country in the vicinity of Old Man Clanton's ranch. That made the first foray in June and the last in August.

Anyhow, in regard to Wyatt's question whether it surprised me I could truthfully tell him, "Not entirely. I recall talk at the time."

Wyatt nodded. "The Clanton boys knew. We had to be on our guard from then on. The big shivaree was only a couple of months coming after that. Before that the fat got in the fire again when we pulled in Stilwell and Spence for robbing the Bisbee stage." He snorted. "Stilwell was Behan's deputy at the time. Clum really roasted Johnny for that in the *Epitaph*."

How well I remembered. It was the beginning of my real serious doubts about my smiling Irish friend.

Wyatt didn't tell me then, or ever, how the Clanton Boys really found out the Earp posse had killed their father; but Jim Earp did, as I'll relate in due time.

One night I asked Wyatt directly about the taking-off of Ike, since he'd brought it up.

He said, "I was going to tell you that. Slipped my mind. I'm glad you brought it up. Did you ever hear of a character named Rawhide Jake Brighton?"

I told him, "I can't say as I have."

"Well, back in the late eighties when Ike cashed in, Brighton was a deputy sheriff up in northern Arizona under Commodore Perry Owens. Brighton wrote me a letter when I was in San Diego. I don't know how he knew I was there — maybe through the newspapers, or maybe because he was a 'scientific detective.' That's how he put it, anyhow."

Wyatt chuckled, which was as close to laughing as he ever came, to my knowledge.

"Brighton told me he took a 'scientific detective' course by mail, and said I ought to if I planned to go back to lawing — but this is getting ahead of my story. I hadn't met him yet then. His letter was to ask me if I knew of any rewards out on Clanton which he figured I might know because he'd heard of our trouble with Ike at Tombstone. I thought he might be a crank, and come to think of it he probably was. He told me Clanton was up in his neck of the woods and a general trouble maker. I wrote back and told him to get in touch with Jim Hume at Wells Fargo. The next I heard of Brighton was in the papers at the time of the Sontag-Evans business. Some time after that somebody pointed me out to him in a saloon in Frisco and he came over and introduced himself. I asked him if he ever got in touch with Jim Hume. He said, 'I sure did, and I owe you a drink.'

"I didn't ask him why and he didn't offer any information, except to tell me he'd beefed Ike with a Winchester when Ike tried to run away after he yelled to him to throw up his hands.

"That was the last I ever saw or heard of Brighton."

Knowing the old time Wells Fargo manner of doing business, I can figure what Brighton owed Wyatt a drink for, and I suppose Wyatt figured the same.

Chapter 13

I Move To Tombstone

Tuesday, August 22, 1881.

There is no finer climate than the Tombstone area. (Some days.) I returned to Tombstone the third and final time in August, 1881. I travelled by stagecoach through a 'gully-washer' between Benson and Contention that day. The teams were barely manageable during the height of the downpour, alternately trying to run away, then dashing off the road into each clump of mesquite to gain some shelter, I suppose. Whether the driver's unbelievable profanity, or God's intercession, averted our being upset, with the possibility of injuries or death, I was grateful to come through with a whole skin.

I recall that my stomach was tied in a knot even while I clung for dear life to anything that I could get hold of to keep from being beaten to death by the coach or the passengers flopping around. Our bodies were like projectiles at times. Those riding on top had a far worse time since they would have been thrown off, and if we upset could have landed under the coach. They were soaked to the skin, and we were a long ways from dry inside.

We were delayed at least an hour while a temporary river subsided. It was roaring down the same wash where Bud Philpot had been killed during the holdup attempt in March.

So much for romantic stage coach travel. We all got out, thankful to be alive, when the driver got the rig stopped just short of inundation at the brink of the rushing transient river. Several men volunteered to hold onto the bridles of the nervous horses and managed to calm them with reassuring talk. I was grateful that a lot of experienced horsemen were around in those days. I wasn't one. It would be hard to find someone who could harness a horse today, but I've learned how since then and a lot more about horses. Then I wouldn't have got near one of those horses on a bet. In fact, I was thinking of walking the rest of the way in if the water ever went down. It was my first experience of an Arizona boulder-roller.

In plain sight over toward the Whetstones was another huge storm, the water pouring down so densely it looked like a black pillar. The departing storm we'd weathered took on the same appearance after it moved away some distance. I prayed that the new deluge over to the west wasn't planning to pay us a visit too. It didn't, but moved off south down the shoulder of the mountains.

Even under the circumstances I savored the incomparable tang of desert air after a rain, a mingling of creosote, always the predominant odor, and other fragrant desert plants and trees that are at their most luxuriant during the rainy season of July and August.

"Welcome home," I said to myself, a little numbly. I was already thinking of that new country as my home. I finally had some money to invest in the exploding economy I'd observed before. **Now, of course, I would really get rich.** Everyone there had similar hopes. It was an optimistic populace for the most part, young and old alike. No one yet had an inkling that the underground water already encountered in the mines in small quantities, and regarded as a blessing, would decree the end of the bonanza days in only a few years.

Tombstone was destined to become another ghost camp, as so many others had, but fortunately for our hopeful frames of mind, none of us suspected that — or that it would happen while a fortune remained in the earth. It is still there. And the town is still there, tottering along like us old timers who thrilled to its flush times.

When I finally got in and put up at the Grand, I opened the windows of my room wide to let in the pungent air which was as cool as any modern air-conditioned building.

The coaches had started to unload right at the main hotels, since the hack business that had been a sort of racket, carrying passengers and transhipping their baggage only a block or two, had been put out of business by public disapproval. I had both a trunk and valise, having come to stay, and a couple more trunks on the way.

My first thought was to look up my **best** friend, Johnny Behan. I hadn't let him know I was coming in, wanting to surprise him — to say nothing of the lovely Mrs. Behan. I was tired and lay down on the bed, planning only to stretch out for awhile, turning over pleasant thoughts about the future, renewing old friendships, getting rich. . . . .

The next thing I knew it was dark out. My ears were serenaded by the sounds of Tombstone waking up to start its evening round of pleasures. At first I had to figure out where I was. When it came to me, a wonderful chill of anticipation circulated through my whole being. Shortly that part of my being where the stomach is located reminded me I was ravenous. Delicious odors were drifting up from the restaurant downstairs. I struck a match and looked at my watch. It was 8:30 P.M.

I got up, lit the gas burner and washed up. Distant voices from the street filtered in the window. The occasional clink of trace chains on passing teams and the soft plod of hoofs reminded me that Tombstone's busy commerce moved day and night. Probably a beer wagon or some merchant getting a late delivery of merchandise to stock up for the next day's trade. Everyone worked long days then and thought nothing of it. Most had to. The unforgettable smell of Mesquite wood smoke from cooking fires added the final nostalgic touch.

A knock on my door really surprised me. I went over and opened it, wondering who it could be and found my friend, the sheriff, standing outside smiling. Johnny Behan himself, at his best and most typical. I could smell the liquor on him at once. He shoved out his hand and I shook it warmly. His first words answered the question in my mind.

"I saw your name on the register."

"Good to see you," I said. It really was good to see him. It still would be, bless him, for all his tricky, questionable ways. I'd even forgive him the murders he undoubtedly condoned, if not actually hired. I'd have swooned then if I knew the real Johnny. But, what the hell, I'm not that innocent kid anymore. It was a tough country. He's been dead for over thirty years. Maybe God has forgiven him by now — and even Morg Earp. They may all be up there somewhere together. Come to think of it, God may have forgiven Johnny, but the Earps weren't the forgiving type, as I well know.

Anyhow, the upshot of Behan showing up was that I must take supper with smiling Johnny — and pay for it and the liquor. His supper was liquor.

"I ate earlier," he explained. I wonder if he had. He eventually drank himself to death.

"How is Mrs. Behan?" I naturally asked.

Today I'd pay more attention to his facial expression, but I didn't yet know there was a possible dividend in watching. My recollection is that he became guarded, but that may be hindsight. I didn't know then that they'd never been legally hitched. His closest associates knew, and half the town probably suspected. The Behans were never invited out by the respectable families, though normally anyone as prominent as the sheriff would have been cultivated. The same can be said for the Earps, who in addition were saloonmen and gamblers. I can imagine what all of their women must have been before they took up with them. I don't think Virg, Wyatt and Morg were ceremonially married, Jim may have been, and Warren never married, though he wasn't 'that way' like Breakenridge.

Anyhow, all Behan said in reply to my question about Josie was, "She's O.K."

Having read her unpublished memoir, I know she tried to convey the idea that she dropped Behan for Wyatt long before that really happened. She had eyes for Wyatt for quite awhile before then, and perhaps for some others as well. The fact that Wyatt was married, or appeared to be, wasn't apt to bother Josie a bit. The problem, since she was hunting a husband, was that Wyatt would have to leave his wife, Mattie, before Josie got serious. Moreover, she wanted a husband she wouldn't have to spend her life reforming. I know that when she finally decided Wyatt was the one, nothing stood in her way.

It was about a month after that night before I saw Josie and Johnny together in public — a scene I'll tell about later.

Johnny got around to pumping me again, as he had upon first meeting him, just as soon as he could gracefully manage it.

He started out with the sympathetic friend act, saying, "I'm sorry about your father."

So was I and didn't want to be reminded. We'd been a close pair. His passing left me well off as his sole heir, but I'd rather he lived even if I had to labor for a living till I was tripping on my beard. I told Johnny I appreciated his concern, and after a pause he asked, "What do you aim to do now?"

"Stick around here and look over the prospects, I guess." That was all I intended to tell him.

He said, "I suppose you'll be needing a job. I know Harry Woods can use a good newsman over at *The Nugget.*"

That was one of his artful fishing trips. Like a ninny I said, "I don't really need a job."

He said, "No sense in draining your bank roll."

"I'm pretty well fixed." An even dumber confession.

Before the evening was over, he dragged me out on a round of the saloons. I met his crowd, the ones I already knew, and a lot more. He was hale fellow to everyone. He even introduced me to Virgil Earp who was by then Chief of Police, a job that required drifting around the joints to be seen, just to let the crowd know he was keeping an eye on things. Surprising how that works, especially with a lawman of the caliber of any of the Earps. The Cowboy rite of shooting up the town went out of fashion when Virg came on as Chief of Police. He had a couple of deputies that could handle the tough ones, too. Jim Flynn, for example. Everyone also knew that Virg had two tough brothers to back him up.

I finally got away from Johnny by midnight, pleading that I was completely worn out from my trip and badly needed sleep. Johnny was still going strong, backslapping the boys and tossing them down. He could punish a lot of whiskey in those days and hold it well. Before I left he hit me up for twenty bucks.

"The County is stingy about paying warrants on time," he explained his fix. "I'll get back to you in a few days."

He didn't, though. Then or ever.

I was dead on my feet when he shook my hand for about the fifth time before he let me go, and clapped me on the back as I turned to leave.

I was panhandled by two down-on-their luck drunks before I made it from Corrigan's to the Grand. I have to say there wasn't all that much difference between them and Johnny. He was a little bit smoother. He spent every cent he made as fast as he got it, if not before.

My diary tells me I slept till almost noon the next day — like the gamblers did.

Chapter 14

It Wasn't Like Hollywood Said

I came back to Tombstone lured by two things that were clear enough to me even then. First of all, it was a wonderful country that had cast a spell on me the first time I clapped my eyes on it, despite its violence. Next, it was a good place to get rich, and no one in that era was bashful about admitting they were pursuing the Almighty dollar to make life more comfortable. Everyone I met in Tombstone had that in mind. My third reason for coming to Tombstone wasn't as clear to me then, or else I was too much of a hypocrite to admit it to myself. I was smitten with Josephine Behan. My innocent attraction was more puppy love than the real thing, but I was a naive young fellow. Despite being at least what we called "of age," and then some, and having squired around a lot of "proper" young ladies, yet I'd never got up my nerve to kiss a female except my mother. People today would laugh at that, but it wasn't so uncommon then.

189

I positively know that seeing Josie again was in my mind that first morning back, because it says so right here in my diary for that date.

When I got up I'm sure breakfast had first priority. I remember being hungry most of the time as a young fellow. A hotel kitchen is a great ad for its restaurant, with savory odors permeating the building. I cleaned up and shaved in a hurry and headed down to eat.

Beyond the thought of eating was the obvious prospect of having to find some place permanent to live, and a copy of *The Nugget* solved that problem. In the ads was one for a furnished set of rooms, almost around the corner from the Grand. Fate may have taken a hand there, since the place was the second door below *The Nugget* office. As I passed the newspaper building, Harry Woods was coming out with a handful of note paper, looking at it, and almost bumped into me. Nothing would do but we go back in and renew old acquaintanceship, which hadn't amounted to all that much. He pulled open his desk drawer and set out a bottle.

"Have an eye opener."

It was a custom of the country. As some observer from the East said, "more common than brushing teeth," and as the Grand Duke Alexis of Russia allegedly said, "more refreshing." I took a good pull. I'd had a little more practice since Curly Bill had inflicted his 'Old Popskull' on me and this was a damn sight better than Curly's brand. Harry had one after me. I wondered how many that left

190

him for the rest of the day, since three was his limit. Maybe none. He looked like he needed it.

"Ah," he exhaled contentedly. I wasn't so used to eye openers yet that I needed one but the habit grew on a man in that country.

Harry brought up my going to work for him. I didn't really want a job and told him so, and why. At least he didn't put the touch on me as soon as he found out I was flush.

He looked disappointed. "Something to do while you look around," he argued. "Besides I'm in a hell of a fix and really need help."

How could I turn down an (almost) old friend? Well, in those days I couldn't. I had a job before I had a place to stay.

About that set of rooms, Harry volunteered, "I'll go down with you. The old gal will treat you better."

The 'old gal' turned out to be a widow about thirty, and a real spring chicken, which was probably the main reason Harry was so obliging. Never mind her name. The last time I visited Tombstone, her daughter was still living there.

The rooms wouldn't have been anything to be ashamed of back home, new, clean, bright, well-furnished and not too expensive — or at least cheaper than a hotel. There were four two-room apartments, two on each side of a hall that went through the building and had a back door. I got the one on the left rear, the northeast corner. The rooms weren't big, but they were cool and cheerful. I still have fond memories of the months I lived there. The windows were deep-set in thick adobe walls. Larger acquaintance with Tombstone, and the Southwest in general, suggested Mexican artisans had designed and built the place. Oddly, my parlor walls were wainscotted, but the natural wood had been painted bright blue, and had a flowered wallpaper above, and the ceiling was painted pale rose. The bedroom was all white except for turquoise-blue window and door casings, the door painted the same blue. It sounds gaudy, but I liked it.

The parlor had a pot bellied stove with a flat top and removable lid, so you could cook on it if you wanted to, and there was a cupboard to keep canned goods in — at least that's what I kept in it (and a little bottled goods). While I stayed there, I made a lot of coffee in a big granite pot on that stove, and sometimes cooked on it, though what I didn't know about cooking in those days is what they printed all those cook books about. Next to the stove was a wood box, lined with tin, empty the day I moved in. When cool fall weather set in the Mexican Mesquite peddlers began to go up and down the streets, carrying stove-length billets in aparejos, piled so high on their little burros you'd have thought it would break their backs. If you wanted wood down in that part of town for cooking in the summer, since few did, you could go to these peddlers and order some, or get on their route. I put in a supply later, just in case, but did most of my eating in restaurants. I kept the wood box full in winter, though. Tombstone

Mrs. Virgil Earp (Aunt Allie), *left,* **with her dear friend, Adelia Earp Edwards** (the Earp boys' sister), 1939, at the time they saw Randolph Scott playing Wyatt in *Frontier Marshal,* and agreed that his poker faced rendition of Wyatt was true-to-life. Aunt Allie still appeared much like this when the author first met her in 1943.

THE BOYER COLLECTION

Adelia Earp Edwards, sister of the Earp boys, whose daughter, Estelle Miller, and her husband, Bill were the author's principal informants and channel to other knowledgeable people.

THE BOYER COLLECTION

The author's most intimate friends in the Earp family,
left to right: Estelle Edwards Miller, Bill Miller (her
husband), Charlie Griffin (their son-in-law) and
LaVonne Griffin, the Miller's daughter. LaVonne did,
with Alvira "Aunt Allie" Earp, Allie's true memoir,
Aunt Allie Remembers now owned by the author.

PHOTO BY THE AUTHOR

The Casons, who provided the author the manuscript
of Josephine Earp's memoir, *I Married Wyatt Earp,*
shown with Josephine Earp in 1944, (as she looked
when the author met her), *left to right:* Josephine
Earp, Rae Cason, Mabel Earp Cason, Ernest
("Wyatt Earp-is-a-dirty word") Cason, Jeanne Cason.

COURTESY JEANNE CASON LAING

Wyatt Earp, as he looked in Tombstone.

THE BOYER COLLECTION

Virgil Walter Earp,
Wyatt's older brother, who
was actually Chief of Police
of Tombstone when the
Earp Boys and Doc Holliday
went down and shot it out
with the Cowboys. Photo
taken in 1882, according
to his wife Alvira's
notation on the back.

THE BOYER COLLECTION

Site of Kinnear Stage Holdup, on March 15, 1881 that was a coverup for the killing of Bob Paul. About a mile north of Contention and a few hundred yards short of what was Drew's Station, now in ruins.

PHOTO BY THE AUTHOR

Morgan Earp, the previous photo accepted as him had the same history as that of James, a very careful pencil rendering of an imaginative concept. This is the only known, authentic photo of him, provided by the grand niece and nephew of Morgan's common-law wife, Louisa Houston Earp.

COURTESY ELEANOR MUELLER AND BRUCE ROBINSON

Will McLaury, who admitted in letters to his father in later years that he'd hired the killings of several people in Tombstone; the only completely successful attempt being that on Morgan Earp; Virgil Earp was crippled in the attempt on his life.

THE BOYER COLLECTION

John H. Behan, Tombstone's venal sheriff, Wyatt Earp's arch enemy, who considered himself a great ladies' man, but lost his mistress to Wyatt and never forgave either of them.

THE BOYER COLLECTION

Josephine Earp, c. 1880. Copy of a photo in the possession of Carmelita Mayhew, photographer unknown, extensively copied after the death of Johnny Behan for whom it was made, according to Carmelita. An identical locket size oval of the face only was given to the author by Mr. Ernest A. Cason. (Authenticity disputed by some, due to the copies, but verified by her family.)

THE BOYER COLLECTION

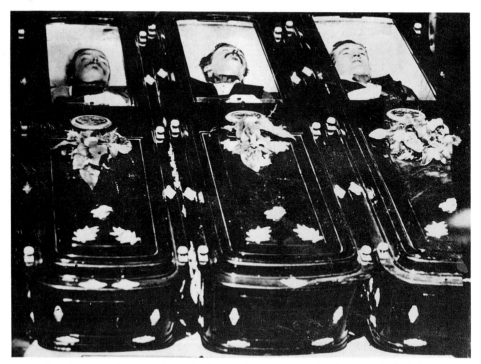

Left to right, in their coffins: **Frank and Tom McLaury and Billy Clanton,** demonstrating the folly of over-confidence.

THE BOYER COLLECTION

Lenhardt House, Oakland, where Wyatt and Josie
spent many months with her widowed sister,
Henrietta, in their later years.

COURTESY MARJORIE MACARTNEY

Dodge City Peace Commission, *back row left to right,*
William H. Harris, Luke Short, Bat Masterson; *front row
left to right,* Charley Bassett, Wyatt Earp, Frank
McLain, Neal Brown. Mrs. Earp relates Wyatt's
clairvoyance while a member of this group.

COURTESY MRS. MERRITT BEESON

Mary Katherine Harony (Big Nose Kate), *center with dark coat,* **with her brother, Alexander's family, 1929, shortly before she entered the Arizona Pioneers' Home where she dictated the memoirs that support this book.**

COURTESY HATTIE MADDOX AND ALBERT HARONY, KATE'S NIECE AND NEPHEW gets plenty cold in the winter, at least at night, and it even snows.

I got my things moved in and sat down in the parlor to take stock of my situation and plan my next move. Best I record here, for a prospective reader of the modern age, something about Western towns like Tombstone.

The first locators of the rich ground, such as the Scheiffelins and Girds, eventually sold out for a lot of money, upward to a million or so apiece. The big moneyed interests who bought them out expected to get their investment back and a lot more, and usually did. They were the ones who made the really big money on mining ventures. But there was a third group — the one that actually made things hum and tick — that is seldom mentioned in Western strikes. The speculators. They were the biggest group of all. Lots of them made big money, too. I intended to try it.

The first ingredient of a good mining camp editor was to be adept at promoting mine prospects. His puffs were reprinted or clipped and sent back East, where stock issues were floated based largely on hopes. A lot of money was taken in that way on worthless pieces of ground. Of course it was a racket. Eventually someone ended up holding the bag. It was usually spread out, however, so the outcry wasn't so loud as to dry up the racket. My father's business associates had warned me away from that sort of game. They also told me to **never, never** buy a mine, no matter how glowing the prospects. The better the prospect, the more

193

apt it was to be salted.

There were producing mines, and profitable dealings in their stocks, but the boom camp editor was expected to puff their prospects far above their true worth. So our papers were full of stories about new drifts, pockets, stopes, levels, veins, etc. Tombstone's "million dollar stope" is a good example. That assured money for the backers who'd originally come in, in case they had decided it was time to cut and run, rather than wait for dividends that might never materialize. Certainly anyone wise to the Western mining business realized that even the best prospects eventually were going to be worked out. The only exception that comes to mind is the Homestake up at Lead, S. Dakota. (Which, incidentally, shows what a long head old George Hearst had for mines. He looked over Tombstone, as I'll tell about in time, and didn't bite. But he was in the Homestake at Lead, S. Dakota big. It's the cornerstone of his son Willy's fortune, the reason he flew high, till he got his wings clipped during the Depression.)

I want to record here for posterity what places like Tombstone **weren't like.** They weren't like the screen products created by historically-ignorant migrants from Brooklyn or the Bronx. (The outpourings they produce are probably the revenge of writers who could do a lot better, but have learned from experience that art or authenticity would only be burned at the stake.) Sooner or later, when the last of us old-timers are gone, I suppose that kind still will be interpreting our

Heritage for a gullible public, that not only believes everything it reads, but especially believes what appears on the silver screen. We'd better start paying more attention to this garbling of history.

I almost never saw an openly armed man on the street in Tombstone, unless he was coming or going. Certainly no cowboys were lounging around in bars, wearing cartridge belts and six-shooters. No sojourner tied a horse to a hitching rail and left it standing with a Winchester propped up in a scabbard. Horses were put up in stables, since they would have created a nuisance otherwise. The jail's prisoners were out daily cleaning up the streets, but had enough to do cleaning up after legitimate drayage business and citizens buggies, either of which, I might add, legally could be tethered on the street while business was conducted.

I never saw a saloon with a woman in it, dance-hall girl or otherwise, and nearby Bisbee had similar rules of conduct, although some Western towns allowed entertainers and B girls, as they'd be called today. (A possible exception would have been such respected gambling women as Poker Alice or Lottie Deno, or even Doc Holliday's woman, Kate, who was a successful gambler in her own right.) But forget Alice Faye warbling, accompanied by a derelict tin-pan-alley piano player, or on the stage singing a nostalgic ballad. That was restricted to the novelty theaters like the Bird Cage, where you could see damn near anything. (I remember the day a transient Holy Fool cast a curse on the place to last a thousand years, muttering that "the toad in the hole" would one day blight it with his presence, whoever he was, and lighting Roman candles and speaking in the tongues. He got a large audience of Mexicans, a band of Indian scouts passing through town with an Army lieutenant, and town loafers. He made a hell of a racket till the Marshal — by then Dave Neagle — netted him.) There were also respectable halls, such as Ritchie's and Scheiffelin's, where you could see legitimate plays, minstrels and that sort of thing.

In movies, and I suspect it will never change, there are two ways for the protagonist to arrive in the never-never Western town; at a saloon where he dismounts and ties his horse at the hitch rail to go inside where everyone is wearing a six-shooter, lounging at the bar or playing poker, with the aforesaid Alice Faye, wearing skimpy chorus-girl tights, rumpling the card players' hair and swivelling her hips around; or at the sheriff's office where he dismounts and goes in to deliver his dismal news about disaster to a venal sheriff who is in cahoots with the baddies whose foul play the hero is reporting.

Tombstone was not primarily a cowboy town. If they came to town, they were a distinct minority. Curly Bill's crowd, known as the Cowboy Gang, came to town rarely, and had to forsake shooting up the town when the Earp regime took over.

Saloons were a man's preserve where it was customary to drop in several times a day for a 'smile.'

They were where ordinary business might be discussed. Most of them had gambling concessions. Faro was the preferred game, and draw poker was played, usually among friends, though big games drew the professionals.

We did have our venal sheriff, every bit the equal of Plummer up at Virginia City, but his office functioned normally unless his associates were concerned. His jail wasn't constructed right to retain them. His deputies, for the most part, weren't shining lights. As Wyatt Earp commented to Lake (one of the few remarks attributed to him by Lake that sound like him): "Breakenridge was a process server." The best of the bunch was Dave Neagle. He worked there because he needed a job. Years after he left Tombstone, while acting as bodyguard for U.S. Supreme Court Justice Field, he killed Judge Terry in California and made national headlines.

I seem to have trouble sticking to the vendetta that this is supposed to be all about, but I've got to digress a little to make crystal clear the kind of conditions that made the Tombstone Vendetta possible, perhaps even inevitable.

The central problem was Behan's refusal to uphold the law. Locals were distracted from noticing that because of their frantic pursuit of wealth. They let him get away with it. In more settled communities the sort of conditions that were tolerated, even ignored, at Tombstone, would have resulted in panic calls for action, and even martial law. (That finally happened at Tombstone as well, but only after the horse was gone from the barn for a long time. Public apathy had let the problem balloon to tremendous proportions.)

The unbridled pursuit of wealth made most boom towns lawless places; after struggling to get rich all day there wasn't much energy left for tidying up the community to resemble a lace-bordered Ivy League town that nurtured sages and poets. Petroleum V. Nasby would have gloried writing about *The Highhanded Outrage at the Bird Cage*, or some such title.

Almost everyone knows that Tombstone was founded by Ed Scheiffelin, and some have heard of his backers, the Girds, experienced mining men with the money to grubstake him. They found their angel in Governor Safford, with Eastern connections who provided the money to develop the discoveries. Miners comprised the backbone of the community and drew top wages while the bonanzas lasted. Following upon their heels came the merchants, saloonmen, gamblers and fast ladies, out to skim the bucks from them.

Sometimes the merchants were less saintly than the others, though they all appreciated appearances and went to church (after there was a church).

Prospectors were still active when I arrived, hoping to make new discoveries or to find new districts, which some did. Everyone else was there to serve the miners, the mining companies and each other. First had been the freighters and teamsters, since everything moved by horses, mules, or oxen. Liverymen naturally followed. Their demands for hay and grain supported a sizeable freighting operation. Hay raising got to be a big business down the river at St. David and Tres Alamos and over East in the Sulphur Springs Valley.

All the professions were present: doctors, lawyers, dentists, bankers, officers from the fort, gamblers (known throughout the West as the profesh), etc. I guess prostitution is sometimes called a profession — it was well represented. (And, from what I heard, represented well. Comparisons of their wares were a frequent topic of discussion among men.)

Add to the above the service people: butchers (often in league with cattle rustlers), bakers — no candlestick makers I can recall — upholsterers, dressmakers, storekeepers of all kinds, cooks, shoe and boot makers, barbers, bookkeepers, carpenters, masons, hotelkeepers, assayers, painters, bartenders (absolutely indispensable), laborers, woodchoppers, farmers, ranchmen, etc.

The latters' need for cheap brood stock to build up their herds helped put Curly Bill and his kind in business. They, of course, sold cheap, wet stock to butchers and sold to the Army and Indian Agency purchasing officers, but their biggest outlet was to ranchers getting their operations started. Some Cowboys became ranchers and their descendants are still around to bugle the perfidy of the Earps, who persecuted jolly Curly Bill and his merry men and evaded the clutches of Honest John Behan. Some of them, of course, recall that Curly rustled the stock again, after they'd bought it, and sold it to the Army. They have a somewhat different view of him.*

Curly's happiest hunting ground was Mexico. It was a circumstance that made even honest Gringos decidedly unwelcome in Mexico. Sonora, just across the border from Cochise County, had a fully justified "show me" attitude toward all Americans. Behan's cultivated blindness was at the root of that. An honest sheriff with guts, such as Pat Garrett in Lincoln County, New Mexico, could have cleaned up Cochise County just as he cleaned up Lincoln County. Of course, killing undoubtedly would have been necessary, but it came to that anyhow. Along with supine Behan, several others were at the root of Mexican hatred for Gringos. (Hard feelings from the Mexican War were still very much alive, but they were aggravated by what was going on along the Arizona border.) Old Man Clanton and John Ringo were also leading lights in the rustler confederation, with the allegiance of some fifty hard-core badmen, most of whom had fronts as ranchers, freighters, cowboys, sometimes miners and even businessmen.†

Lots of other small ranchers kowtowed to this band because they had little choice. As one of them observed, if he complained to the law over the theft of one horse or a few cows, they'd clean out

---

* The Mormons called them the scum of the earth, referring specifically in this case to the Clantons — **GB.**

† Sadly, Ten Eyck didn't cite an example of the latter — **GB.**

all the rest. This raiding in Arizona had its potential penalties. Colonel Henry Hooker of the huge Sierra Bonita Ranch, and the moving spirit of the incipient Stock Growers' Association, put a one thousand dollar reward on Curly Bill's head. He obviously recognized the futility of looking to Arizona sheriffs and courts.

Speaking of Curly and the leniency of Behan, it wasn't uncommon for old Curly to drop into *The Nugget* office after hours — always at night, as a matter of fact, by the back door. He'd appropriate an unoccupied desk chair, put his feet up, swig from Harry's office bottle and smoke our cigars. He liked to gab. The first time he dropped in and discovered me there, he looked as surprised as I must have.

"Hi, keed." he said. "You still huntin' them lost explorers?"

That was a giveaway that he'd actually known who Dr. Livingstone was, or at least that he remembered what I'd told him.

One night I got brave and asked him where his horse was.

He gave me a sharp look for a minute, then decided I'd made the team, I suspect, and said, "Down in the gulch."

"How in the hell do you find him in the dark?" I'd discovered by then it helped to throw in a cuss word or two with him to appear more like one of the boys.

"I know my way around Tombstone better in the dark than the daytime. It's the way I usually come to town **anymore.**"

I knew what he meant — **after the Fred White killing.** Fred still had friends who might have fetched Curly with a scattergun. Come to think of it, one of them finally did.

The first time he came in, I wasn't shocked to see him there. I knew Behan and Woods let him get away with plenty and were nominally his friends; at least his bedfellows. It just took me unawares. I was doing a quick adaptation to the customs of that country. You might shake hands with a fellow one minute and shoot him the next.

Parsons' Journal has a note on that exact subject. He was hand wringing because Virgil Earp shook hands with Curly when an Indian-chasing posse from Tombstone ran into Curly at the McLaury ranch. George thought it was altogether too friendly for a lawman and an outlaw. (Curly wasn't under indictment for anything at the time; simply had a hard reputation.) George would have swooned if he saw two other lawmen, Behan and Woods, carrying on with Curly. The connection to what I said about shaking hands one minute and shooting the next is that a later journal entry of George's opines that Curly Bill was one of the party that ambushed Virgil with shotguns some two months later.

What did the boys gas about at *The Nugget?* When Johnny wasn't there a prime subject was the fact that he and Josie's relationship had never been embarrassed by clergy — or J.P. either. I was shocked to the core when I first heard that.

"Are you sure?" I asked.

That got me a pitying look. Of course they were sure. Obviously that made her a loose woman. A lot of personal aspirations were expressed by various men that didn't please me in my then pure state, even though theirs differed from mine only in method. I'd have brought flowers and candy first, then squired her like a son of a gun, prepared to make an honest woman of a fallen angel. What a simp I was. She probably wouldn't have laughed openly, but it wouldn't have done me much good. She was still hoping Johnny would be the one to make her an honest woman, or at least hanging in because she couldn't bear to part from young Albert, whom she loved. What would happen to Albert if she threw Johnny out or stalked out herself? (On second thought she wasn't about to stalk out of "her house"; she was still renting it to Dr. Goodfellow in 1887.)

Being a provident soul, as that indicates, she had Johnny's replacement in her sights. At first, I'm convinced, she merely used Wyatt Earp to make Johnny jealous in hopes it would drive him to the altar. It didn't work. All her obvious eye-batting at Wyatt accomplished was that it helped Behan decide to break his agreement with Wyatt to make him under-sheriff. (Of course that wasn't the only reason he did it, or even the most compelling, as I'll mention, but Josie didn't help.) Regardless, she had her role in turning the wolves loose on Cochise County. It is certain that after her open break with Johnny in favor of Wyatt,

Behan's resentment helped Cochise County remain a land of turmoil and terror a lot longer than it had to. The types Johnny finally hired as deputies, unlike Wyatt Earp's kind, reminded me of the Keystone Cops, or maybe the Three Stooges.★

Alongside Wyatt, Behan was a yipping terrier compared to a wolf.

The sheriff of Cochise County never cleaned up that country, not Behan, not Slaughter, who is given credit for doing that. Wyatt Earp cleaned up Cochise County. When he departed, leaving corpses strewn around the desert waterholes, **organized crime was dead.** His circuit had created a condition of uneasiness in the dregs of Curly Bill's Boys; they didn't like to live with the realization that a temporarily-half-crazed dead shot, with ice for blood, and nerves of steel, was on the revenge trail, that he and a like-minded posse of gunmen, might ride up to one's camp at some isolated water hole and, if they even suspected you'd said good morning to the other faction, cut loose with Winchesters. The riff raff cut for greener pastures, never to return, and did it **muy pronto.**

The idea that John Slaughter cleaned up Cochise County makes old timers laugh. He was a back shooter, just like the Clanton crowd. In fact I've often wondered if he wasn't the real Kingpin of the outlaw fraternity. He brought most of their

★ Ten Eyck lived till 1946, so these were well known movie characters of his latter days — **GB.**

204

bright ornaments into that country: Curly Bill, Ringo, the McLaurys, Billy Claiborne, Gus Gildea, Joe Hill, Dick Lloyd, Pony Diehl, George Turner and some others I can't recall right now. There were warrants out on all of them in Texas and New Mexico.

Slaughter had the reputation of never hiring an honest man if he knew it, since they blighted the phenomenal fertility of his cows which all tended to have twins or triplets every year.

Aside from the Kinnear stage holdup the previous March, the first incident of the Vendetta of which I had personal knowledge was the "standing up" of the Bisbee Stage on Thursday, Sept. 8, 1881.

The basic facts were that two men stopped the stage about four miles beyond Hereford at about 10 P.M. They took the Wells Fargo box with about $2,500.00 in it and went through the passengers. One of the passengers, Ed Hardy, I got to know pretty well later. They took his gold watch and a little money.

After I got to know him, Ed volunteered some information, which was, "Did you ever have a stage robber point a forty-five right at you, about two feet away?"

I said, "I can't say as I have. Why?"

I record his reply as being worthy of going down for posterity: "I almost shit my pants."

I suppose I might have, too.

The posse that went after them consisted of Billy Breakenridge and Dave Neagle from the sheriff's office, and Wyatt and Morg Earp and Marshall Williams, representing Wells Fargo, and Fred Dodge, a gambler. (Somehow Walter Noble Burns in his book *Tombstone* had already pegged Fred as an under-cover man for Wells Fargo, as confirmed in Lake; maybe Wyatt told them both.) Based on distinctive bootprints of one of the robbers, and the circumstance that Frank Stilwell had such a pair of heels removed from his boots by a Bisbee bootmaker, the posse, which had tracked the robbers to Bisbee, arrested Stilwell, and Pete Spencer, who was with him. They were brought to Tombstone for a hearing and released on bond. They were rearrested on Federal warrants and taken to Tucson for another hearing, and again released on bond.

The Cowboy fraternity took this as another affront by the Earps, since the second arrest was by Virg Earp as U.S. Deputy Marshal. Naturally they didn't blame the sheriff's office, since they recognized any arrests of gang members they made were for appearances sake.

A comic aspect of this was that Stilwell was one of Johnny Behan's Keystone Cop deputies. When Johnny got the word, he burst into Woods' office shortly after, ignoring me, if he saw me, and blurted out, "Do you know what that dumb son of a bitch, Stilwell, did?"

"I'll bite," Harry said, knowing Stilwell might do almost anything.

The scene tells a lot about the degree to which Behan had come to trust me in a very short time.

Why I trusted him so long, I can't imagine. I guess I should face the fact that I was an innocent simpleton.

Johnny had already sweated Stilwell and got the whole story. Frank was guilty as sin. So was Spencer, or Spence as he was commonly called.

Johnny said, "If that bastard Stilwell didn't like the ladies so damn well he wouldn't always need money."

Talk about the pot and the kettle. That whole situation says a lot about the condition of law and order around Tombstone; also about the general uselessness of the ethics course I'd had in college. My mother would have swooned over the people I was accepting as respectable. Moral pliability was the local norm. It was contagious. I thought I was simply adapting to a new set of community standards.

A lot else was happening in my business affairs at that time, but not pertinent to Wyatt Earp's story. For one thing George Parsons kept trying to sell me — or anyone else — a **real good** mine. He should have stuck to working for Milton Clapp at the bank. Or got any steady job. He was almost always desperate for money due to his get-rich-quick schemes. But so were most of his sort around there.

The thing that stands out to me today as really strange is how long it took me to find out Johnny Behan. I had some company there, but never got brave enough to discuss it with Josie.

Chapter 15

Ike Clanton's Game

If Wyatt Earp told John Flood Ike Clanton's fear of retaliation for double-crossing his own gang was the cause of the street fight with the Cowboys, it wasn't because Wyatt didn't know better. Of course Lake picked it up and repeated it in his book. But Wyatt was a mighty close-mouthed man and did a lot of things for reasons that are not clear even to me. I'd bet Flood and Bill Hart cooked that story up for a movie, and Wyatt went along with it, if he even saw it.

I know that whoever dreamed it up didn't know the inside story. Ike thought he had no reason to fear his own gang before the shootout. His plan may have started out as a genuine double-cross of Leonard, Head and Crane, and probably did, but when Ike suspected he was going to be found out, the plan then became one to entrap Wyatt Earp. He told Curly Bill his plausible lie about what he was doing with Wyatt. A little bird named Curly Bill told me the latter personally, but he didn't know the full story of Ike's scheming. If he had, he'd have killed Ike.

Why Wyatt didn't suspect something like that might have been in Ike's mind, I can't say. I forbore ever asking, since the implication occurs that if he didn't, he was pretty dense in this instance, which wasn't like him. It doesn't seem to have occurred even to Lake's fertile mind that Ike's deal with Wyatt Earp could have been a golden opportunity to lure the Earps to some remote spot on the pretext of throwing Leonard, Head and Crane into their net.

Ike certainly suspected that Wyatt knew he was one of the other four stage robbers present when Philpot was killed. He desperately wanted Wyatt and his brothers and Doc out of the way. If an ambush was unsuccessful, what did Ike have to lose? He didn't plan to be there and the finger wouldn't necessarily point at him if it turned out that the Earps survived the fuss. Everyone knew the Cowboys had spies all over the country. If Crane were killed in such an ambush, Ike might still collect the Wells Fargo rewards, provided the set-up wasn't suspected by the Earps.

What Ike overlooked was the possibility that he had more to fear from Wyatt Earp than anyone if such a suspicion arose in Wyatt's mind. When Wyatt got the picture, that became obvious. "Finding-out" Ike explains Wyatt's course of action. He discovered Ike's treachery the night before the gunfight. And vice versa. This fact explains everything that Ike and Wyatt **really** said and did the next day, which is getting ahead of my story, but it looks to me like it fits here as well as anywhere. I'm too old to be a perfectionist.

I learned a lot sitting around *The Nugget* not saying much. I even met Ike Clanton there. He sure wasn't a beauty, constantly chewing tobacco, needing a bath and being loud. I hated to see him come in. Harry Woods and the others felt the same way. Fay detested Ike, but Art wasn't around much, spending a lot of time in Tucson and on the coast. He wasn't actually running *The Nugget*; Harry Woods was. What the real deal was there I never discovered.

A good question is what Ike was **really** mad about when his deal with Wyatt came out. If he thought he had nothing to fear from his own gang, then something else ailed him. What? And why blame Wyatt? Billy Breakenridge, who had good reason to know what was going on, probably blabbed all over the country. Josie Earp called him Billy Blab. (We mustn't forget, either, that Ike half-suspected he, himself, caused his father's death at the hands of the Earps and was sore about it. There was talk about the Earps not being seen around Tombstone at the time it happened, and of having a motive.) It is also possible that Ike suspected, since Wyatt no longer needed him after the three rustlers were all killed, that he was trying to get Ike's own gang to dispose of him. Even Ike was smart enough to reason that Wyatt, being in the dark, might think that would happen.

EDITORIAL COMMENT:

When Ike changed his plan to turn Wyatt's proposal into a way to decoy the Earps into an ambush, there was no need for Crane, or anyone, as genuine bait. That being so, it was provident that the Earps went out on a reconnaissance into the country where Hill had told them earlier they'd find Crane, and by sheer accident, located and killed him.

Ten Eyck continues:

As I said, since Wyatt had no idea of Ike's real intentions, maybe Ike was mad because Wyatt seemed to be trying to throw him to the wolves **now that he could no longer use him.** Knowing Ike, he may simply have been tender about his general reputation. He wasn't smart enough to recognize until too late that it wasn't his reputation in the community that was at stake but his life. Oddly, "reputation" had bothered Frank McLaury over Capt. Hurst's allegation that he'd stolen some government mules. Neither the Clantons or McLaurys had reputations in that country worth two cents. In Frank's case he was blinded by a puffed up ego.

Ike's life went on the line for sure when Doc Holliday got word of his scheme to put Doc and the Earps out of the way. I'll tell how that happened shortly. Again, Ike's stupidity was to blame — not to mention Doc's temper.

In the month or more after the Bisbee stage holdup — before the street fight took place —

I was reasonably busy with my own affairs and giving Harry a hand at *The Nugget.* I wrote a lot of the stories that are in the old files of that paper. I was learning to be a propagandist for the mining interests, and since it helped me personally, really took to it.

My social life picked up as soon as the mamas of the town discovered that I might be a good catch for their daughters. Word got out I was a lot more than the usual penniless, hard-drinking newsman of that day, and I got a lot of invitations to home-cooked meals and whist parties. Parsons also saw that I got involved with his set, mostly the Clapps, Ecclestons, John Clum and his wife and other respectable people of the town. On the other hand, I got to know the Dunbars well, both John and Tom, and have always liked them. I can't imagine how they got mixed up with Behan, and I don't think they could either, though they remained loyal to him to the day he died. Johnny, as I said, was a likeable blackguard. I usually find more to chuckle about than deplore when I remember him.

I never again was out with Johnny and Josie socially, since they weren't going out together, and she wasn't entertaining. It must have been hard for Josie to be cooped up day and night with Albert Behan. I met her out shopping a time or two, but was afraid to present myself to her under the circumstances, since she didn't seem to notice me, or remember who I was.

I forgot to mention how fast the town was rebuilding after the big fire that had eaten up a full block of the main part of town in June. In fact George Parsons' unnecessary heroics fighting the fire got his nose mashed and he was not a pretty sight until Doc Goodfellow rebuilt it. George basked in his martyr's role and gloried in his suffering. As a matter of fact, George was a stuffy ass, though well intentioned. We all know what the road to hell is paved with.

George was also a leading light in the Citizens' Safety Committee, which was Tombstone's milktoast vigilante band. They were more of a Rotary Club, interested in Roberts' Rules of Order instead of law and order. Judging from Parsons' Journal, they loved secret meetings. If they had worked like Vigilantes had in earlier, less civilized, communities, they'd have hung Behan, Clark and Gray, and Curly Bill and most of the trouble in that country soon would have gone away. In fact, just hanging Johnny and replacing him with an honest sheriff would have done the job. A likely choice for sheriff would have been one of the Earps.

It shouldn't surprise anyone, but it probably will, to learn that The Citizens' Safety Committee regularly delivered the Earps a "bag" to do their work for them. John Clum got out an injunction restraining Clark and Gray from entering on any lots in Tombstone till a court decided the title question, and it had exactly the effect of writing on water. The Earps, on the other hand, were paid to visit C&G's lot jumpers at night and did what my young G.I. friends would term, "Kicked the shit out of them!" Shades of the Ku Klux Klan. Were the Earps running a protection racket? Not really. They didn't muscle in. They were invited. There's a difference.

In any case it, and their other pursuits, which included speculation in mining, town lots and water sites, in addition to gambling, made Tombstone a prosperous home for them and, **as long as they stayed,** a safe place for businessmen and law abiding citizens. Big money was the only reason they stayed after the heat was turned up, long after almost anyone with discretion would have pulled out. (Of course Wyatt had personal reasons that influenced them all, which I'll get to.)

The monthly Earp Protection Fund must have been substantial. I conjecture that at least a hundred business men chipped in an average of five dollars a month. Divided equally between the three brothers who were active in law work, that comes to half again what a first class miner was making; this in return for merely being on hand like a fire department. The Cattlemens' Association was also ante-ing up, and Wells Fargo was the Boys' biggest backer behind the scenes. (What they would have lost without the deterrent of the Earps is staggering compared to the little they did lose.) Tombstone was a bonanza for the Earp Clan. After Virgil became Chief of Police, the kitty sweetened. Marshals were expected to issue unofficial licenses for a **sub rosa** fee. These things were understood. Anyone with the notion that Wyatt and his brothers were self-sacrificing public-spirited citizens, risking their lives **pro bono publico,** needs his head examined.

They all became my friends over the years and they were brave, likeable people, but they were human. Like everyone else in Tombstone they had money and the main chance uppermost in their minds.

1914

Jim Earp and I are out to dinner — on me, of course. He wasn't cheap, he just didn't have much money to spend. Jim is feeling good from a few snorts, and we are having a good cigar with our coffee after the main course is cleared away.

Jim opens with, "That son of a bitch Ike Clanton was what we called a Jonah in the Army. He botched up every God damned thing he tried to do."

We get an outraged look from a matron at a nearby table and I would like to crawl under our table. "Not so loud," I plead, knowing I'm wasting my breath.

"Loud, my ass," he says, and the matron's companion glares at us. If he's thinking of coming over and reproving Jim, the thought goes through my mind that Jim might, even now, have a six shooter in his back pocket. I make a note to check for a bulge when he gets up. Challenging any Earp wasn't a healthy pursuit right up to the day they died.

I know he has something he wants to get off his mind, and suspect it must be something interesting, so I don't want to shut him up. It sure as hell is interesting. It is the key to the puzzle of what **really** happened, and why, on October 26, 1881, between the Earps and their enemies.

Before telling the rest of Jim's remarks, I need a little background. The Citizens' Safety Committee was good for one thing besides ponying up the "bag" to pay a semi-official police force that actually got the job done. That one thing was that nothing happened but some member got wind of it. They all could keep secrets, too. The best kept one was who the members were. They had to be good at that to protect their own necks. Even Behan wasn't sure who they were. I have a pretty good idea today of about ninety-five percent of them. John Clum was the head of the thing. (For all of George Parsons' jealous remarks, Clum was a fellow who had a lot of guts; he just didn't give a damn or he wouldn't have taken on the job as Apache Agent up at San Carlos when he was just past twenty-two years old, appointed February 27, 1874.)

Some member of the Citizens' Safety Committee got a tip that the Cowboys were going to stage a showdown with the Earps in the near future. Wyatt sent Morg down to Tucson to round up Doc Holliday. It's possible he only wanted Doc to mollify Ike Clanton and avoid a fuss, since it looked like Ike was the moving spirit behind the brewing trouble. A shootout might ruin the Earps' sweet deal in Tombstone, which was exactly what happened.

My educated guess about what happened next is based on Jim Earp's revelations and what I heard at *The Nugget*:

Doc was half crocked when he looked up Ike to give him the word. Instead of accomplishing what Wyatt wanted, Doc said to Ike, "I hear you've been telling Wyatt Earp lies about me." You can imagine the effect that had.

Ike said, "I told Wyatt I heard you've been spreading around the word that Wyatt and I were in a deal to get Billy Leonard, Harry Head and Jim Crane killed and I'd get the rewards on them for giving them away." (Doc hadn't been informed of the double-cross before then, but he certainly was now.)

It was news to Doc, but it sounded just like something Ike would do, so Doc said, "Were you in such a deal?"

Ike's expression probably gave him away. He was a damned poor liar. (I can vouch for that, having watched and listened to him in court later.)

"I sure as hell wasn't!" Ike weaseled.

"You're a God damned liar!" Doc said, reading the truth in Ike's eyes. Lake alleged that Doc got mad because Billy Leonard, who was Doc's friend, might have got killed in a genuine double-cross. I doubt that. Doc was simply goading Ike because he didn't like him.

This, as I said, so far as the word-for-word conversation goes, is pure conjecture on my part, but

217

I'll vouch for the sense of it based on what Jim Earp told me that night at dinner.

Jim continued, "Wyatt was in the Alhambra eating at the lunch counter when Ike and Doc started a cussing match. Morg was in there, too. Wyatt told Morg, since he was on the police force, to break it up. It finally took both of 'em to get the two separated, Doc with his hand on his six-shooter daring Ike to jerk his. Ike swore he didn't have one on him. If he did, he used good sense not to try jerking it. Doc wasn't really much of a shot, but he was quick and wasn't apt to miss at that range. They dragged Doc outside.

"Like the damn fool he was, Ike followed them outside and said, 'I had a deal going all right, Holliday, but it wasn't to get the boys killed, it was to get you bastards out where we could fill you with lead.'

"A light went on in Wyatt's head about then, and Doc's too. Doc said, 'That's just your yellow speed, you son of a bitch. Well, all you did was get your old man killed — I did him up myself with a Winchester, and I'm going to do the same to you.'

"Doc spilled the beans before Wyatt could shut him up. The fat was in the God damned fire for sure. Ike left like a shot before Doc perforated him. He said, 'I'm going now — don't shoot me in the back!' Hell fire, not even Doc would do that."

I said, "No wonder Ike got himself heeled and was around breathing fire after that. He probably sent someone for his brothers. I can see why Wyatt gilded the lily about it at the hearing after the fight. Ike too, for that matter."

Jim said, "What did you figure he'd say — that he was suckered by the dumbest bastard in the Tombstone District? If he told the straight story, any bright kid could figure out the Earps had a first class reason for killing Ike and those other sons of bitches, even if Virg and Morg did pass up a good chance to do up Ike the morning before the showdown."

I, of course, knew about that. The whole town did. Ike was making the rounds of the saloons the morning after his cussing match with Doc, that is the day of the fight, October 26, 1881, packing a six-shooter and rifle and yelling for blood. The first blood he got was his own. Virg and Morg sneaked up on him on Fourth, and when he swung around trying to get his Winchester in position to fire, Virg knocked him down with the barrel of his six-shooter. They dragged him off to Judge Wallace's Court, which was almost across the street from where I lived.

What I witnessed personally was the aftermath of what had gone on inside the court room. I heard about that later from Wyatt's and Ike's testimony at the hearing. In view of what had happened the night before, it is easy to understand Wyatt's attitude in Wallace's court while they were waiting for the justice to show up.

Wyatt said to Ike, "You damned dirty cow thief, you have been threatening our lives and I know it. I think I would be justified in shooting you down* any place I should meet you, but if you are anxious to make a fight I will go anywhere on earth to make a fight with you, even over to the San Simon among your crowd."

Shortly after that Wyatt ran into Tom McLaury outside the court and assumed someone had told him what had been said, and that Tom was rushing to Ike's assistance, armed. Tom **probably** wasn't armed at the time, but Wyatt had every reason to suspect he was.

I saw Tom McLaury coming toward the court as Wyatt stepped outside. Without too much preliminary talk, or at least nothing I could distinguish, Wyatt stiff-armed Tom, like a football player, jerked a six-shooter and clubbed Tom to his knees. I could hardly believe my eyes. Tom crawled around for awhile, then tried to get up and Wyatt knocked him down again. It was the first time I was an eye-witness to real violence and it scared hell out of me. I thought, "My God, he's going to kill him!" But he didn't. Instead he looked around, taking me into his appraisal of the crowd, and his face was something I hope I never see again. His eyes glowed like a cornered wolf's. He growled to no one in particular, loud enough for me to hear across the street, "I should have

---

* Generations of readers have passed over this remark in print without recognizing that it's the essence of the Code of the West, with roots in the days of knighthood when the gauntlet was thrown down for personal offenses. It seeks an Old Testament justice — **GB.**

killed the son of a bitch."

I was too stunned to join the others who helped
Tom up. I stayed out on the sidewalk, wondering
what else might happen, and watched Wyatt go
into Hafford's Saloon a half block up the street
across Allen and come out in a short while calmly
puffing on a cigar.

Before I tell what really happened at that
"shootout" an hour or so later (told by Wyatt Earp
himself among friends when he had no motive to
be evasive) I will sketch in the events of that in-
tervening hour from what I saw and what I've
heard, as well as a sifting of the testimony of the
witnesses at the J.P. Court hearing that lasted almost a month following the killings.

Regarding that Court testimony, here is my con-
cluding diary entry and it will serve as a caution
to anyone depending on the Court record alone
to arrive at the truth:

November 28th
    I've been listening to this hogwash for al-
most a month. What a parade of liars. And
how different from what some of them say
off the record. The Cowboy crowd is trying
to railroad the Earps, and the Earps are trying
to save their skins. I can guess why Johnny
is lying. It's all over town. She went out to
Ritchie's Hall with Wyatt before this whole
thing came to a head. I was there when they
ran into Johnny. She just smiled, but with
a really wicked look, and said, "You never

take me out, Johnny." He tried to laugh it off and put a good face on it. He said, "That's all right, pet. I don't mind." Wyatt just grinned like the cat that ate the canary. Harry Jones told me he walked her home too. Johnny has sent her to San Francisco with Albert to get her out of temptation's way.

Chapter 16

Many Conflicting Motives

The battle lines were drawn in Tombstone by the morning of October 26, 1881. Ike Clanton's and Doc Holliday's drunken mouths had seen to that. The showdown would have come sooner or later, anyhow.

Why? Because determined men of two factions had no intention of yielding the field.

An outlaw confederation of hardened criminal types, some of them psychopaths, who had held sway in unorganized parts of Texas and New Mexico only to be driven out by hot lead and nooses, thought they'd finally found utopia in southeastern Arizona and adjoining New Mexico and Old Mexico. They refused to acknowledge that their sweet deal had to end here, too, due to the arrival of the commercial interests of a mining boom camp.

They brooded at the injustice of it, smoldered over **their majesties** being opposed by determined men in the Earp clan, were encouraged by Behan's support, and made bold enough by it to challenge their enemies, even in broad daylight in open combat in the enemy's own keep.

How demented they became due to lack of opposition before then! I now see clearly that all of that can be laid at the door of one man — morally pliable Johnny Behan. Why he allowed it, why he did or did not do the various things of which I learned, is the whole key to the vendetta that he abetted.

I know the motives of everyone who met on that battleground on the fateful day.

The McLaurys had hated the Earps from the time they accompanied Capt. Hurst to recover stolen government mules at their ranch. Frank openly threatened Virg shortly afterward. In addition, both brothers suspected that the Earps now knew they had been involved in a conspiracy to lure an Earp posse to some isolated spot and ambush them. Ike knew for sure he'd put the Earps fully on guard as a result of his drunken blabbing. He probably wanted to kick himself, even though he found out what had really happened to his father which made him even hotter under the collar. Ike certainly didn't tell Tom what he'd blurted out to Doc in front of the Earps. If he had, Tom would have given him hell. In any case, they naturally sent word to Frank and Billy Clanton to come side them in a showdown, with as many others as they could bring.

There definitely were to have been others, or at least Ike thought so. At minimum: Curly Bill,

Pete Spence, Frank Stilwell, Ringo if he could get there in time.

How do I know that? I'm not sure any more, but I was certainly a trusted adjunct of the Behan faction. I heard so much, and it was sufficiently blameworthy, that I stopped writing it down. Some of what I wrote I later destroyed, recognizing that it was actually incriminating and that I should have bowed out long before I did. (When I did, I had to be damn careful to convince them the only reason was that my real business interests took too much time — I knew too much, and felt nervous for a long while. Another case of getting in over one's head.)

I learned a lot from many sources and my memory is clear on the pattern of events, and I have informed hunches about what I didn't learn directly. For example, the expectation on the part of the Earps that others of the Cowboy Gang would be at the fight was the reason Doc Holliday was carrying a shotgun — to even the odds.

Those others who didn't show up, all had a motive to be there or at least to dispose of the Earps. (On the other hand, they may have had a motive not to be there.) Whether discretion, ulterior motives, or being too far away to reach the scene in time prevented their presence or not, I don't know. Perhaps Curly Bill decided to throw Ike Clanton to the wolves as Josie thought, and claimed to know. He certainly had reason enough. Ike was the gang's Achilles Heel, just as Doc was Wyatt's.

Ike Clanton, Spence, Stilwell, and Curly Bill

were all aware that Wyatt worked for Wells Fargo as a **detective,** that he had reason to know they'd been the four who rode away from the Kinnear stage holdup, concealed by darkness, and never openly suspected. That, alone, was enough to make them extremely apprehensive, because they knew that when all else failed, Wells Fargo simply paid hard men to kill for them, whether the victims had been indicted by a Grand Jury or not. All had ample reason, therefore, to fear Wyatt Earp. As it was, he eventually killed two of them, and would have killed the rest if he'd come up on them in the right circumstances. Certainly after Morg was murdered, he'd have taken a year off from a high paying job and ridden a thousand miles to kill any of that gang.

The Earps, in addition, had been the constant fly in the gang's ointment. They'd come pounding on the McLaurys' door after the stolen mules; Wyatt had raised a lump on Curly Bill's head after the White shooting and used Curly's predicament to get the testimony that put Wells Fargo's man, Bob Paul, into office as sheriff of Pima County in place of Behan's lifelong pal, Charley Shibell. The Earps had closely pursued the perpetrators of the sham stagecoach robbery that had been a coverup to kill Paul, kept on the trail for weeks, and the Earps and Paul (which is to say, Wells Fargo) knew the inside story of that plot. All that they lacked was firm knowledge that either Behan or Shibell had been behind it. The final blow had been the accidental killing of Old Man Clanton by an Earp posse. The more recent arrests of Stilwell and Spence for the Bisbee stage robbery were just the icing on the cake. The Earps were cramping the **Boys'** style. They had to go.

How about the motives of my old friend, smiling Johnny? Where would he end up if Curly Bill, Ike, Spence, Stilwell sung? He had engineered the botched attempt on Bob Paul's life. He gave the most treacherous one of them, Stilwell, a job as deputy sheriff to keep him quiet. (And look what it got him.) Behan was in the power of any or all of that crowd. If anything happened to any of them, it was possible he could be a suspect for having conspired to dispose of them. He had the motive. No wonder Behan was drunk every night. He had a lot to blot out. He must have shook in his boots when his boys had to go in pursuit of the Bisbee stage robbers, and actually had to take them in with the Earps watching. And it was the damned Earps again who were responsible. When one of those arrested turned out to be Stilwell, one of his own deputies, Johnny almost had apoplexy, as I witnessed. Talk about getting in over your head.

As soon as Ike blabbed on the night of the 25th, the Earps could not mistake the handwriting on the wall. They knew the deadly motives of all the others better than anyone. Before then they had simply recognized the Cowboy Gang as a general threat to law and order, and the natural enemies of any honest lawmen. That explained why the Cowboys were all antagonistic and mouthy, threatening the Earps whenever they came to town and got tanked up in the saloons.

Now it was obvious that they fully intended to carry out those threats and had to or leave the country. (There is plenty of indication that the McLaurys were planning to slip out of the country anyhow. They weren't quite quick enough.) Yet, even after Ike Clanton walked around Tombstone, armed with both rifle and six-shooter, bellowing his threats to kill them, Virg and Morg couldn't bring themselves to take the ready-made opportunity to kill him in an arrest attempt, for which no one could have criticized them under the circumstances. (Later Ike boasted in public that if he'd been a little quicker, the coroner would be working on Virg's case.) Virg and Morg were simply too amiable and forebearing. Wyatt was forebearing till pushed too far. Doc Holliday was neither amiable nor forebearing.

The foregoing circumstances and the personalities involved explain the bloody confrontation that followed on the streets of Tombstone on the afternoon of October 26, 1881. They explain the aftermath as well, up to a point. The difference was that the gunfight itself created additional threatening complications. Ike had acquired another motive for revenge, since his brother Billy was killed. The two McLaury boys who were killed had a brother, Will, who demonstrated the inherent Scottish clan predilection for revenge.*

* I asked Bill's grandson what he had meant by a remark he once made to me that his father (Will's son) had been "one of the **more stable** McLaurys." He said, "For one thing he didn't believe in harboring a grudge all his life, like his father." — **GB.**

Chapter 17

Street Fight With The Cowboys

EDITORIAL COMMENT:
It is obvious from the voluminous, unorganized notes and many heavily revised manuscript pages on this affair, that Ten Eyck had so much information about the preliminaries of the fight, since he witnessed some of them, and listened to testimony about all of them in court later, that he never decided what to put in the final version. Accordingly, I have selected several items and an order in which to put them that I think fits the need of a coherent story of the events leading up to the shooting.

Ten Eyck Continues:
I didn't see the morning's happenings on October 26th, during which Ike was circulating around Tombstone threatening the Earps, but they were amply attested by Roderick Hafford, Ed Boyle and Julius Kelly, witnesses who had no reason to lie about it. Virgil and Wyatt Earp also

testified to Ike's threats.

At the hearing after the gunfight, in Judge Wells Spicer's court, Boyle testified that he met Ike in the vicinity of the telegraph office about 8:30 or 9:00 A.M. and that Ike had a pistol in sight and said when the Earps or Doc hit the street, "the ball will open." Kelly saw Ike between 9 and 11 A.M., both on the street and in the saloon where he worked, and Ike said the Earps and Doc had threatened him and when they showed up they'd have to fight. Hafford saw Ike in his saloon about 12:05. Ike had a pistol and rifle and stated the Earps had agreed to meet him before noon, but they hadn't yet shown up.

Virg Earp said Ike had told him the same thing about 7 A.M. as he went home to bed after staying on duty all night. Ike first said he wanted Virg to take a message to Doc that he had to fight. When Virg refused to do that, Ike said Virg himself might have to fight before he knew it. Wyatt Earp testified that Ike had said virtually the same thing to him the night before.

With that background, Ike, himself, later testified regarding the high-handed outrage that was perpetrated on an unoffending citizen, such as he, at about half past one o'clock:

"As I was walking up on Fourth St. between Fremont and Allen Street, Virgil and Morgan Earp came up behind — don't know where they came from. Virgil Earp struck me on the side of the head behind the ear with a six-shooter and knocked me up against the wall. Morgan Earp cocked his pistol and stuck it at me. Virgil Earp took my six-shooter and Winchester from me. I did not see or know that they were about there, until I was struck. I did not know who struck me until after I recovered from my fall against the house. They pulled me along and said, 'You damn son-of-a-bitch, we'll take you up here to Judge Wallace.' "

In Wallace's court, according to R.J. Campbell, Clerk of the Board of Supervisors, Ike said to Morgan Earp: "If you fellows had been a second later, I'd have provided a coroner's inquest for the town."

I mention these things to establish the fact that Ike was definitely around begging for trouble. There wasn't much argument about that. Boyle added that he went down and told Wyatt Earp that Ike was hunting the Earps and Doc with blood in his eye.

I repeat that I, myself, witnessed what happened outside Wallace's court right after that, when Wyatt was still hot under the collar from his exchange in the court room with Ike. The testimony of several of the witnesses in Wells Spicer's J. P. Court after the shooting shed some added light on that difficulty between Wyatt and Tom McLaury.

A. Bauer, J. H. Batcher and Tom Keefe testified about it. However, they couldn't agree as to the number of blows Wyatt struck, or which way the two were travelling. Maybe they hadn't paid any attention till the scuffle started. At any rate I can vouch for the fact that Wyatt was going out and Tom coming into Wallace's court. Wyatt knocked him down twice, with which Keefe agreed. Bauer heard words to the same effect that I did, which were that Wyatt said something about killing the son of a bitch. Only I heard him say, he "should" have, and Bauer heard him say he "could" have. (Bauer was probably afraid to tell the truth. I didn't have to.)

The next incident of note occurred maybe a half hour later, after Frank McLaury and Billy Clanton reached town. They got together with Ike and Tom and had a talk, then went down to Spangenberg's Gun Shop on Fourth, passing Wyatt Earp as they did, where he was still standing on the front stoop of Hafford's. He followed them down to see what they were up to. The key to his frame of mind can be seen in his later testimony at the J.P. Hearing, which I extract here, and will repeat again in context when I include his entire court statement:

"I was tired of being threatened by Ike Clanton and his gang and believe from what he said to me and others, and from their movements that they intended to assassinate me the first chance they had, and I thought that if I had to fight for my life with them I had better make them face me in an open fight."

Wyatt told me later he followed them down to Spangenbergs, intending to goad them into just such an open fight. He said, "I was satisfied I could kill them all before they got started. None

232

of them had the nerve for a real face to face shootout."

Obviously true, as proven by events. A witness to what Wyatt was doing down at Spangenberg's was Bob Hatch, later sheriff, in whose saloon Morg would be killed a few months later. Hatch was no fighting man, and he didn't understand what Wyatt was doing. He saw Wyatt backing Frank McLaury's horse off the sidewalk in front of Spangenberg's and ran to get Virg, saying, "Wyatt is down there alone, they'll murder him." Virg then went to join Wyatt, carrying a shotgun. So Wyatt didn't get the fuss started then as he'd hoped to.

The Cowboys, that is Frank and Tom McLaury and Ike and Billy Clanton, then went down to the Dexter Corral on the south side of Allen St., opposite the O.K. Corral. They were observed at the Dexter having an "earnest" conversation in one of the stalls. Shortly thereafter they were seen crossing into the O.K. Corral, at which time they were heard saying they were going to clean out the Marshal and all of the Earps. This was overheard by a newcomer to town, H.F. Sills, and by Rube Coleman, our town gossip and old lady. Both carried word to Virg, since he was Chief of Police.

Meanwhile, Johnny Behan told Virg he was going down to disarm the Cowboys, since he'd been told they were below the O.K. Corral on Fremont St. He was down with them twenty minutes. One wonders what was under discussion all that time. In any case he didn't disarm them, assuming he tried. As our G.I.'s would put it today, Frank McLaury told him to "blow it out his barracks bag" and to disarm the Earps first and then he'd think about it. Disarming the police was a proposition as Judge Spicer later wrote: "Both monstrous and startling." It didn't seem to occur to anyone that Behan apparently agreed to try to do it, "a proposition even more monstrous and startling."

The fact that the Cowboys were just below Flys was significant in itself, since Doc Holliday was staying at Flys. Ike had been down there with his rifle earlier, looking for Doc, and Doc had come uptown to borrow a shotgun, intending to face Ike alone. Doc told me this in Denver years later. A shotgun loaded with buckshot would overcome Ike's advantage of using a rifle at any range at which a shootout was apt to take place. This, and the fact that the Earps expected the Cowboys to have some reinforcements on hand in case of a fight, explains the presence of the shotgun hidden under Doc's overcoat when they all went to Fly's.

After waiting in vain for Johnny Behan to return, and having been visited by irate citizens suggesting that he do something about the threatening presence of the Cowboys, Virg called on his brothers and Doc to go with him to see what was going on. Virg may have had some notion of arresting the Cowboys, and perhaps Morgan did too. I have already covered Wyatt's frame of mind.

I insert at the end of this, the testimony of Behan given at the Coroner's hearing, at which I was present, from which I concluded at the time that the Earps and Doc Holliday had murdered Frank and Tom McLaury and Billy Clanton. My eyes were soon opened up, however.

I heard the shooting and got there in time to see the bodies still lying where they fell. Billy and Tom were still alive. No one seemed to know exactly what had happened. I saw a surrey being run up from the O.K. Corral by some men, and Virg and Morg Earp, both wounded, were put into it. Rather than hitch it up, a number of enthusiastic supporters of the Earps (no doubt members of the Citizens' Safety Committee) rolled it the couple of blocks down to Virg's house.

A wagon was procured and the three corpses were taken down to the Dexter Corral where they were laid out on planks on saw horses. I don't know whose idea that was, but anyone in town who wished to was allowed to look at them. A lot of boys paraded down to see dead men. (Shades of Huck Finn.) Matthews, the coroner, had them stripped to the waist and examined their wounds while I watched. I expected to be sick to my stomach, but was hardly affected at all. I left and don't know if he convened the coroner's jury and held the hearing there, or later up at Ritter and Ryan's funeral parlor, where he had them taken.

As an interesting aside, Allie Earp told me years later that she was on Allen Street when she heard the firing start, and knowing the trouble brewing might lead to shooting, ran down Third over to Fremont to see what had happened and find out if Virg was all right. Rounding the corner building on Third and Fremont, holding her skirts high, she almost tripped on Tom McLaury, who was still moving a little. She said she stopped, startled, leaned down and looked at him, and said, "Well, what son of a bitch shot you?"

She laughed when she told it, and said, "Wasn't that foolish? Didn't make a lick of sense." Allie cussed a lot, but coming out of her on the occasions it did, cussing was usually like poetry.

Without any more fuss, this is what Johnny Behan said at the Coroner's Jury hearing:

Document #48
CORONER'S INQUEST

District Court of the First Judicial District, County of Cochise

Inquest on the body (sic) of William Clanton, Frank McLowery (sic) and Thomas McLowery (sic), deceased. Filed December 1st, 1881. George H. Daily, Clerk, H.M. Matthews, Deputy Clerk.

EDITORIAL COMMENT:
The names of the McLaury boys are consistently misspelled as McLowery in the original document and appear so below.

TERRITORY OF ARIZONA

COUNTY OF COCHISE

} ss

Inquest on the bodies of William Clanton, Thomas McLowery, and Frank McLowery. List of Jurors: T.F. Hudson, D. Calisher, M. Garrett, B.F. Goodrich, John C. Davis, Thomas Moses, Harry Walker, C.D. Reppy, R.F. Hafford, George H. Haskill.

John H. Behan being duly sworn deposes and says his name is John H. Behan and that he resides in the city of Tombstone, County of Cochise, Arizona Territory, and is Sheriff of Cochise County, Arizona Territory.

Q. Were you present on Fremont Street when the encounter took place during which the deceased were killed?
A. I was.
Q. Do you know all of them?
A. I do. I know all of them.

STATEMENT

I slept late the day of the shooting. Got up about one or half-past one o' clock. I went to the barber shop to get shaved. While I was being shaved someone said, "There is (likely) to be trouble between the Clanton boys and Earp boys." There was a good deal of conversation going on in the barber shop about the trouble that happened in the morning. I asked the barber who was shaving me to hurry — I wanted to get out and disarm the parties. I meant all of them — everybody who had arms, except the officers. After I got through in the barber shop (I) went out across the street to Mr. Hafford's Corner.

I asked the Marshal, Earp, what was the excitement. He said there was a lot of (I think sons-of-bitches) who wanted to make a fight. I said to him he had better disarm them. He said he would not do it — if they wanted to fight he would give them a chance. I said to him, "It is your duty as a peace officer★ to stop this thing, and I want you to do it. I am going to try." I said, "I am going down the street and disarm the cowboys," meaning McLowery and any of the boys that was armed and showing a disposition to make trouble.

I left Earp and came down to the corner of Fourth and Fremont. There I met Frank McLowery standing in the street holding a horse. I told him I wanted him to give up his arms. He said he would not, without those other people being disarmed. I suppose he

★ To get this admonition in focus, one must recall that, as a peace officer, Behan hired the murder of Bob Paul — **GB.**

meant the crowd; Holliday, Earp and others. He said he had done nothing and did not want to make any fight. I looked down Fremont Street and saw the Clanton brothers and Tom McLowery and I said to Frank, "Come on down with me." We went along down to where the boys were standing — two of the parties who were killed and Ike Clanton. I said to them, "I want you to come up to the Sheriff's Office and lay off your arms." Frank McLowery rather demurred from going up, and gave as his reason that he wanted the other party, the Earp party, disarmed.

EDITORIAL COMMENT:

What a delightful phraseology: "demurred." Moreover, in that the Marshal was one of the Earp party, and his brother, Morgan, was a paid city policeman, one can readily see how Judge Wells Spicer later termed Frank's desire to have them disarmed: "A proposition both monstrous and startling," particularly in view of the fact that the evidence showed the intention of Frank and his comrades was to kill the Earps and Doc Holliday, especially the latter.

About that time I saw Marshal Earp, Doc Holliday, Wyatt Earp, and Morgan Earp coming down the street. Expecting that there would be some trouble if they met, I walked up the street toward them and ordered them back; told them not to go any further. They passed me, said something, I forgot what it was, but it was to the effect they would not go back.

EDITORIAL COMMENT:
One could safely bet that such a proposition (i.e.: to desist from going to arrest belligerent parties threatening to kill the police force) was never before or since presented by a county sheriff to the city police, in any jurisdiction, in the entire history of the United States.

When they got to the party of cowboys, they drew their guns and said, "You sons-of-bitches, you have been looking for a fight and you can have it!"

EDITORIAL COMMENT:
Seldom have truer words been spoken.

Someone of the party, I think Marshal Earp, said, "Throw up your hands! We are going to disarm you!" Instantaneously with that, the fighting commenced. They fought around there, and there was from 25 to 30 shots fired.

All the time before the shots were fired, I was talking to all parties, saying, "Put up your guns!" Not to shoot. I heard Billy Clanton say, "Don't shoot me! I don't want to fight," or something to that effect. I afterwards saw Billy Clanton shooting whilst he was on the ground. He was lying on the ground with his legs crossed and his pistol resting on his knee.

Tom McLowery said, "I have got nothing," and threw his coat back to show that he was not armed. This was instantly with the shooting, almost at the same time. The order to throw up their hands and this remark and the shooting were almost simultaneous. After the fight was over, Wyatt Earp said to me, "You threw me off my guard. You have deceived me. You told me that you had disarmed them." I said, "I did nothing of the kind," and I repeated what I had said to their party.

Several questions were asked of Behan and his answers follow:

A.   When I went down to disarm them, I put my hands around Ike Clanton and found he had no arms. He showed me he had nothing on him. Ike Clanton said that they were just getting ready to go out of town. Frank McLowery and Billy Clanton were armed. Frank McLowery had his horse, holding him down there. I think Billy Clanton had his horse with him — am not positive.

A.   There were six of us standing around including myself. I said, "How many is there of you?" and they said, "Four." Claiborne said he was not in the party.

A.   I can't say who fired the first shot. It appears to me that it was fired from a nickel-plated pistol. There was two shots very close together. I know that the nickel-plated pistol was on the side of the Earps. I won't say which one of the Earp crowd fired first.

A. The only thing I saw when the order to "Throw up your hands," was given was Tom McLowery throwing open his coat, taking hold of the lapels of his coat and holding it back.

EDITORIAL COMMENT:
Tom McLaury was wearing a blouse, not a coat.

A. There was a shotgun in the Earp party. Holliday had it. He was putting it under his coat, so as to get it more effectively concealed. That was when they were coming down the street.

A. I cannot say that I saw the shotgun go off. There was a scramble. I don't know whether the shotgun was fired or not. I think it was — did not see it.

A. I saw Billy Clanton fall first, and then I saw Frank McLowery fall, on the north side of Fremont Street, almost exactly opposite Fly's place, after the fight commenced.

A. No, I did not see Tom McLowery fall. I did not see him until the fight was over. Then I saw him on the ground.

A. The fight commenced in a vacant lot or space between Fly's Photograph Gallery and a little board house below it, on the south side of Fremont Street near the corner of Third Street. This was in Tombstone, Cochise County, Arizona Territory

A. It was at this spot where I met Tom McLowery and Ike and Billy Clanton:, when I went down with Frank.

A. I am satisfied that two of the parties were not armed — I mean Ike Clanton and Tom McLowery.

A. When I went to disarm the McLowerys and Clantons, I understood that there was likely to be a row between the Earp brothers and Holliday, and the Clanton crowd, and that is my reason for going to disarm them.

A. No one refused to give up their arms, except Frank McLowery. He said that he came on business, and did not want any row. He never refused to go to my office.

EDITORIAL COMMENT:
True — instead he, "rather demurred," see Behan above.

A. When I met the Earp party, I did not tell them that I had disarmed the other party. I did tell them that there would be trouble if they went down. I told them I did not want any trouble, and would not allow it if I could help it, and not to go down.

A. Frank McLowery did not have his pistol drawn when Marshal Earp told him to

243

throw up his hands.

A. At the time I left the McLowerys and Clantons and met the Earps, I considered the Clanton party under arrest, but I doubt whether they considered themselves under arrest or not after I turned to meet the other party.

EDITORIAL COMMENT:
This must be considered one of the most fantastic, to say nothing of evasive, statements ever made.

A. I left them for the purpose of stopping the Earp party.

A. Nothing was said to (lead) me to believe they were acting in an official capacity. After the fight was over, Wyatt Earp said, "We went there to disarm that party." I think I heard Virg say the same thing. The horses were saddled, but Frank McLowery, Bill Clanton and Old Man Frink had just come into town. During my conversation with them, Ike Clanton said, "We are going out of town." But Frank McLowery said, "I am not, I am here on business."

CORONER'S VERDICT
William Clanton, Frank and Thomas McLowery, came to their deaths in the town of Tombstone on October 26, 1881, from the effects of pistol and gunshot wounds inflicted

by Virgil Earp, Morgan Earp, Wyatt Earp and one — Holliday, commonly called "Doc" Holliday.

EDITORIAL COMMENT:

As the newspapers commented, the verdict didn't meet with community approval because it didn't indicate whether the deceased were killed by the Marshal in the line of duty. It is strange that none of the Earp party were called as witnesses. Behan, in his later testimony at the Justice Court Hearing, convened for the purpose of determining whether the Earps should be bound over for murder, denied that he had said to Charlie Shibell, shortly after the fight, that it was a "dead square fight." If he had made such a remark at the Coroner's Hearing it would have been the end of the matter. In a jurisdiction where the sheriff wasn't a partisan of the criminal element, the blacksmith would have been striking off two pound silver "hero" buttons for each of those who killed the McLaurys and Billy Clanton, as having performed a public service. One wonders if the coroner shouldn't have found that the deceased met their deaths from an excess of overconfidence and a lack of common sense.

Johnny was substantially corroborated at the Coroner's hearing by Ike Clanton and Billy Claiborne. They all expanded on their testimony when the Justice Court hearing took place before Wells Spicer. It lasted almost a month.

I had dinner the night of the coroner's hearing with Johnny and Harry Woods. By midnight Johnny was in his cups. He usually held his liquor pretty well before his liver was shot, but had a lot more than he usually did. I figured the strain of events was eating at him. He looked nervous.

"You're lucky you didn't get caught by a stray bullet," I said.

He looked at me a little cockeyed and said, "You don't really think I was standing out there like an ass waving my hands around? I knew at least the Cowboys meant to shoot it out."

I said, "I mean, you said you saw. . . . ."

He interrupted me, "I didn't see a damn thing. I ran around Fly's and **didn't see a damn thing.** I bumped into Ike Clanton running out the back door as I was coming in. He almost knocked me down. He was white as a sheet and almost incoherent." Then he laughed, joined by Harry.

At the time I felt just like they did about Wyatt Earp and all the Earps for that matter. I didn't give a damn what happened to them. I hadn't liked the idea of seeing Wyatt with Josie, with her batting her big brown eyes at him. I laughed, too. I hoped they'd hang them all.

Chapter 18

Free To Tell The Full Story

January 5, 1945.

Now I'm free to do the full story, at last. I'd rather not be.

The war seems to go on interminably. (WWII.) So does the war with my diary and scrapbooks.

The thing is, Josie is gone. Died the 19th of last month. I was there. She wanted me there. Me, John (Flood), Bessie (Nevitt). Josie wanted to be alone with me for awhile and everyone went out. She died while I held her hand, and I cried like a baby. I loved her all these years. I don't want anyone who reads this to mistake my meaning — I loved my wife too, and felt the same when she died in childbirth in 1900 (a late pregnancy; we should have known better, but wanted a kid too much). Life can be heartbreaking. After Wyatt died, I'd have married Josie, just to look after her better, but knew she wouldn't have me — she almost died of grief when Wyatt went, and never got over it.

We took her ashes up to Colma and buried them next to his.

I stood there at the grave after everyone left — alone and lonely — on a mountain of memories. Only Allie and I are left now.

Standing at the grave, Wyatt's voice came back to me as he read his statement in the J.P. court back there in 1881. It seemed only a few short years before. Actually it was sixty-three years.

Few of the other's statements were truthful, as I finally have come to recognize after all these years, because they couldn't be, for one reason or another. Mostly because the other side wanted to railroad the Earps, or had something to conceal. Wyatt had both the least to conceal and the most. His statement, given under oath, not subject to cross examination, as the law permitted, was written for him by attorney Tom Fitch.

All of the testimony at that hearing as reported in the *Nugget* is in my scrapbooks. It and the court record weren't worth the paper they were printed on. I didn't know that at the time, but began to suspect as I listened to the day to day testimony.

I am giving Wyatt's testimony here, which, as I said, comes closer to the truth than anything else stated. Following it, I will record what he said off the record, many years afterward. The two are not hard to reconcile, in view of what I learned was going on. Much of it I have written here before now. It began to dawn on me during the hearing that I had jumped to some wrong conclusions about the Earps.

Wyatt Earp's statement as reported in the *Nugget* follows:

On this sixteenth day of November, 1881, upon the hearing of the above entitled action, on the examination of Wyatt Earp and J. H. Holliday, the prosecution having closed their evidence in chief, and the defendants, Wyatt Earp and J. H. Holliday, having first been informed of his rights to make a statement as provided in Section 133, page 22 of the laws of Arizona, approved February 12, 1881, and the said Wyatt Earp having chosen to make a statement under oath and having been personally sworn, makes such statement under oath in answer to interrogatories as follows:

(Q) What is your name and age?

(A) My name is Wyatt Earp: 33 years old last March the 19th.

(Q) Where were you born?

(A) In Monmouth, Warren County, Illinois.

(Q) Where do you reside and how long have you resided there?

(A) I reside in Tombstone, Cochise County, Arizona: since December 1, 1879.

(Q) What is your business and profession?

(A) Saloon keeper at present. Also have been a Deputy Sheriff and also a detective.

(Q) Give any explanations you may think proper of the circumstances appearing in the testimony against you, and state any facts which you think will tend to your exculpation.

(A) The difficulty which resulted in the death

of William Clanton and Frank McLaury originated last spring, [Objection made by prosecution against the defendant, Wyatt Earp, in making his statement, of using a manuscript from which to make statement without limit as to its relevancy. Objection overruled.] and at a little over a year ago, I followed Tom and Frank McLaury and two other parties who had stolen six government mules from Camp Rucker. Myself, Virgil Earp, and Morgan Earp, and Marshall Williams, Captain Hurst, and four soldiers; we traced those mules to McLaury's ranch. [Prosecution moved to strike out the foregoing statement as irrelevant. Objection overruled.]

While at Charleston I met a man by the name of Dave Estes. He told me I would find the mules at McLaury's ranch. He said he had seen them there the day before. He said they were branding the mules "D.S.", making the "D.S." out [of] "U.S." We tracked the mules right up to the ranch. Also found the branding iron "D.S." Afterwards, some of those mules were found with the same brand.

After we arrived at McLaury's ranch, there was a man by the name of Frank Patterson. He made some kind of a compromise with Captain Hurst. Captain Hurst come to us boys and told us he had made this compromise, and by so doing, he would get his mules back. We insisted on following them up. Hurst prevailed on us to go back to Tombstone, and so we came back. Hurst told us two or three weeks afterwards, that they would not give up the mules to him after we left, saying that they only wanted to get us away, that they could stand the soldiers off. Captain Hurst cautioned me and my brothers, Virgil and Morgan, to look out for those men, as they had made some threats against our lives.

About one month after we had followed up those mules, I met Frank and Tom McLaury in Charleston. They tried to pick a fuss out of me down there, and told me if I ever followed them up again as close as I did before, they would kill me. Shortly after the time Bud Philpot was killed by the men who tried to rob the Benson stage, as a detective I helped trace the matter up, and I was satisfied that three men, named Billy Leonard, Harry Head, and James Crane were in that robbery. I knew that Leonard, Head, and Crane were friends and associates of the Clantons and McLaurys and often stopped at their ranches.

It was generally understood among officers that Ike Clanton was sort of chief among the cowboys, that the Clantons and McLaurys were cattle thieves and generally in the secrets of the stage robbers, and that the Clanton and McLaury ranches were meeting places and places of shelter for the gang.

I had an ambition to be Sheriff of this County at the next election, and I thought it would be a great help to me with the people and businessmen if I could capture the men who killed Philpot. There were rewards offered of about $1,200 each for the capture of the robbers. Altogether there was about $3,600 offered for their capture. I thought this sum might tempt Ike Clanton and Frank McLaury to give away Leonard, Head, and Crane, so I went to Ike Clanton, Frank McLaury, and Joe Hill when they came to town. I had an interview with them in the back yard of the Oriental Saloon. I told them what I wanted. I told them I wanted the glory of capturing Leonard, Head, and Crane, and if I could do it, it would help me make the race for Sheriff at the next election. I told them if they would put me on the track of Leonard, Head, and Crane, and tell me where those men hid, I would give them all the reward and would never let anyone know where I got the information.

Ike Clanton said he would like to see them captured. He said that Leonard claimed a ranch that he claimed, and that if he could get him out of the way, he would have no opposition in regard to the ranch. Clanton said that Leonard, Head, and Crane would make a fight, that they would never be taken alive, and that I must find out if the reward would be paid for the capture of the robbers dead or alive. I then went to Marshall Williams, the agent of Wells Fargo & Co., in this town and at my request, he telegraphed to the agent, or superintendent, in San Francisco to find out if the reward would be paid for the robbers dead or alive. He received, in June, 1881, a telegram, which he showed me, promising the reward would be paid dead or alive.

The next day I met Ike Clanton and Joe Hill on Allen Street in front of a little cigar store next to the Alhambra. I told them that the dispatch had come. I went to Marshall Williams and told him I wanted to see the dispatch for a few minutes. He went to look for it and could not find it, but went over to the telegraph office and got a copy of it, and he came back and gave it to me. I went and showed it to Ike Clanton and Joe Hill and returned it to Marshall Williams, and afterwards told Frank McLaury of its contents.

It was then agreed between us that they were to have all the $3,600 reward, outside of necessary expenses for horse hire in going after them, and that Joe Hill should go to where Leonard, Head, and Crane were hid, over near Yreka, in New Mexico, and lure them in near Frank and Tom McLaury's ranch near Soldier Hole, 30 miles from here, and I would be on hand with a posse and capture them.

I asked Joe Hill, Ike Clanton, and Frank McLaury what tale they would make up to get them over here. They said they had agreed upon a plan to tell them there would be a paymaster going from Tombstone to Bisbee, to pay off the miners, and they wanted them to come in and take him in. Ike Clanton then sent Joe Hill to bring them in. Before starting, Joe Hill took off his watch and chain and between two and three hundred dollars in money, and gave it to Virgil Earp to keep for him until he got back. He was gone about ten days and returned with the word that he got there a day too late; that Leonard and Harry Head had been killed the day before he got there by horse thieves. I learned afterward that the thieves had been killed subsequently by members of the Clanton and McLaury gang.

After that, Ike Clanton and Frank McLaury claimed that I had given them away to Marshall Williams and Doc Holliday, and when they came in town, they shunned us, and Morgan, Virgil Earp, Doc Holliday and myself began to hear their threats against us.

I am a friend of Doc Holliday because when I was city marshal of Dodge City, Kansas, he came to my rescue and saved my life when I was surrounded by desperados.

About a month or more ago [October 1881], Morgan Earp and myself assisted to arrest Stilwell and Spence on the charge of robbing the Bisbee stage. The McLaurys and Clantons were always friendly with Spence and Stilwell, and they laid the whole blame of their arrest on us, though the fact is, we only went as a sheriff's posse. After we got in town with Spence and Stilwell, Ike Clanton and Frank McLaury came in.

Frank McLaury took Morgan Earp into the street in front of the Alhambra, where John Ringo, Ike Clanton, and the two Hicks boys were also standing. Frank McLaury commenced to abuse Morgan Earp for going after Spence and Stilwell. Frank McLaury said he would never speak to Spence again for being arrested by us.

He said to Morgan, "If you ever come after me, you will never take me." Morgan replied that if he ever had occasion to go after him, he would arrest him. Frank McLaury then said to Morgan Earp, "I have threatened you boys' lives, and a few days later I had taken it back, but since this arrest, it now goes." Morgan made no reply and walked off.*

Before this and after this, Marshall Williams, Farmer Daly, Ed Barnes, Old Man Urrides, Charley Smith and three or four others had told us at different times of threats to kill us, by Ike Clanton, Frank McLaury, Tom McLaury, Joe Hill, and John Ringo. I knew all these men were desperate and dangerous men, that they were connected with outlaws, cattle thieves, robbers, and murderers. I knew of the McLaurys' stealing six government mules, and also cattle, and when the owner went after them finding his stock on the McLaury's ranch; that he was drove off and told that if he ever said anything about it, he would be killed, and he kept his mouth shut until several days ago, for fear of being killed.

I heard of John Ringo shooting a man down in cold blood near Camp Thomas. I was satisfied that Frank and Tom McLaury killed and robbed Mexicans in Skeleton Canyon, about three or four months ago, and naturally kept my eyes open and did not intend that any of the gang should get the drop on me if I could help it.

Ike Clanton met me at the Alhambra five or six weeks ago and told me I had told Holliday about this transaction, concerning the capture of

* McLaury was obviously drunk. — **GB.**

255

Head, Leonard, and Crane. I told him I had never told Holliday anything. I told him when Holliday came up from Tucson I would prove it. Ike said that Holliday had told him so. When Holliday came back I asked him if he said so.

On the night of the 25th of October, Holliday met Ike Clanton in the Alhambra Saloon and asked him about it. Clanton denied it. They quarreled for three or four minutes. Holliday told Clanton he was a damned liar, if he said so. I was sitting eating lunch at the lunch counter. Morgan Earp was standing at the Alhambra bar talking with the bartender. I called him over to where I was sitting, knowing that he was an officer and told him that Holliday and Clanton were quarreling in the lunch room and for him to go and stop it. He climbed over the lunch room counter from the Alhambra bar and went into the room, took Holliday by the arm and led him into the street. Ike Clanton in a few seconds followed them out. I got through eating and walked out of the bar. As I stopped at the door of the bar, they were still quarreling.

Just then, Virgil Earp came up, I think out of the Occidental, and told them, Holliday and Clanton, if they didn't stop their quarreling he would have to arrest them. They all separated at that time, Morgan Earp going down the street to the Oriental Saloon, Ike going across the street to the Grand Hotel. I walked in the Eagle Brewery where I had a faro game which I had not closed. I stayed in there for a few minutes and walked out to the street and there met Ike Clanton. He asked me if I would take a walk with him, that he wanted to talk to me. I told him I would if he did not go too far, as I was waiting for my game in the Brewery to close, and I would have to take care of the money. We walked about half-way down the brewery building, going down Fifth Street and stopped.

He told me when Holliday approached him in the Alhambra that he wasn't fixed just right. He said that in the morning he would have man-for-man, that this fighting talk had been going on for a long time, and he guessed it was about time to fetch it to a close. I told him I would not fight no one if I could get away from it, because there was no money in it. He walked off and left me saying, "I will be ready for you in the morning."

I walked over to the Oriental. He followed me in and took a drink, having his six-shooter in plain sight. He says, "You must not think I won't be after you all in the morning." He said he would like to make a fight with Holliday now. I told him Holliday did not want to fight, but only to satisfy him that this talk had not been made. About that time the man that was dealing my game closed it and brought the money to me. I locked it in the safe and started home. I met Holliday on the street between the Oriental and Alhambra. Myself and Holliday walked down Allen Street, he going to his room, and I to my house, going to bed.

I got up the next day, October 26, about noon. Before I got up, Ned Boyle came to me and told me that he met Ike Clanton on Allen Street near the telegraph office, that Ike was armed, that he said, "As soon as those damned Earps make their appearance on the street today, the ball will open, we are here to make a fight. We are looking for the sons-of-bitches!" I laid in bed some little time after that, and got up and went down to the Oriental Saloon.

Harry Jones came to me after I got up and said, "What does all this mean?" I asked him what he meant. He says, "Ike Clanton is hunting you boys with a Winchester rifle and six-shooter." I said, "I will go down and find him and see what he wants." I went out and on the corner of Fifth and Allen I met Virgil Earp, the marshal. He told me how he heard Ike Clanton was hunting us. I went down Allen Street and Virgil went down Fifth Street and then Fremont Street. Virgil found Ike Clanton on Fourth Street near Fremont Street, in the mouth of an alleyway.

I walked up to him and said, "I hear you are hunting for some of us." I was coming down Fourth Street at the time. Ike Clanton then threw his Winchester rifle around toward Virgil. Virgil grabbed it and hit Ike Clanton with his six-shooter and knocked him down. Clanton had his rifle and his six-shooter in his pants. By that time I came up. Virgil and Morgan Earp took his rifle and six-shooter and took them to the Grand Hotel after examination, and I took Ike Clanton before Justice Wallace.

Before the investigation, Morgan Earp had Ike Clanton in charge, as Virgil Earp was out at the time. After I went into Wallace's Court and sat down on a bench, Ike Clanton looked over to me and said, "I will get even with all of you for this. If I had a six-shooter now I would make a fight with all of you." Morgan Earp then said to him, "If you want to make a fight right bad, I will give you this one!", at the same time offering Ike Clanton his own six-shooter.

Ike Clanton started to get up and take it, when Campbell, the deputy sheriff, pushed him back in his seat, saying he would not allow any fuss. I never had Ike Clanton's arms at any time, as he stated.

I would like to describe the positions we occupied in the courtroom. Ike Clanton sat on a bench with his face fronting to the north wall of the building. I myself sat down on a bench that ran against and along the north wall in front of where Ike sat. Morgan Earp stood up on his feet with his back against the wall and to the right of where I sat, and two or three feet from me.

Morgan Earp had Ike Clanton's Winchester in his hand, like this, with one end on the floor, with Clanton's six-shooter in his right hand. We had them all the time. Virgil Earp was not in the courtroom during any of this time and came there after I had walked out. He was out, he told me, hunting for Judge Wallace.

I was tired of being threatened by Ike Clanton and his gang and believe from what he said to me and others, and from their movements that they intended to assassinate me the first chance they had, and I thought that if I had to fight for my life with them I had better make them face me in an open fight. So I said to Ike Clanton, who was then sitting about eight feet from me, "You damned dirty cow thief, you have been threatening our lives and I know it. I think I would be justified in shooting you down any place I should meet you, but if you are anxious to make a fight, I will go anywhere on earth to make a fight with you, even over to the San Simon among your crowd!"

He replied, "I will see you after I get through here. I only want four feet of ground to fight on!"

I walked out and then just outside of the courtroom near the Justice's Office, I met Tom McLaury. He came up to me and said to me, "If you want to make a fight, I will make a fight with you anywhere." I supposed at the time that he had heard what had just transpired between Ike Clanton and myself. I knew of his having threatened me, and I felt just as I did about Ike Clanton and if the fight had to come, I had better have it come when I had an even show to defend myself. So I said to him, "All right, make a fight right here!" And at the same time slapped him in the face with my left hand and drew my pistol with my right. He had a pistol in plain sight on his right hip in his pants, but made no move to draw it. I said to him, "Jerk your gun and use it!" He made no reply and I hit him on the head with my six-shooter and walked away, down to Hafford's Corner. I went into Hafford's and got a cigar and came out and stood by the door.

Pretty soon after I saw Tom McLaury, Frank McLaury, and William Clanton pass me and went down Fourth Street to the gunsmith shop. I followed them to see what they were going to do. When I got there, Frank McLaury's horse was standing on the sidewalk with his head in the door of the gun shop. I took the horse by the bit, as I was deputy city marshal, and commenced to back him off the sidewalk. Tom and Frank and Billy Clanton came to the door. Billy Clanton laid his hand on his six-shooter. Frank McLaury took hold of the horse's bridle and I said, "You will have to get this horse off the sidewalk." He backed him off into the street. Ike Clanton came up about this time and they all walked into the gun shop. I saw them in the gun shop changing cartridges into their belts. They came out of the shop and walked along Fourth Street to the corner of Allen Street.

Virgil Earp was then city marshal; Morgan Earp was a special policeman for six weeks or two months, wore a badge and drew pay. I had been sworn in in Virgil's place, to act for him while Virgil was gone to Tucson on Spence's and Stilwell's trial. Virgil had been back several days but I was still acting and I knew it was Virgil's duty to disarm those men. I expected he would have trouble doing so, and I followed up to give assistance if necessary, especially as they had been threatening us, as I have already stated.

About ten minutes afterwards, and while Virgil, Morgan, Doc Holliday, and myself were standing on the corner of Fourth and Allen Streets, several people said, "There is going to be trouble with those fellows," and one man named Coleman said to Virgil Earp, "They mean trouble. They have just gone from Dunbar's Corral into the O.K. Corral, all armed, and I think you had better go and disarm them." Virgil turned around to Doc Holliday, Morgan Earp, and myself and told us to come and assist him in disarming them.

Morgan Earp said to me, "They have horses, had we not better get some horses ourselves, so that if they make a running fight we can catch them?" I said, "No, if they try to make a running fight we can kill their horses and then capture them."

We four started through Fourth to Fremont Street. When we turned the corner of Fourth and Fremont we could see them standing near or about the vacant space between Fly's photograph gallery and the next building west. I first saw Frank McLaury, Tom McLaury, Billy Clanton and Sheriff Behan standing there. We went down the left-hand side of Fremont street.

When we got within about 150 feet of them I saw Ike Clanton and Billy Clanton and another party. We had walked a few steps further and I saw Behan leave the party and come toward us. Every few steps he would look back as if he apprehended danger. I heard him say to Virgil Earp, "For God's sake, don't go down there, you will get murdered!" Virgil Earp replied, "I am going to disarm them," he, Virgil, being in the lead.

When I and Morgan came up to Behan he said, "I have disarmed them." When he said this, I took my pistol, which I had in my hand, under my coat, and put it in my overcoat pocket. Behan then passed up the street, and we walked on down.

We came up on them close; Frank McLaury, Tom McLaury, and Billy Clanton standing in a row against the east side of the building on the opposite side of the vacant space west of Fly's photograph gallery. Ike Clanton and Billy Claiborne and a man I don't know were standing in the vacant space about halfway between the photograph gallery and the next building west.

I saw that Billy Clanton and Frank and Tom McLaury had their hands by their sides, Frank McLaury and Billy Clanton's six-shooters were in plain sight. Virgil said, "Throw up your hands, I have come to disarm you!" Virgil said, "Hold, I don't mean that! I have come to disarm you!" Then Billy Clanton and Frank McLaury commenced to draw their pistols. At the same time, Tom McLaury threw his hand to his right hip, throwing his coat open like this, [showing how] and jumped behind his horse.

I had my pistol in my overcoat pocket, where I had put it when Behan told us he had disarmed the other parties. When I saw Billy Clanton and Frank McLaury draw their pistols, I drew my pistol. Billy Clanton leveled his pistol at me, but I did not aim at him. I knew that Frank McLaury had the reputation of being a good shot and a dangerous man, and I aimed at Frank McLaury. The

263

first two shots were fired by Billy Clanton and myself, he shooting at me, and I shooting at Frank McLaury. I don't know which was fired first. We fired almost together. The fight then became general.

After about four shots were fired, Ike Clanton ran up and grabbed my left arm. I could see no weapon in his hand, and thought at the time he had none, and so I said to him, "The fight had commenced. Go to fighting or get away," at the same time pushing him off with my left hand, like this.

My first shot struck Frank McLaury in the belly. He staggered off on the sidewalk but fired one shot at me. When we told them to throw up their hands Claiborne threw up his left hand and broke and ran. I never saw him afterwards until late in the afternoon, after the fight. I never drew my pistol or made a motion to shoot until after Billy Clanton and Frank McLaury drew their pistols. If Tom McLaury was unarmed, I did not know it, I believe he was armed and fired two shots at our party before Holliday, who had the shotgun, fired and killed him. If he was unarmed, there was nothing in the circumstances or in what had been communicated to me, or in his acts or threats, that would have led me even to suspect his being unarmed.

I never fired at Ike Clanton, even after the shooting commenced, because I thought he was unarmed. I believed then, and believe now, from the acts I have stated and the threats I have related and the other threats communicated to me by other persons as having been made by Tom McLaury, Frank McLaury, and Ike Clanton, that these men last named had formed a conspiracy to murder my brothers, Morgan and Virgil, Doc Holliday, and myself. I believe I would have been legally and morally justified in shooting any of them on sight, but I did not do so, nor attempt to do so. I sought no advantage when I went as deputy marshal to help disarm them and arrest them. I went as a part of my duty and under the direction of my brother, the marshal, I did not intend to fight unless it became necessary in self-defense of my own life and the lives of my brothers and Doc Holliday.

I have been in Tombstone since December 1, 1879. I came here directly from Dodge City, Kansas. Against the protest of businessmen and officials, I resigned the office of city marshal, which I held from 1876. I came to Dodge City from Wichita, Kansas. I was on the police force in Wichita from 1874 until I went to Dodge City.

The testimony of Isaac Clanton that I ever said to him that I had anything to do with any stage robbery or giving information to Morgan Earp going on the stage, or any improper communication whatever with any criminal enterprise is a tissue of lies from beginning to end.

Sheriff Behan made me an offer in his office on Allen Street in the back room of a cigar store, where he, Behan, had his office, that if I would withdraw and not try to get appointed sheriff of

Cochise County, that he would hire a clerk and divide the profits. I done so, and he never said another word about it afterwards, but claimed in his statement and gave his reason for not complying with his contract, which is false in every particular.

Myself and Doc Holliday happened to go to Charleston the night that Behan went down there to subpoena Ike Clanton. We went there for the purpose to get a horse that I had had stolen from me a few days after I came to Tombstone. I had heard several times that the Clantons had him. When I got there that night, I was told by a friend of mine that the man that carried the dispatch from Charleston to Ike Clanton's ranch had rode my horse. At this time I did not know where Ike Clanton's ranch was.

A short time afterwards I was in the Huachucas locating some water rights. I had started home to Tombstone. I had got within 12 or 15 miles of Charleston when I met a man named McMasters. He told me if I would hurry up, I would find my horse in Charleston. I drove into Charleston and saw my horse going though the streets toward the corral. I put up for the night in another corral. I went to Burnett's office to get papers for the recovery of the horse. He was not at home having gone down to Sonora to some coal fields that had been discovered. I telegraphed to Tombstone to James Earp and told him to have papers made out and sent to me. He went to Judge Wallace and Mr. Street. They made the papers out and sent them to Charleston by my youngest brother, Warren Earp, that night. While I was waiting for the papers, Billy Clanton found out that I was in town and went and tried to take the horse out of the corral. I told him that he could not take him out, that it was my horse. After the papers came, he gave the horse up without the papers being served, and asked me if I had any more horses to lose. I told him I would keep them in the stable after this, and give him no chance to steal them.

I give here, as part of the statement, a document sent me from Dodge City since my arrest on this charge, which I wish attached to this statement and marked "Exhibit A".

[Here counsel for the Prosecution objects to this paper being introduced or used for, or attached as an exhibit as a part of this statement, on the grounds that the paper is not on its face, a statement of the defendant, but a statement of other persons made long after the alleged commission of this crime. Counsel for the Defense objects to any objections interpolated by counsel for the prosecution in a statutory statement made by the party charged with crime, for the reason that the law contemplates such statement shall not be interrupted by the court, the counsel for the prosecution, or the counsel for the defense, or for the further reason that it is perfect evidence of character lacking only the absurd formality. Objection of counsel for prosecution overruled and the paper ordered to be filed as part of this statement.]

In relation to the conversation that I had with Ike Clanton, Frank McLaury, and Joe Hill was four or five different times, and they were all held in the backyard of the Oriental Saloon.

I told Ike Clanton in one of those conversations that there were some parties here in town that were trying to give Doc Holliday the worst of it by their talk, that there was some suspicion that he knew something about the attempted robbery and killing of Bud Philpot, and if I could catch Leonard, Head, and Crane, I could prove to the citizens that he knew nothing of it.

In following the trail of Leonard, Head, and Crane, we struck it at the scene of the attempted robbery, and never lost the trail or hardly a footprint from the time we started from Drew's ranch on the San Pedro, until we got to Helm's ranch in the Dragoons. After following about 80 miles down the San Pedro River and capturing one of the men named King that was supposed to be with them, we then crossed the Catalina Mountains within 15 miles of Tucson following their trail around the foot of the mountain to Tres Alamos on the San Pedro River, thence to the Dragoons to Helm's ranch.

We then started out from Helm's ranch and got on their trail. They had stolen 15 or 20 head of stock, so as to cover their trail. Virgil Earp and Morgan Earp, Robert H. Paul, Breakenridge the deputy sheriff, Johnny Behan the sheriff and one or two others still followed their trail to New Mexico.

Their trail never led south from Helm's ranch as Ike Clanton has stated. We used every effort we could to capture those men or robbers. I was out ten days. Virgil and Morgan Earp were out sixteen days, and [we] all done all we could to catch those men, and I safely say if it had not been for myself and Morgan Earp they would not have got King as he started to run when we rode up to his hiding place and was making for a big patch of brush on the river and would have got in it, if [it] had not been for us two.

[signed] Wyatt Earp

DEFENSE EXHIBIT "A"

To All Whom It May Concern, Greetings:

We, the undersigned citizens of Dodge City, Ford County, Kansas, and vicinity do by these presents certify that we are personally acquainted with Wyatt Earp, late of this city; that he came here in the year 1876; that during the years of 1877, 1878, and 1879, he was Marshal of our city; that he left our place in the fall of 1879; that during his whole stay here he occupied a place of high social position and was regarded and looked upon as a high-minded, honorable citizen; that as Marshal of our city he was ever vigilant in the discharge of his duties, and while kind and courteous to all, he was brave, unflinching, and on all occasions proved himself the right man in the right place.

Hearing that he is now under arrest, charged with complicity in the killing of those men termed "Cow Boys," from our knowledge of him we do not believe that he would wantonly take the life of his fellow man, and that if he was implicated, he only took life in the discharge of his sacred trust to the people; and earnestly appeal to the citizens of Tombstone, Arizona, to use all means to secure him a fair and impartial trial, fully confident that when tried he will be fully vindicated and exonerated of any crime.

R.M. Wright	Representative, Ford County
Lloyd Shinn	Probate Judge, Ford County, Kansas
M.W. Sutton	County Attorney, Ford County
George F. Hinkle	Sheriff, Ford County, Kansas
G.M. Homer	Chairman, County Board
J.W. Liellow	Ford County Commissioner
F.C. Zimmerman	Ford County, Treasurer and Tax Collector
G.W. Potter	Clerk of Ford County
Thomas S. Jones	Police Judge and Attorney at Law
A.B. Webster	Mayor, Dodge City, Kansas
C.M. Beeson	City Council, Dodge City, Kansas
Geo. Emerson	City Council, Dodge City, Kansas
P.F. Sughrue	City Council, Dodge City, Kansas

A.H. Boyd City Council, Dodge City, Kansas
J.H. Philips Deputy County Treasurer, Ford County
R.G. Cook U.S. Commissioner
Wright, Beverly & Co. Dodge City Merchants
Herman F. Fringey Postmaster, Dodge City, Kansas
O.W. Wright Pastor, Presbyterian Church
Marsh and Son Merchants
W.W. Robins Groceries
H.P. Weiss Shoemaker
Fred T.M. Wenir Notary Public and Insurance Agent
R.C. Burns Attorney
H.M. Bell Deputy United States Marshal
T.L. McCarty M.D.
D.E. Frost ex-Police Judge
Beeson and Harris Liquor Dealers
W.E Petillon Register of Deeds, Ford County
J.Ormond Bookkeeper
N.B. Klaine Editor, [Dodge City] *Times*, City Treasurer, School Director, and Notary Public
Walter Straeter _____?
J.H. Kelley ex-Mayor, Dodge City
Jim Anderson Livery Man
J. McGinnis R.R. Agent, and Agent, Wells Fargo & Co. Express
D.C. Kane Mgr. Western Union Tel. Co.
P.G. Reynolds and Son _____?
Tom Bugg Deputy Sheriff
Coe and Boyd Props., Dodge House

Oscar Tsevallee	Boots and Shoes
B.C. Vanderburg	City Marshal
T. Coller	Merchant
Ed. Cooley	Constable and Dep. Sheriff
R.E. McAnulty	Cattle Dealer
Bond and Nixon	Liquor Dealers
John Mueleer	Cattle Dealer
H.F. Wray	_____?
Jno. T. Lytle	Cattle Dealer
R.W. Evans	
[And 13 others on paper]	

Notarized or acknowleged by; H.P. Myton, Clerk of the District Court, Ford County, Kansas. [With Seal]

DEFENSE EXHIBIT "B"

STATE OF KANSAS

COUNTY OF SEDGEWICK } ss

We, the undersigned citizens of Wichita in the County and State aforesaid are well acquainted with Mr. Wyatt S. Earp and that we were intimately acquainted with him while he was on the Police force of this city, in the years A.D. 1874,

1875 and part of the year, 1876. We further certify that the said Wyatt S. Earp was a good and efficient officer, and was well known for his honesty, and integrity, that his character while here was of the best, and that no fault was ever found with him as an officer, or as a man.

Geo. E. Harris, Mayor in 1875
M. Zimmerly, Councilman in 1875
C.M. Garrrison, Councilman in 1875
R.C. Ogdell, ex-City Marshal
J.M. True, ex-City Treasurer
Fred Sclattner, City Clerk
James Cairns, City Marshal

Sworn and subscribed to and before me this fourth day of November A.D. 1881.

CHARLES HATTON, NOTARY PUBLIC

I hereby certify that I knew personally Wyatt S. Earp during his residence in the city of Wichita. That I served four years as city attorney of said city and have known personally all of the officers of said city for the past ten years. I take great pleasure in saying that Wyatt S. Earp was one of the most efficient officers that Wichita ever had and I can safely testify that Mr. Earp is in every sense reliable and a trustworthy gentleman.

[signed] Chas. Hatton

EDITORIAL COMMENT:
There were many more witnesses than those quoted. What they said can be partially reconciled

to other statements, but for a coherent narrative, including all pertinent facts, I have been selective, not to slant the readers' conclusions, but to avoid interminable speculation, and also to keep this narrative manageable. (A full coverage of all of the testimony appears in the book "The O.K. Corral Inquest", edited by Alford Turner; Creative Publishing Company, College Station, Texas. The transcript is fairly accurate since it was Stuart Lake's copy, passed to the editor of "The Tombstone Epitaph" by Lake and later to me by that editor. In turn I loaned it to Turner since he wanted to annotate and publish it, which he did with my blessing. It may provide centuries of joy for generations captivated by Chinese Puzzles, and clubs of Western buffs whose principal attraction to joining seems to be an opportunity to antagonize one another, but the transcript does not provide much unarguable insight.)

Ten Eyck continues his story:

The defense attorneys were fully aware that neither Behan nor Billy Claiborne had seen the actual shooting, and that Ike's view of it had been so brief and terror stricken that he couldn't be sure what he'd seen. Before adding what Wyatt said of the shooting years later, I will insert the defense's questioning that showed they knew the main prosecution witnesses had seen next to nothing. It is important to put this in here, because knowledge of that makes Wyatt's later story entirely credible.

274

Bob Hatch, later sheriff, was on the stand. Wyatt's attorney, Fitch was questioning him:

Q. Are you not satisfied from all you saw that Behan and Claiborne saw nothing of this difficulty?

(The question was objected to by the prosecution, objection sustained, but the defense's desired reply was obtained from a restatement of the question.)

Q. When last did you see Sheriff Behan at that difficulty?

A. I did not see him while the shooting was going on at all. . . . .

I always marvelled at what a wonderful euphemism "difficulty" was to describe what sometimes amounted to a "hog butchering."

I suspect a lot of people have been waiting to hear Wyatt on the subject of the shooting, off the record. They will not have to wait any longer.

He got around to it during the previously related visit I made to the Happy Day in 1910.

Anyhow the following is the substance of what Wyatt said in his own words as I remember them:

"When we first got down below Fly's and filed into the empty lot facing that crowd, I knew that Behan lied to us about disarming them. I said, 'You sons of bitches have been looking for a fight.' Virg said, 'Throw up your hands.' I don't know why he said that after what I said and since Frank and Billy already had their hands on their sixshooters and had cocked them. I had mine out, cocked. I shot those two as quick as I could do

275

it without missing. I'd have got Ike too, but the son of a bitch was too close and grabbed me. I tried to twist my six-shooter around to gut shoot him, but he was strong as an ox. He pushed me into a little ditch they'd dug to put in water pipes, and I didn't get my balance quick enough to plug him while he ran."

I couldn't help but ask Wyatt, "How come they said Doc and Morg fired the first shots?"

"Maybe they didn't know. Ike must have known though. I figured he told Johnny and that's why he tried to arrest me right after the shooting."

EDITORIAL COMMENT:
Behan probably tried to arrest Wyatt because of Wyatt's previous actions that indicated he was looking for a fight, and because he wasn't technically a member of the police force. And certainly because Behan hated his guts — GB.

I said, "But even Ike testified that Doc and Morg shot first."

"I always wondered about that. I guess he was after them for the night before."

Wyatt had some more to say on that subject that is illuminating:

"We expected some of the other Cowboys might show up at the fight; in fact had a tip that they would. On the way down to Fly's I said to Doc, 'If you see any of those s.o.b.'s, use that scattergun and let 'em have it.' Some damn woman caught the tail end of it and almost sunk our boat when she repeated it in court.

"Before that I'd told Doc, 'It's going to be up to us to get rid of those bastards. Neither Morg nor Virg would kill a fly.'

"Doc agreed that we were going to have to get rid of them sooner or later.

"If we didn't they'd only ambush us somewhere else, the way it looked to me. That's what the rest of that gang did, anyhow. I should have hunted them down and shot them like mad dogs.

"We'd have been better off in that fight, if Virg and Morg stayed down at Hafford's and had a beer. We only needed Virg along for his badge. All Morg did was manage to get shot standing around with his mouth open. I let him take credit for finishing Frank McLaury because he thought he did. Hell, neither Morg nor Frank knew which end was up after they were plugged. I saw Morg's shot at Frank go into the ground about five feet in front of him, just after I drilled Frank through the head and finished him. Morg said, 'I got him.'

"Billy was strong as a bull, though, and kept right on shooting after I plugged him in the brisket. I'd have finished Billy, too, if Virg wasn't dodging around in the way. There wasn't time to do it when I first shot him. I figured we had to get a slug in them all as quick as we could. I didn't see any gun on Ike, but the son of a bitch could have had one in his back pocket and was too yellow to jerk it.

"Tom back-shooting Morg was what spoiled the whole affair. He got a chance to do that when somebody tried to shoot some of us from Fly's back porch."

It made sense to me. In court during Ike's testimony, Harry Woods leaned over and whispered to me, "Remember what Behan said about Ike running into him coming out the back door of Fly's? Remind me to tell you the rest of it."

That was tantalizing. I reminded him all right. Harry told me, "Behan said, 'It was pretty plain that Ike had pissed his pants. He bounced off me and I could see he was wet all down one leg. He managed to say, 'The Earps shot Billy and Frank. Wyatt almost got me.' Then he pulled his freight, so scared he couldn't see straight. He even threw away his six-shooter.' "

So Ike had a six-shooter and Behan knew it. Ike had probably bought it when they were all in Spangenberg's after Billy and Frank came to town.

This is 'enough said.' I'm going to leave it at that.

Chapter 19

"A Proposition Both Monstrous And Startling"

I knew that neither Ike nor Johnny had seen much of the shooting, and was therefore amused at their testimony. Behan, being smarter, was a much cleverer liar. Nonetheless, he tripped himself up and the defense didn't seem to notice. Johnny's obvious contradiction of himself related to questions about when Ike departed the shooting.

Johnny and Ike hadn't got their stories together, though it was obvious to me that all the prosecution witnesses had been rehearsed — as I said, by Harry Woods, for the most part.

Ike testified prior to Johnny and had been asked:

Q.   At what period of the shooting did you run?

A.   There had been four or five shots fired.

Q.   Where did you retreat from? State the course of your retreat.

A.   I ran through the front door of Flys lodging house, through the hall to the open space between the lodging house and the daguerrian gallery, then into the open space west of the daguerrian gallery, thence southerly to Allen Street. . . . .

EDITORIAL COMMENT:
If Ike jumped off the west side of the stoop and ran, he was panicked so badly that he was totally disoriented because that course put him right back in the path of the gunfire.

Ten Eyck continues:

Recall that Ike said he left after the fifth shot, let's see what Johnny said with a bearing on that. He testified:

"I suppose there was as many as eight or ten shots before I saw arms in the hands of any of the McLaury or Clanton party. Frank McLaury is the first man of that party in whose hands I saw a pistol. Ike Clanton broke and ran after the first five shots were fired." (So far so good, for the coaching.) "I saw him at the back corner of Fly's house, the last I saw of him there. I should judge he ran into an addition on the back of Fly's building." (Johnny got a failing grade here.)

We know Johnny left before any shots were fired, by his own admission. Those who heard him in court should have known that. If Johnny saw Ike out back, and Ike left after the fifth shot, then everyone should have realized that Johnny could not have been out front at the tenth shot as he said he was. If I hadn't already known where he was, I'd have wondered if he were a lightning runner, or able to see through walls. Of course he was lying. Too bad the defense didn't notice that.

They did pretty well anyhow. They even had asked Ike what he was down at that particular spot for in the first place. Naturally the prosecution objected. They knew too, that the Cowboys were all there to shoot down Doc Holliday when he came home. It must have been a rude shock for Ike to look up the street and see Doc coming home with three grim-faced friends.

If the actors had been up to their parts as well as Harry Woods had been up to creating them, perhaps the Earps would have gone to the pen or been hung.

I have filled in the background motives for the fight and they throw light on Ike Clanton's involved self-justification of his agreement to sell out his outlaw associates, in return for the rewards.

He thought he'd cleared himself, but began to feel he was in hot water again during the hearings. He'd told Curly Bill about the Earp's offer, but came clean a couple of months too late. The first offer had been made in early June but he didn't come clean to the gang until late July. That suggested to anyone even half-bright what the real situation had been — he'd accepted Wyatt's deal until it looked like there was no longer enough money in it. About then he had also concluded that his part in it might become public knowledge. Ike couldn't help but admit in court that some deal had existed and told a comical story.

Regarding Wyatt's offer of the rewards, covered in Wyatt's statement in full (which hadn't yet been presented to the court) Ike said:

". . . . . I then asked him why he was anxious to capture these fellows. He said that his business was such that he could not afford to capture them. He would have to kill them or else leave the country. He said he and his brother Morgan had piped off to Doc Holliday and William Leonard the money that was going off on the stage. . . . ."

This is so transparently ridiculous I'm surprised Ike was induced to say it. And I am confounded to even imagine why the defense never asked Ike questions such as:

Q. Mr. Clanton, you say that Wyatt Earp admitted to you he'd "piped off" the money from the stage — can you suggest to us why, if that were so, Wells Fargo, which is usually careful in such matters, never missed the money?

Q. In that you could have been considered an enemy of the Earps, why in the world would Wyatt Earp put himself and his brother Morgan in your power by making guilty confessions to you, of all people?

Q. Why would Wyatt and Morgan Earp "pipe off" money to Doc Holliday and William Leonard, at considerable risk to themselves, rather than keep it?

And why didn't the defense put on Wells Fargo agent, Marshall Williams, to testify that no money had been lost?

After that Wyatt worked on and off for Wells Fargo for many years, perhaps till after the turn of the century. He certainly continued in their confidence till the day he left Tombstone. His supervisor was Jim Hume, one of the shrewdest and most effective detectives that any express company ever employed. Hume would have had to be a real dunce to be deceived by the Earps if they had actually done what Ike said. The robbery, as Ike had to know, was a cover for an attempt to kill Bob Paul, and Ike had been one of the participants, may have been the man who actually killed Bud Philpot by accident. Although Wells Fargo knew this, it would not have done to bring it out in court. Ike would have left the country. They undoubtedly still hoped to get something on him, or kill him.

No more wonderfully stupid piece of testimony than this of Ike's was ever presented in a court. I always wondered why Harry Woods put him up to it. Maybe Behan wanted Ike's mob to get rid of him and sicced Harry on him. Harry was clever enough to create a part for Ike that could get him killed, and even to convince him it made sense. Ike wasn't too smart. And he certainly had been an embarrassment to them all. As one of those still alive who knew Behan was behind the attempt on Paul's life, Ike was most dangerous to Johnny. Behan would have preferred to see Ike dead.

On the other hand, with respect to Wyatt Earp's testimony, which had the ring of truth in the whole affair, the defense produced in court a copy of the Wells Fargo telegram Wyatt said he had sent for at Ike's request to verify that the rewards would be paid, dead or alive. Except for the reason Wyatt gave, why else would he have sent for such a telegram?

Of that telegram, Ike earlier had stated in court: "I never heard anything about the telegram to Wells Fargo before today. . . . ."

I certainly didn't believe that after the telegram was produced in court. Few did. Why his own crowd didn't do him up for sure after that I can't imagine. He may have been useful in some manner I can't conceive. Another thought just occurred to me. Rather than Behan wanting Ike rubbed out by his own gang, it may have occurred to Johnny that such an event would confirm, in the public mind, everything to which Wyatt Earp had testified. If Wyatt's testimony were fully accepted by the public, it would advance his chances of successfully running against Johnny for sheriff in the fall of 1882. Curly Bill would leave Ike alive at Johnny's request in such a case; Curly also would realize that Wyatt Earp as sheriff of Cochise County spelled an end to the outlaw gang for sure. It sounds a little complicated in the telling, but knowing the people involved, it makes sense.

In addition to Ike, other witnesses who were not necessarily hostile to the defense were not dependable. Rube Coleman, for example, said:

"Wyatt Earp stood and fired in rapid succession, as cool as a cucumber, and was not hit."

Fired? At what? Did he hit it? Depending on the answers to those questions, either the defense or prosecution might have wished to ask them.

Or did the lawyers think, as I did, that Coleman,

284

a notorious gossip and standing joke as such in the community, was not too convincing, acting like he'd been a calm spectator on the third base line, when anyone with sense knew he ran like hell, saw very little, then **spread and blew** later.

Claiborne was a similar case. If he had actually seen the shooting commence, he'd have known that Wyatt fired the first shots. Why then did he later testify that Morgan and Doc did? (Doc was on the northwest corner of Fly's with the shotgun just as Wyatt asked him to be, alert to pick off any others who might be in ambush to aid the Cowboys.) More perplexing yet, if Claiborne had seen Wyatt open the ball, he may have told Behan that, after they were both in Fly's, accounting for Behan's attempt to arrest Wyatt right after the fight; but if that were so, Claiborne's later testimony to the contrary is even more inexplicable. Surely Claiborne would want to sink Wyatt's boat with the truth, if he knew it. The more tenable belief is that Claiborne ran, panic stricken, and saw nothing. Even more tenable, is the assertion that all this is simply impossible to untangle.

Before throwing up my hands, I've got some more questions that were never asked, that should have been:

Q. Mr. Behan, you were down there talking to the deceased for twenty minutes before the shooting; what were you talking about for such a length of time, since you said you simply went down to disarm or arrest them?

Q. Mr. Behan, Ike Clanton testified that you

said you wanted to disarm his party to avoid trouble. What sort of trouble did you anticipate and why?

Q. Mr. Behan, you testified that you told Frank McLaury that you were going to disarm the other party; doesn't it strike you as rather odd that you proposed to disarm the Chief of Police and his men, when it was obvious from your other testimony that you expected trouble, and in fact stated that you earlier had invited the Chief of Police to accompany you in arresting these men? Did you propose to the Chief of Police at that time that he go with you unarmed to avoid trouble?

Q. Mr. Behan, you've testified that these men defied you when you tried to arrest them. Why didn't you pull your six-shooter and force them to comply?

Q. Mr. Behan, in that you hadn't previously been able to force these men to submit to arrest, why didn't you avail yourself of the re-enforcement provided by the arrival of the Chief of Police and go back with him to enforce your authority?

Q. Were you aware that Ike Clanton was earlier down at Mr. Fly's lodging house with a rifle, looking for Doc Holliday who is stopping there?

Q. Do you see any relation between the fact that you found these men, Ike Clanton and his friends and associates, waiting where Ike Clanton earlier had been looking for Doc Holliday with the obvious intention of killing him?

Q. Don't you think it is likely that these men

were contemplating the murder of Doc Holliday before the Chief of Police and his men came to disarm them?

Q. Isn't it true that these men told you why they were there and you encouraged them in their intent, which is why you didn't disarm them.

Q. Isn't it true that you wished to see these men kill the Earp party, which is why you gave them the advantage by telling Chief of Police Earp you had disarmed them?

Whatever the case may have been, the elaborately rehearsed, yet comically conflicting testimony, did not deceive Judge Wells Spicer, whose decision follows as printed in *The Nugget*:

TERRITORY OF ARIZONA vs. **MORGAN EARP, et al** **DEFENDANTS**	**Judge Wells Spicer's** Decision

Defendants Wyatt Earp and John Holliday, two of the defendants named in the above entitled action, were arrested upon a warrant issued by me on the 29th day of October, on a charge of murder. The complaint filed, upon which this warrant was issued, accuses said defendants of the murder of William Clanton, Frank McLaury, and Thomas McLaury on the 26th day of last month, at Tombstone, in this County.

This case has now been on hearing for the past thirty days, during which time a volume of testimony has been taken and eminent legal talent employed on both sides.

The great importance of the case, as well as the great interest taken in it by the entire community, demand that I should be full and explicit in my findings and conclusions and should give ample reasons for what I do.

From the mass of evidence before me — much of which is upon collateral matters — I have found it necessary for the purposes of this decision to consider only those facts which are conceded by both sides or are established by a large preponderance of testimony.

Viewing it in this manner, I find that on the morning of the 26th day of October, 1881, and up to noon of that day, Joseph I. Clanton or Isaac Clanton, the prosecuting witness in this case, was about the streets and in several saloons of Tombstone, armed with revolver and Winchester rifle, declaring publicly that the Earp brothers and Holliday had insulted him the night before when he was unarmed, and now he was armed and intended to shoot them or fight them on sight. These threats were communicated to defendants, Virgil Earp and Wyatt Earp.

Virgil Earp was at this time the chief of police of Tombstone and charged as such officer by the city ordinance with the duty of preserving the peace, and arresting, with or without warrant, all persons engaged in any disorderly act, whereby a breach of the peace might be occasioned, and to arrest and disarm all persons violating the city ordinance which declares it to be unlawful to carry on the person any deadly weapon within the city limits, without obtaining a permit in writing.

Shortly after noon of October 26th, defendant Virgil Earp, as chief of police, assisted by Morgan Earp, who was also at the time a special policeman in the pay of the city and wearing a badge, arrested and disarmed said Isaac Clanton, and in such arrest and disarmament, inflicted upon the side of his head a blow from a pistol — whether this blow was necessary is not material here to determine.

Isaac Clanton was then taken to Justice or Recorder Wallace, where he was fined and his arms, consisting of a revolver and Winchester rifle, taken from him and deposited at the Grand Hotel, subject to his orders.

While at Justice Wallace's court and awaiting the coming of Judge Wallace, some hot words passed between Isaac Clanton and Wyatt Earp. Earp accused Clanton of having previously threatened to take his life, and then proposed to make a fight with him anywhere, to which Isaac Clanton assented, and then declared that "Fight was his racket," and that when he was arrested and disarmed, if Earp had been a second later, "there would have been a coroner's inquest in town."

Immediately subsequent to this, a difficulty occurred in front of Judge Wallace's courtroom, between Wyatt Earp and the deceased Thomas McLaury, in which the latter was struck by the former with a pistol and knocked down.

In view of these controversies between Wyatt Earp and Isaac Clanton and Thomas McLaury, and in further view of this quarrel the night before between Isaac Clanton and J.H. Holliday, I am of the opinion that the defendant, Virgil Earp, as chief of police, subsequently calling upon Wyatt Earp, and J.H. Holliday to assist him in arresting and disarming the Clantons and McLaurys — committed an injudicious and censurable act, and although in this he acted incautiously and without due circumspection, yet when we consider the conditions of affairs incident to a frontier country; the lawlessness and disregard for human life; the existence of a law-defying element in [our] midst; the fear and feeling of insecurity that has existed; the supposed prevalence of bad, desperate and reckless men who have been a terror to the country and kept away capital and enterprise; and considering the many threats that have been made against the Earps, I can attach no criminality to his unwise act. In fact, as the result plainly proves, he needed the assistance and support of staunch and true friends, upon whose courage, coolness and fidelity he could depend, in case of an emergency.

Soon after the conclusion of proceedings at Judge Wallace's court, Isaac Clanton and Thomas McLaury were joined by William Clanton and Frank McLaury, who had arrived in town. In the afternoon these parties went to [the] gun shop, where they were seen loading their guns and obtaining cartridges. These proceedings were seen by Wyatt Earp, who reported the same to Virgil Earp, chief of police, said Wyatt Earp at the time being a sworn policeman.

After this, the Clantons and McLaurys went to the Dexter Stables, on Allen Street, and shortly after, crossed the street to the O.K. Corral and passed through to Fremont Street. With what purpose they crossed through to Fremont Street will probably never be known. It is claimed by the prosecution that their purpose was to leave town. It is asserted by the defendants that their purpose was to make an attack upon them or at least to feloniously resist any attempt to arrest or disarm them that might be made by the chief of police and his assistants.

Whatever their purpose may have been, it is clear to my mind that Virgil Earp, the chief of police, honestly believed [and from information of threats that day given him, his belief was reasonable], that their purpose was, if not to attempt the deaths of himself and brothers, at least to resist with force of arms any attempt on his part to perform his duty as a peace officer by arresting and disarming them.

At this time Virgil Earp was informed by one H.F. Sills, an engineer from the A.T. & S.F. R.R., then absent from duty, on a lay-off furlough, and who had arrived in town only the day before and totally unacquainted [with] any person in town, or the state of affairs existing here. Sills had overheard armed parties just then passing through the

O.K. Corral say, in effect, that they would make sure to kill Earp, the marshal, and would kill all the Earps.

At the same time, several citizens and a committee of citizens came to Virgil Earp, the chief of police, and insisted that he should perform his duty as such officer and arrest and disarm the cowboys, as they termed the Clantons and McLaurys.

Was it for Virgil Earp as chief of police to abandon his clear duty as an officer because its performance was likely to be fraught with danger? Or was it not his duty that as such officer he owed to the peaceable and law-abiding citizens of the city, who looked to him to preserve peace and order, and their protection and security, to at once call to his aid sufficient assistance to arrest and disarm these men?

There can be but one answer to these questions, and that answer is such as will divest the subsequent approach of the defendants toward the deceased of all presumption of malice or of illegality.

When, therefore, the defendants, regularly or specially appointed officers, marched down Fremont Street to the scene of the subsequent homicide, they were going where it was their right and duty to go; and they were doing what it was their right and duty to do; and they were armed, as it was their right and duty to be armed, when approaching men they believed to be armed and contemplating resistance.

The legal character of the homicide must therefore be determined by what occurred at the time and not by the precedent facts. To constitute the crime of murder there must be proven not only the killing, but also the felonious intent. In this case, the *corpus delicti* or fact of killing, is in fact admitted as well as clearly proven. The felonious intent is as much a fact to be proven as the *corpus delicti*, and in looking over this mass of testimony for evidence upon this point, I find that it is anything but clear.

Witnesses of credibility testify that each of the deceased or at least two of them yielded to a demand to surrender. Other witnesses of equal credibility testify that William Clanton and Frank McLaury met the demand for surrender by drawing their pistols, and that the discharge of firearms from both sides was almost instantaneous.

There is a dispute as to whether Thomas McLaury was armed at all, except with a Winchester rifle that was on the horse beside him. I will not consider this question, because it is not of controlling importance. Certain it is that the Clantons and McLaurys had among them at least two six-shooters in their hands, and two Winchester rifles on their horses. Therefore, if Thomas McLaury was one of a party who were thus armed and were making felonious resistance to an arrest, and in the melee that followed was shot, the fact of his being unarmed, if it be a fact, could not of itself criminate the defendants, if they were not otherwise criminated.

It is beyond doubt that William Clanton and Frank McLaury were armed, and made such quick and effective use of their arms as to seriously wound Morgan Earp and Virgil Earp.

In determining the important question whether the deceased offered to surrender before resisting, I must give as much weight to the testimony of persons unacquainted with the deceased or the defendants, as to the testimony of persons who were companions and acquaintances, if not partisans of the deceased. And I am of [the] opinion that those who observed the conflict from a short distance and from points of observation that gave them a good view of the scene, to say the least, were quite as likely to be accurate in their observation as those mingled up in or fleeing from the melee.

Witnesses for the prosecution state unequivocally that Willam Clanton fell or was shot at the first fire and Claiborne says he was shot when the pistol was only about a foot from his belly. Yet it is clear that there were no powder burns nor marks on his clothes. And Judge Lucas says he saw him fire or in the act of firing several times before he was shot, and he thinks two shots afterwards.

Addie Bourland, who saw distinctly the approach of the Earps and the beginning of the affray, from a point across the street, where she could correctly observe all their movements, says she cannot tell which fired first — that the firing commenced at once, from both sides, on the approach of the Earps, and that no hands were held up;

that she could have seen them if there had been. Sills asserted that the firing was almost simultaneous. I could not tell which side fired first.

Considering all the testimony together, I am of the opinion that the weight of evidence sustains and corroborates the testimony of Wyatt Earp, that their demand for surrender was met by William Clanton and Frank McLaury drawing or making motions to draw their pistols. Upon this hypothesis my duty is clear. The defendants were officers charged with the duty of arresting and disarming armed and determined men who were expert in the use of firearms, as quick as thought and as certain as death and who had previously declared their intention not to be arrested nor disarmed. Under the statutes [Sec. 32, page 74 of Comp. Laws], as well as the common law, they have a right to repel force with force.

In coming to this conclusion, I give great weight to several particular circumstances connected with [the] affray. It is claimed by the prosecution that the deceased were shot while holding up their hands in obedience of the command of the chief of police, and on the other hand the defense claims that William Clanton and Frank McLaury at once drew their pistols and began firing simultaneously with [the] defendants. William Clanton was wounded on the wrist of the right hand on the first fire and thereafter used his pistol with his left. This wound is such as could not have been received with his hands thrown up, and the wound received by Thomas McLaury was such as could not have been received with his hands on his coat lapels. These circumstances being indubital [indubitable] facts, throw great doubt upon the correctness of the statement of witnesses to the contrary.

The testimony of Isaac Clanton, that this tragedy was the result of a scheme on the part of the Earps to assassinate him and thereby bury in oblivion the confessions the Earps had made to him about "piping" away the shipment of coin by Wells Fargo & Co. falls short of being a sound theory, [on] account of the great fact, most prominent in this matter, to wit: that Isaac Clanton was not injured at all, and could have been killed first and easiest, if it was the object of the attack to kill him. He would have been the first to fall; but, as it was, he was known or believed to be unarmed, and was suffered and, as Wyatt Earp testified, told to go away, and was not harmed.

I also give great weight in this matter to the testimony of Sheriff Behan, who said that on one occasion a short time ago Isaac Clanton told him that he, Clanton, had been informed that the sheriff was coming to arrest him and that he, Clanton, armed his crowd with guns and was determined not to be arrested by the sheriff — or words to that effect. And Sheriff Behan further testified that a few minutes before the Earps came to them, that he as sheriff demanded of the Clantons and McLaurys that they give up their arms, and that they "demurred", as he said, and did not do it, and that Frank McLaury refused and gave as a reason that he was not ready to leave town just then and would not give up his arms unless the Earps were disarmed — that is, that the chief of police and his assistants should be disarmed.

In view of the past history of the county and the generally believed existence at this time of desperate, reckless and lawless men in our midst, banded together for mutual support and living by felonious and predatory pursuits, regarding neither life nor property in their career, and at the same time for men to parade the streets armed with repeating rifles and six-shooters and demand that the chief of police and his assistants should be disarmed is a proposition both monstrous and startling! This was said by one of the deceased only a few minutes before the arrival of the Earps.

Another fact that rises up preeminent in the consideration of this said affair is the leading fact that the deceased, from the very first inception of the encounter, were standing their ground and fighting back, giving and taking death with unflinching bravery. It does not appear to have been a wanton slaughter of unresisting and unarmed innocents, who were yielding graceful submission to the officers of the law, or surrendering to, or fleeing from their assailants; but armed and defiant men, accepting their wager of battle and succumbing only in death.

The prosecution claims much upon the point, as they allege, that the Earp party acted with criminal haste — that they precipitated the triple homicide by a felonious intent then and there to kill and murder the deceased, and that they made use of their official characters as a pretext. I cannot believe this theory, and cannot resist the firm conviction that the Earps acted wisely, discretely, and prudentially, to secure their own self-preservation. They saw at once the dire necessity of giving the first shots, to save themselves from certain death! They acted. Their shots were effective, and this alone saved the Earp party from being slain.

In view of all the facts and circumstances of the case, considering the threats made, the character and positions of the parties, and the tragical results accomplished in manner and form as they were, with all surrounding influences bearing upon res-gestae of the affair, I cannot resist the conclusion that the defendants were fully justified in committing these homicides — that it is a necessary act, done in the discharge of an official duty.

It is the duty of an examining and committing magistrate in this territory to issue a warrant of arrest in the first place, whenever from the depositions given there is reasonable ground to believe that the defendant has committed a public offense [Sec. 87, page 111 of Comp. Law].

After hearing evidence, however, the statute changes the rule, and he is then required to commit the defendant only when there is "Sufficient cause to believe" him guilty. [Sec. 143, page 111 of Comp. Laws].

My interpretation is that the rule which should govern an examining magistrate is the same as that which should govern the conclusions of a Grand

Jury. That such as prescribed by statute [Sec. 188, page 121 of Comp. Laws] is: "The Grand Jury ought to find an indictment when all the evidence before them, taken together, is such as in their judgment will, if unexplained or uncontradicted, warrant a conviction by the trial jury."

The evidence taken before me in this case, would not, in my judgment, warrant a conviction of the defendants by trial jury of any offense whatever. I do not believe that any trial jury that could be got together in this territory, would, on all evidence taken before me, with the rule of law applicable thereto given them by the court, find the defendants guilty of any offense.

It may be that my judgment is erroneous, and my view of the law incorrect, yet it is my own judgment and my own understanding of the law as I find it laid down, and upon this I must act and decide, and not upon those of any other persons. I have given over four weeks of patient attention to the hearing of evidence in this case, and at least four-fifths of my waking hours have been devoted, at this time, to an earnest study of the evidence before me, and such is the conclusion to which I am forced to arrive.

I have the less reluctance in announcing this conclusion because the Grand Jury of this county is now in session, and it is quite within the power of that body, if dissatisfied with my decision, to call witnesses before them or use the depositions taken before me, and which I shall return to the district court, as by law required, and to thereupon disregard my findings, and find an indictment against the defendants, if they think the evidence sufficient to warrant a conviction.

I conclude the performance of this duty imposed upon me by saying in the language of the Statute: "There being no sufficient cause to believe the within named Wyatt S. Earp and John H. Holliday guilty of the offense mentioned within. I order them to be released."

[signed] Wells Spicer, Magistrate

Chapter 20

Mysterious Will McLaury

I see that I haven't yet emphasized the role of
the McLaury boys' older brother, Will. He came
to Tombstone as soon as he got word of the killings, and being an attorney, joined in the prosecution.

EDITORIAL COMMENT:
*Will McLaury's later letters confirm that he not
only joined the prosecution team, but was ready
to knife Wyatt or Doc right in court, and later
hired assassins to kill them and their supporters.
What follows is Ten Eyck's description of the aftermath of the Spicer hearing, drastically edited
down to all that is really necessary to understand
why Wyatt eventually launched his vendetta.*

The failure of both defense and prosecution attorneys to go for the jugular during the hearings
reveals something I should have emphasized. Attorneys on both sides couldn't help but recognize

they were dealing with a dangerous factional war. If the Earps were cleared, the prosecution attorneys faced rubbing elbows with them in the community. It was obvious they were dangerous men, capable of shooting to kill. (This prospect was particularly scary in the case of Doc Holliday, who everyone knew was apt to force someone into a fight if he thought he owed them something — such as he tried to do with Ike Clanton. This undoubtedly explains the prosecution's failure to place Doc on the witness stand. He probably would have refused to testify under the Constitutional clause that prohibits self-incrimination, but why force him into such a public embarrassment, and perhaps order oneself a set of funeral clothes in the bargain?)

Another wrinkle gave the prosecution something to think about. The Citizens' Safety Committee, which is to say the big money in the community, was behind the Earp faction. That had been pretty obvious when they showed up a hundred strong right after the shooting, and wheeled the two wounded Earps down home in a carriage, pushed by several men, accompanied by cheers. The 'late unlamented' were just that, Behan or no Behan. (In effect, Wyatt and his brothers and Doc had been hired to do just what they finally had done. I've often wondered how much they were paid under the table — look what Wells Fargo had been willing to pay for Leonard, Head and Crane. The Earps, at the least, were paid for their silence regarding their backers.)

The prosecution attorneys had to reflect that the vigilantes had been a supine outfit for the most part; "but would that always be true?"

On the other hand, everyone was aware that Curly Bill's gang was a ruthless crew, capable of anything, such as murdering a town marshal under the guise of an innocent shooting at the moon. Certainly the defense attorneys had taken that into consideration. The aftermath of the Spicer hearing, which I am about to relate, proves that apprehensions regarding retaliation from the Cowboy Gang were well founded.

Will McLaury succeeded in putting a little stiffening into the prosecution, but he didn't have to live in the community afterward. He was from Ft. Worth. He had Wyatt and Doc stuck back in jail and they had to post additional bond to get out. While they were in, as he had the first time, John Clum saw that extra guards were placed around the jail, whether Behan liked it or not. Everyone knew Johnny would just as soon let the Cowboy Gang kill the Earps in their cells. In fact he might have paid to have it done.

At that stage, Behan was a desperate man, driven by insane jealousy and fear of his outlaw associates, as well as of the Earps. What would happen if they were freed? They certainly were aware he was trying to railroad them for having performed a community beneficence. Harry Woods, of course, was Johnny's executive arm in achieving that. I wonder why. He actually held Behan in contempt because anytime there

303

was a tough arrest or process serving, Johnny sent Harry. Harry didn't even carry a six-shooter, and everyone knew it.

I abetted Harry, but with less and less enthusiasm. The hearing had begun to open my eyes good. What followed finished the job.

The first public evidence that revenge might be impending was a letter Wells Spicer had received which he placed in the newspapers, and his reply. The text of both follow:

"Editor Epitaph: On Saturday morning I received the following spirited letter from the postoffice at this place, viz:

Tombstone, A.T Dec. 13, 1881

"To Wells Spicer — Sir, if you will take my advice you will take your Departure for a more genial Clime as I don't think this One Healthy for you much longer. As you are liable to get a hole through your coat at any moment. If such sons of Bitches as you Are allowed to dispense justice in this Territory, the Sooner you depart from us the better for yourself And the community at large you may make light of this but it is only a matter of time you will get it sooner or later So with those few gentle hints I Will Conclude for the first and Last time."

[signed] A Miner

In his reply Spicer stated, among other things:

304

"There is a rabble in our city who would like to be thugs, if they had courage; would be proud to be called cow-boys, if people would give them that distinction; but as they can be neither they do the best they can to show how vile they are, and slander, abuse and threaten everyone they dare to. Of all such I say, whenever they are denouncing me they are lying from a low, wicked and villainous heart; and that when they threaten me they are low-bred, arrant cowards, and know that "fight is not my racket" — if it was they would not dare to do it. (Dec. 18, 1881.)

Similar threats were sent to all of the defense attorneys, John Clum and the Earps. Josie tells in her memoir how, a few days following the shooting, a man, clumsily disguised in womens' dress, knocked on the door of Virgil Earp's house one dark night. When Jim Earp answered the door, the person mumbled something about having the wrong house and moved off in the darkness. The Earps figured if Wyatt or Doc had come to the door, they'd have been shot. It's a wonder the man didn't shoot Jim on general principles. They suspected it had been Frank Stilwell, since only he was that wild and daring.

Following that, the Earps all moved to the Cosmopolitan Hotel where they could arrange to guard themselves better. They lived there until their departure from Tombstone — from about the first of November till late March. Strange no one ever inquired how they could afford such an expense, and the expense of twenty-four hour guards on duty. Who paid for that? Of course Billicke was their friend, but he couldn't afford to tie up rooms and provide meals free, although he may have provided it all at close to cost. In any case the cost wasn't borne by the Earps, I'm sure.

At about the same time that Wells Spicer received his threatening letter, the Benson stage carrying John Clum was attacked, and John heard someone yell, "Get the old bald-headed s.o.b."

They fired a volley at the stage and hit a horse that dropped dead in the harness after running quite a way. In the confusion of cutting the horse out of the harness, John decided it would be safer to proceed on foot, which he did, to the Grand Central Mill at Contention. He caught a few hours sleep and borrowed a horse to ride to Benson and catch his train. The attack hadn't been pressed and could have been more an attempt to scare him than kill him. Or the attackers didn't have the stomach for a close encounter. They were aware Clum would be armed and had lived three years among the Apaches and survived.

As was to be expected, tension and death were in the air in Tombstone. Respectable people avoided going out after dark if they could. It gave me a bad taste for the place for the first time. I recall Josie commenting that evil seemed to rise out of the ground at Tombstone. There was a pall over the Christmas season, which I, for one, resented. It was supposed to be a joyous time.*

I jumped at an invitation from John Dunbar to celebrate Christmas with them at his brother Tom's ranch up at Tres Alamos. (That was a few miles below Benson on the San Pedro.)

John said, "I need to get out of this damn place, Ted. You should, too, for awhile. I have the willies around here lately."

It occurs to me today that he figured it would be healthier to clear his skirts of what he knew — or at least suspected — was about to happen. Will McLaury was still in town lusting for revenge. Everyone in the know was aware of that. I never once talked to the man, but others I knew did, and Dunbar was one of them. Was John warning me that I should get away from any possible tar-daubing from an impending crime? I was associated with the Behan circle in the public mind. Clum hardly spoke to me any more, though Parsons was cordial still; also still trying to sell me something.

EDITORIAL COMMENT:

John Dunbar's required notice as County Treasurer to the County Board of Supervisors regarding an impending absence from the county of over thirty days was submitted at that time, and A.E. Harley appointed his replacement, with a posted

---

* It appears to have been a joyous time for those less in the know than Ten Eyck since there was a big Christmas party at Scheiffelin Hall, with even Chris Billicke there. He said his present, a doll, didn't have enough clothes on — GB.

307

bond on record. I don't know if Dunbar actually left the county or lay low at his brother's ranch, and Ten Eyck didn't say.

What Dunbar warned me to be well clear of took place right after Christmas. As a member of the Citizens' Safety Committee, Parsons was on the inside of the event and I quote his Journal to cover the affair:

PARSONS' JOURNAL:
"Wednesday 28th (Dec. 1881)

". . . . . Tonight about 11:30 Doc G (Goodfellow) had just left and I thought couldn't have crossed the street — when four shots were fired in quick succession from very heavily charged guns, making a terrible noise and I thought were fired under my window under which I quickly dropped, keeping the dobe wall between me and the outside till the fusillade was over. I immediately thought Doc had been shot and fired in return, re-membering a late episode and knowing how pronounced he was on the Earp-Cow-boy question. He had crossed though and passed Virgil Earp who crossed to West side of Fifth and was fired upon when in range of my win-dow by men two or three concealed in the timbers of the new two story adobe going up for the Huachuca Water Company. He did not fall, but recrossed to the Oriental and was taken from there to the Cosmopolitan being hit with buck shot and badly wounded in left arm with flesh wound above left thigh . . . . . Doc had a close shave. Van and I went to hospital for Doc and got various things. Hotel well guarded, so much so that I had hard trouble to get to Earps room. He was easy. Told him I was sorry for him. "It's hell, isn't it!" said he. His wife was troubled, "Never mind, I've got one arm left to hug you with," he said. . . . ."

PARSONS' JOURNAL:

"Thursday December 29th (1881)

"Got to bed about 2:00 A.M. Crowds this morning looking at buck shot and bullet marks on the walls. I was just retiring, taking off stockings — when firing commenced and dropped under the window. A bullet passed very close to me striking near the window, probably passing within a foot or two of my position. Longitudinal fracture, so elbow joint had to be taken out today and we've got that and some of the shattered bone in room. Patient doing well. It is surmised that Ike Clanton "Curly Bill" and McLowry (Will McLaury) did the shooting. Bad state of affairs here. Something will have to be done. . . . ."

Allie Earp is my best source for what happened right after Virg was ambushed. They helped Virg to his room at the Cosmopolitan Hotel, still able to walk, put him to bed and the doctors tried to get the bleeding stopped.

Allie told me, "Virg leaked blood for quite awhile and ruined the mattress and bedding. I had a fit, wondering if he was gonna bleed to death, but worried almost as much what Chris Billicke would say about ruining his things. He never said a word. He was a strong Earp man, as good a friend as us Earps had in town.

"They kept Virg pretty well doped up for the first week or so. He hardly ate. He was so weak he had trouble using the pot. He said he'd be damned if he was gonna piss the bed like a kid, so I had to help him to the thundermug and hold him up on the damn tippy thing so he wouldn't fall off. I never heard of a bed pan in those days. We sure could have used one."

Wyatt Earp was appointed U.S. Deputy Marshal immediately following this, and the federal authorities, prodded no doubt by Wells Fargo and the money powers in Tombstone, decided to turn up the heat on the Cowboy Gang.

I never saw Will McLaury around Tombstone again, a significant fact. He may have scared himself half to death when he realized what he'd done, or hired done.

EDITORIAL COMMENT:
Not likely. His later letters confirm he hired the murder of Morgan Earp, and other Earp associates. He may have returned to Tombstone undetected at the time Morgan was shot. It is a wonder that he didn't try to kill Wyatt or have

310

him killed when Wyatt and Josie visited his home-
town of Ft. Worth a few years later. Maybe he
tried. One wonders, on the other hand, why Wyatt
didn't kill him when he was in Ft. Worth. Maybe
the fire of revenge had burned out of him by then.

Chapter 21

Cupid Fires A Shot

There was a lighter side to this period from before Christmas in 1881 until Wyatt left in 1882. Josie returned to Tombstone, bringing young Albert Behan, both elated at the thought of surprising Johnny and of a happy reunion. Her attempt to surprise Johnny surprised everyone. She found more people in her bed than she expected. Johnny was entertaining in his inimitable fashion. The explosion was audible down the street a half block at Harry Jones'. In fact, she shortly arrived down there dragging Albert with her and spent the night. Johnny got a loud horse laugh all over town behind his back.

Those close to Johnny were certainly all aware of the kind of life he led, and I was one of them. He had an elephantine ego, like all of his kind, in need of conquests to keep it inflated, although they all try to keep their needs a secret. Among Johnny's **stable** were Harry Jones wife, Kitty, which might have got him killed, and his partner

Dunbar's wife, Bert, a nice warm-hearted person. Good old John Dunbar didn't have the faintest inkling of what was going on, or even he might have loaded Johnny up with buckshot. (Some years after we left Tombstone, I ran into Johnny between trains at Deming, and he showed me a letter from a friend in El Paso, where he was employed by the customs service. As I recall, it read roughly, "You'd better come home and lock up your stud. He has your trouble, Johnny, and is jumping all the fences after mares and might get shot." He laughed as I read it. So did I. But not as heartily.)

Josie then moved out and into Mrs. Young's boarding house, which was a short way down the street. By coincidence (maybe) I moved up there after Virg was ambushed. I definitely severed relations with the Behan-Woods crowd. If I'd stayed where I was I could not have avoided running into the *Nugget* crowd all the time. For the first time in months, I felt myself breathing freely.

My stay at Mrs. Young's gave me an unparalleled insight into Josie's and Wyatt's early courtship. He was somewhat like Miles Standish. Regardless, without his growing interest in Josie, the whole Earp clan probably would have left Tombstone and found a healthier clime.

Many years later Virg made an illuminating comment regarding that. He said, "We were getting of a mind to shake the dust of Tombstone, when Wyatt fell in love like a sick calf. You know how it was with his wife." (I didn't, but I didn't let on for fear of drying him up.) "Wyatt told us we could leave if we wanted to, but he was sticking. Jim said he'd stay if Wyatt did. So we all hung on. Besides we were pretty well invested in a lot of stuff and we sure as hell hated to look like we'd been run out." He looked at his crippled arm when he said it, probably thinking it wouldn't have happened if they'd had sense enough to leave.

Jim put it a lot more to the point when he said, "If Wyatt didn't have his brains in his prick we'd all've done a hell of a damn sight better."

He didn't say that Virg wouldn't have been crippled and Morg killed, but he was thinking it. Nonetheless, Jim and Wyatt were the closest — or maybe that was only later when they were the only two blood brothers left.

Allie said it a lot clearer, "Us Earps would have been a sight better off if Wyatt had never laid eyes on Sadie."

Allie and Sadie detested one another. They were natural opposites, Allie a good old boot, Sadie (as the family always called Josie) a patrician in her blood, regardless of her background.

Allie added, "That woman was a schemer."

I can vouch for that. The advances she could make to Wyatt to stiffen his resolve were limited at Mrs. Young's, and in a town like Tombstone, "affairs" weren't conducted in hotel rooms as they are today. She was getting desperate over her lack of progress with Wyatt and made one of her usual determined moves to do something about it. She moved back into "her" house, which Johnny had left empty. Johnny had sent Albert to live with

Tom Dunbar up at the ranch. (I met Albert up there at Christmas time and found him a well-mannered kid. Josie, and probably his mother before her, had done a good job on him.)

Following is what I lifted directly from Josie's memoir on the subject of her netting of Wyatt Earp:

"I had a problem. As the weeks went by it began to look like Wyatt would never kiss me. He'd stand on one foot and another outside Mrs. Young's, trying to get his nerve to kiss me good-night.

"Even Mrs. Young, who ruthlessly chaperoned all the young women under her keeping, kidded me about my bashful beau. Harry and Kitty ribbed me unmercifully. Kitty said, 'You don't need a chaperon where he's concerned, he does.'

"I was soon taking another ribbing over hiring a big fat Mexican woman as housekeeper and body guard and moving back into my own house. By then I was having some desperate doubts regarding my charms, having failed to get Johnny to marry me (thank goodness) and now unable to get the apple of my eye even to kiss me goodnight. I vowed to get him into my sitting room or die trying, but naturally proposed to rebuff him an appropriate number of times to satisfy the demands of maidenly modesty and social propriety What fools young girls are. I'd laid my plans so carefully, even making

315

it clear to Tia Bertha — everyone but me called her Fat Bertha (or Bertha Gorda) — that she wasn't a **duenna** where Wyatt was concerned. She laughed and assured me, 'Yo savvy.'

"Somehow things didn't work out quite like I planned. I inveigled him into my net alright, filling him with Tia's cookies and coffee by candlelight, then got him somehow onto the unimaginably uncomfortable horsehair sofa that was an indispensable appendage of all Victorian sitting rooms then. Lord knows what we talked about. A good deal of the time he simply looked at me, but warily, as though he was afraid I'd break if he touched me. Years later I asked him why. He said, 'You were the prettiest woman I'd ever seen. Besides you smelled a whole lot better than any of the women I'd met up to that time.'

"I'm not so sure I care so much about the last part, but come to think of it there was probably a lot of truth in it and Wyatt had a disconcerting honesty and directness. If I'd known that was what he was thinking then, I'd have giggled and blushed.

"When he finally did try to kiss me I put my girlish plan into such effective action, pretending to struggle away so that it nearly scared him to death. He was on his feet and already had his hat in his hand before I had the rehearsed words, 'What kind of a girl do you think I am?' fairly out of my mouth.

"He said, 'I'm sorry I forgot my manners.

I don't know what got into me. You're so pretty.' His face was red, but almost sad enough to make me cry. He galloped out the door.

"When I realized what I'd done, I felt like crying. How could I run after him and admit I'd really wanted him to kiss me? Can't you imagine me saying something like, 'Please don't go. I dearly wanted you to do that,' and appearing just like the hypocrite I was? I hated the way girls were raised then, and from what I can see, it's changed mighty little since.

"I was in love with him, and up till then he hadn't touched more than my hand. He was so gentle and considerate, clean and upright and manly in his appearance and manners. Any woman would have loved him. Most of my female acquaintances during our marriage were always mooning at him, more than halfway in love with him. You can imagine my panic at driving him away.

"He was outside and almost running away before I could think of a thing to say. I threw a tea cup at the wall.

" 'What a ninny I am,' I kept telling myself, as I lay awake half the night. But in characteristic fashion I went to sleep secure in the thought that he'd come back. I knew men. They were all alike. A week went by. Two. Three. It was unbearable. Was it possible he didn't care for me? The thought never occurred to me what the trouble was. **Here was a real man.** Not a Johnny Behan, willing to do or say anything to get his way. Even I, young as I was, knew Wyatt was a special man. It stuck out all over him. Men as well as women felt the strong pull of his character. But I was too young to know that a preeminent characteristic of such a man was honesty.

"He cared for me too much. But he took my actions for what they were intended to display and had no choice but to believe I didn't really care much for him. Why should I? He was a married man and had no call on me. To believe otherwise he would have to believe me the deceitful schemer I really was, and his gallant nature forbade this.

"I had sense enough to swallow my pride and send a note to him with Harry as my messenger. He appeared tickled to carry a note. Later he told me that Wyatt was really down in the dumps. His marriage had been a farce for years and I was the first other woman he'd looked at. He'd probably have stayed with her for years if we hadn't fallen in love. He sent her money till the day she died.

"Returning to my state of agitation, I recall that my note to Wyatt asked the reason for his prolonged avoidance of me, his forgiveness if I'd done something to offend him, and his early presence at my humble dwelling. It got the desired effect.

"As he told me later, 'I trotted right over.'

"I was very contrite (and wily) standing as close as possible with my hands on his lapels, eyes averted just enough to be able to observe his reaction, and I'm sure my heart was going furiously by the time he was nerved to start again where he left off.

"I'll never forget that first kiss. I'd waited so long and wanted so hard. It was a gentle kiss, then harder as we clung together.

"I knew I was in love. That merely sealed it."

That took place after Virgil had been ambushed. Josie was the reason Wyatt waited too long to leave Tombstone. By then it was too late. Virgil wasn't able to travel. Besides Virgil had got his back up in true Earp fashion and wanted to stay around and recover, then go after the "bastards" who'd shot him. I can't exactly blame him.

Chapter 22

I Pump Doc Holliday

1885

Doc Holliday is talking in his Georgia drawl and says to me, "Wyatt Earp was as good a friend as a man ever wanted. All the Earp boys were pure gold except that young son of a bitch, Warren."

This remark is typical Doc. He is almost as profane as Jim Earp, and might outdo him if he puts his mind to it.

We are in Denver. Doc doesn't look good. He's lost a lot of weight and coughs too much. His face is haggard and anyone can see the coughing fits exhaust him. This is not the dapper Doc I remember from that night at the Maisson Doree, flush from a winning streak at the Oriental.

Doc is down on his luck. He came up from Silver Cliff with me on the D. and R.G. and mentioned that it almost ate up his last nickel. On the other hand, I'm flush and trying to figure out a way to help him without hurting his feelings.

In the past few weeks I've looked over Gunnison, Aspen, Leadville, Telluride, Central City,

Silverton, and a lot more, such as Rosita and Silver Cliff, and talked to dozens of schemers and a few real bricks.* The latter showed me some good stuff and I've bought into a couple.

Doc gets touchy when I bring up the subject of setting him back on his feet, since I just ask him right out, "Could you use a loan?" I should have known better.

He gives me a look that makes me wonder if he's about to plug me.

"For old time's sake," I add quickly.

Finally the frost comes out of those ghostly blue eyes and he laughs, then coughs awhile.

"A loan," he finally manages to say, and smiles, but his words belie the smile, "I don't need anybody's goddam charity."

"A loan," I emphasize.

My motives aren't exactly eleemosynary. It's the newsman still in my blood. I'd like to pump him before he dies.

I've already got five hundred dollars in an envelope and take it out and hand it to him.

He says, "I reckon you were pretty damn sure I'd take this?" Again I wonder if he's thinking of filling me with a little lead, but he grins and takes it.

"Where can I send it back?" he wants to know.

"I'll be around Denver, most likely at the Windsor," I tell him.

---

* Brick was a term used then to denote a solid, dependable man — **GB.**

321

Doc gets tired pretty easy these days and the bottle isn't doing him any good, either.

I'm really getting to know him and he doesn't hesitate to talk. What I want to know about, of course, is the inside story of what happened at Tombstone.

I've told Doc I may do an article on him for the *Police Gazette* or *Leslie's*, since I still have some connections back there, and he doesn't seem to mind, in fact thinks it may do him some good on the local scene where they figure to run his kind out of town every so often when the reform crowd gets worked up. Of course, the article idea is to help get him talking, but I might do one just to keep my hand in.

Well, yesterday we were in the bar at the Windsor, having a drink, of course. I'm staying here. I'm afraid the Western custom of an eye-opener has hold of me for good. It was just a few years ago I was a kid back in New York who'd hardly had a drink in his life. It seems like a hundred years ago. But with Doc here I am living in Tombstone again. With a few drinks in him, here's what Doc has been telling me:

"I knew things would come to a head in Tombstone sooner or later. Finally Ike Clanton spilled the beans about how his gang planned to rub out me and the Earps, so I thought I'd tell him we already rubbed out his Old Man. That got him plenty hot. Maybe he really liked the old bastard."

Doc's expression shows he doesn't understand

how anyone could have liked Old Man Clanton. He starts to laugh and ends up almost choking instead.

When he finally recovers he says, "I tried to get Ike to jerk his six-shooter, but he claimed he wasn't heeled. Maybe he wasn't. He was down to Fly's boarding house the next morning looking for me with a rifle. Kate told him I wasn't there. When I got up, I went looking for him. I borrowed a shotgun from Virg Earp, but he wanted to know why I wanted it. That's when I found out what'd been going on all morning. Ike was looking for trouble earlier and Virg and Morg put a lump on his head and ran him down to Wallace's court. A little later Wyatt ran into Tom McLaury and knocked him on his ass."

"I saw it," I put in here.

Doc grins and says, "I heard he did a good job of it," then goes on, "Wyatt had word Ike sent for some reinforcements. Sure enough, in a little while Frank McLaury and Billy Clanton showed up. We expected some more of them, maybe Curly Bill, Ringo, Spence and Stilwell. I shook hands with Billy Clanton just to throw the bastards off guard. I'd seen him around. I'd seen all of 'em around, though they didn't come to town much when Virg was running things.

"Wyatt followed them down to Spangenberg's after they got together. By then he could see the way things were headed, regardless. He told me later he figured to pick a fight with them if he could and shoot them down. I told him he should have taken me down there with him; that's my kind of game.

"Virg thought that would have looked a little obvious, but he was on the prod, too, and told Behan he wasn't going to arrest those sons of bitches, but shoot them on sight. We'd have been a lot better off after we did it, if he'd kept his lip buttoned. Anyhow, he got word they were down on Fremont Street, making a gun talk against us, so we headed down there.

"Wyatt wasn't sure of either Morg or Virg in a fight after they had a chance to beef Ike and let him get off that morning. Warren was the one mean enough to kill.*

"The way Wyatt put it was, 'Hell, Virg and Morg had their chance to burn down Ike this A.M. and didn't. It'll be up to us.' He was a cool one with a fight brewing and had it all figured out ahead of time. He told me, 'You keep us all covered with the scattergun in case some of those others are down there. I'll handle Ike and his crowd.' He did too. If Ike had been five feet further away when it started, he wouldn't have had time to grab Wyatt and he'd have got him too.

"We walked down the middle of the road and saw them down there with Behan. That little yellow son of a bitch skedaddled before the shooting started. There wasn't any grit in him. Then he lied and said he saw the whole thing. He didn't

* Warren was still home in Colton, healing the wound he'd received when they killed Old Man Clanton — **GB.**

see a damn thing unless he had eyes in the back of his head.

"Wyatt said, 'You sons of bitches have been looking for a fight and now you can have it.' They had their hands on their six-shooters and started to draw them when Wyatt plugged Frank and Billy so quick they didn't know what happened. I remember how both their mouths popped open when the slugs knocked the wind out of them. One of them farted. That probably wasn't all he did either."

He laughs here, and so do I. I expect his laughing to start off another coughing fit, but it doesn't. Doc warms up to his story. It hasn't occurred to me before that someone shot probably shits their pants, but it figures.

"Wyatt tried to plug Ike too, but the bastard grabbed him and threw him off balance. That testimony of Wyatt's about telling Ike to get the hell out of there was all bullshit to make it look good. Fitch thought that up for him. Wyatt told me he'd have burned down Ike whether he had a gun or not. Anyhow Ike got away. He ran in the front of Fly's. By then I'd stepped out further in the road or I might have got him, but I figured I'd better hang onto that buckshot in case we needed it and didn't have time to shift the gun around and jerk my Colt before Ike was inside.

"There wasn't any fight left in that crowd till somebody took a pot shot at us from behind Fly's somewhere and Morg turned that way and gave

Tom McLaury a chance to shoot him in the back over the horse he dodged behind. It was Frank's horse and he must have trained that son of a bitch for shooting off of, like the cavalry, because he didn't run when the shooting started and was still there. The other horse ran. So did Frank's horse when Tom shot his six-shooter practically in its ear. It jumped away and that's when I let Tom have it — both barrels.

"Up till he saw a chance to sneak off a shot, Tom didn't even have a gun in his hand, or I'd have shot him before I did. He was standing there with his mouth open, about like Morg. And Virg still had my cane in his hand like an idiot, even after Wyatt got the job done for him.

"By then Billy Clanton was slumped down at the corner of that little building next to Fly's, but still trying to shoot; Morg was thrashing around on the ground, and Frank was headed across the road; Christ knows how he did it with a big lead pill in his gut. I don't think I could. He even managed to take a shot at me, but he could hardly hold up his pistol. Wyatt and I both shot him at the same time, I guess. I tossed that scattergun down as soon as I emptied it and had my pistol out. Frank's shot went wild and hit me in the pistol scabbard on my left hip and left a hell of a bruise.

"That was about the end of it. Behan tried to arrest us and Wyatt told him to go to hell. You know as much as I do about the rest of it. You heard it in court.

"After that they tried to get us any way they could. Went after Clum and pot shot Virg.

"That ambush of Virg really burned Wyatt up. But, like a damn fool he still thought we could get the courts to do something. Christ Almighty! The sons of bitches we were after alibied each other out of everything. If you didn't have witnesses — and who the hell could you get to testify against that bunch of cut throats? — it turned out they were in church when they bumped somebody off. Me and the Earp boys, and a few others, were the only people with guts enough to buck Behan's gang.

"The law stalled around, as usual after Virg was shot. Naturally Behan didn't do a damn thing, but Wyatt and I took a posse out, with Wells Fargo mainly footing the bill at first, and started to make it hot for those bastards. We even took over Charleston one day and kicked hell out of a bunch of Cowboy lovers. The gang knew they either had to get us out of the way after that, or leave the Territory. After that a bunch of that scum came to town and started hanging around the Grand, loafing around there and shooting their mouths off, looking for a chance to catch one of us alone and do us up. We went out in pairs, at least. Just common sense.

"Wyatt wanted me to say out of trouble and not rock the boat. He was still planning to run for sheriff in the fall and everybody knew we were pretty thick, so he thought any trouble I got in would reflect on him. He was dead right, but I was tired of that bunch of cow thieving pricks shooting off their mouths. I figured Wyatt would come around pretty soon, but it took the killing of Morg to bring him to his senses. Before then a lot of other things happened. The government finally woke up after Wyatt's backers prodded hell out of them."

I think maybe Doc is going to die on me here, since he goes into a real coughing fit. He's coughing up his lungs in pieces and his bloody handkerchief shows it.

"Maybe we'd better quit this. It's aggravating your cough," I say when he finally settles down and gets to breathing fairly normally.

"Hell, no," he says. "I'm going to get this story out to someone. There's been enough lying about it."

So I ask him what he means about Wyatt's backers. He looks at me like I'm a little dim.

"Wells Fargo, the local big bugs," he says. "Who the hell did you think?"

I hadn't thought. I don't think even Behan knew what the Earps were really up to or the power and extent of their backing, or if he did, not until it was too late. I never got more than a glimmering of it before Doc mentioned it. Then the light went on.

Doc goes on, "The goddamn governor and that toss pot, Dake, came down to Tombstone along with Judge Stillwell, and gave Wyatt a hand full of warrants. Wyatt was U.S. Deputy Marshal after Virg got plugged."

EDITORIAL COMMENT:

Before continuing with what Doc recalled, it is pertinent to know a couple of preliminary facts:

1) It is apparent that the territorial authorities and Washington D.C. were fully aware of the lawlessness in Cochise County, and had been for some time, but were prevented by political obstacles from dealing actively with it until it was too late. As today, the executives were willing to act, but were frustrated by Congress playing to pressure groups.

2) John Clum had been agitating for federal action to suppress lawlessness in Cochise County almost as long as he had the Epitaph, which was since May 1, 1880. He was whistling into a hurricane. Finally in late September 1881, John Gosper, acting as governor in the absence of Gov. Fremont, started to look into the Tombstone situation. He was probably prodded by Wells Fargo, who had lost a shipment of specie on the Bisbee stage, held up earlier in the month.

3) On December 6, 1881, President Arthur had asked Congress for an amendment to the Posse Comitatus Act to permit use of the military to enforce the laws in territories, with a specific eye on the Cochise County situation. He was not accommodated by congress, which — as usual — was playing politics, with a view toward re-election, rather than doing a job that needed doing, regardless of whose steer was gored.

4) So there was no help in sight from that quarter. Arizona, and particularly Tombstone, was on its own.

Doc's remarks continue:

"Ringo got brave one day — whiskey guts — and decided to brace me on Allen Street. I was ready to oblige when the police stuck their nose in. We got hauled off to court and fined. Wyatt told me there were some of Ringo's gang upstairs in the Grand ready to get me with rifles. They aimed to plug me from up there, if I jerked a six-shooter and hope it looked like Ringo got me. They'd have had to be damn quick. I'd have loved to gut shoot that drunken, flute-playing* loud mouth.

"After that we kept pushing the sons of bitches, making the rounds out in the country, with a fist full of warrants, but mostly just scaring the shit out of them. It was a big drain on old Curly Bill's organization. He had somebody on almost every piece of water in that country when we started, ready to feed his boys and keep an eye on wet stock till the brands healed over. There were a lot less of them when we finished. It's a cinch Behan wasn't out looking for rustled stock. I never heard of him running in a rustler in all the time I was down there, yet you couldn't throw a rock around Tombstone without hitting a rustler. Most of the honest ranchers were afraid to complain anyhow. The only complaints Behan got were from his own crowd — about us."

I took Doc in to dinner here and he had a pretty

---

* 'Flute playing' was a wry reference to a type of sexual deviation in Doc's day. One wonders if he was simply being insulting, or if Ringo really was 'that way.' — **GB.**

good appetite. Sometimes lungers★ don't. I was a little surprised. It's a good sign. I'm really getting to like Doc. We got on other subjects for awhile, then I suggested we take a bottle up here to my room. I open the window and ask Doc if my smoking a cigar will bother his lungs.

"Hell no, I'll have one myself," he says, and it doesn't seem to bother him. I wonder if he'll get better if he goes back to Arizona. I think, 'Maybe I should ask him.'

He looks over my place and says, "So this is what the rich live like?"

It is a big room with comfortable chairs besides a bed. Why not live well if you can afford it? I notice he doesn't complain and sinks into one of the chairs, looking fairly happy, considering. He gets back around to his story.

"Finally Behan got desperate. I'll bet the gang really had the pressure on him, and he knew he was holding a busted flush, so he had Ike Clanton sign another murder complaint about us killing his baby brother, who outweighed me by about forty pounds. They got their J.P. down in Contention to swear out warrants on Ike's complaint. They knew none of 'em in Tombstone would. It was plain they planned to disarm us and prod us down the road to Contention and have some of the Cowboys shoot us like sitting ducks. Behan actually told us to drive ahead of him in a buggy all by ourselves. What a sweet deal. Wyatt ar-

★ Lungers — a term in the West for tuberculars — **GB.**

ranged for a bunch of his backers to show up —
about thirty of 'em — armed to the teeth and
Behan looked like a trapped rat. That blew up
the ambush he had in mind. The J.P. down below
took one look and referred our case back to
Tombstone. We finally got off in Judge Lucas's
court after he found out there wasn't a damn bit
of new evidence.

"I would have killed Behan by then, but he was
damn careful never to be out alone. Usually he
had a couple of his deputies with him as body-
guards. He needed 'em. Even Wyatt came around
to seeing we had to get him, like burning the heart
of the **Hydra**."

(Yes, Doc wasn't above using a reference to
Greek mythology. He was well-educated for that
day.)

Doc works on our bottle regularly while he's
recalling the vendetta. He seems to drift away at
times and not even realize I'm there, but I'm not
sure whether it's the whiskey or his disease. His
words never slur though. An average person putting away as much as he does would have trouble
talking at all, much less clearly.

He says, "After the hearing in Lucas's court,
we went right back at it, scouring the desert. That
crowd was getting plenty desperate because their
pot of gold was about to empty. They laid low
for a few weeks, then they killed Morg. Shot him
through the window in back of Hatch's, damn near
got Wyatt. That was one goddam big mistake. It
changed Wyatt into a different fellow.

"I was playing faro at the Alhambra and didn't pay any attention. Hell, someone was shooting all the time at night in Tombstone. As soon as I heard what happened, I went over there and saw Morg breath his last. I guess I went a little berserk. I knew who was behind it. Behan. Morg had knocked him on his ass a little before that for messing around Wyatt's girlfriend while Wyatt was out of town with Senator Hearst." (Here's an example of what I mean about Doc — he should have known I knew about that myself — I wonder if he doesn't know who's with him sometimes, or if he even knows anyone is.) He seems to realize where he is and who I am and says, "What the hell am I tellin' you this for? You were there. My mind is getting a little foggy. Anyhow, I was about to say Behan got the ha ha for that all over town. In case you didn't know, it happened right in front of the house where she lived with Behan before she tossed him out and Wyatt moved in."

(I know it didn't happen quite that suddenly on the moving in, but don't tell Doc. I want to keep him talking.)

"That bastard Will McLaury could have come back and been in on Morg's murder too. If he wasn't, he put up money. It was a paid job. Behan was too yellow to kill his own beef.

"I hunted all over Tombstone where I thought I might find Behan, scared a bunch of his lily-white friends half out of their wits, but he must have left town, expecting me or Wyatt would go for him. Wyatt finally collared me and told me we

333

were going after them all — together. That began to look more like my game so I cooled down.

"We knew who the hell we wanted even before Pete Spence's wife spilled the beans at the coroner's hearing. We wanted Spence, Stilwell, Curly Bill, Indian Charlie, Swilling, and a guy who dealt faro for Behan, whose name slips my mind.* She didn't say Curly Bill was in on it, but we had other ways of finding out.

"Wyatt talked Virg into leaving town so we'd be free to go after those murdering bastards. We sent Morg's body out Sunday. I bought him a new set of clothes to be buried in — the least I could do. Virg and his missus left Monday, with us riding behind their buggy to Contention. Me, Wyatt, Warren, Turkey Creek Jack, and Sherm McMasters. Some of the Cowboys prowled around our back trail but were damn careful not to get in rifle range. We left our nags at Contention and went on the train to guard Virg. It was a good thing we did. Wyatt planned to go with him all the way to his folks home to be at the funeral, but it didn't work out that way.

"We got word Ike Clanton, Stilwell and a couple of others were in Tucson and knew we were on the train. Wyatt had the connections to know such things. Sure enough they were hanging around the railroad station. We went in to watch while Virg and the Mick ate." (Doc always called Allie the Mick. They didn't like each other.)

* Listed as John Doe Fries by the Coroner's Jury — **GB.**

334

"When we got Virg back on the train, we spotted some of them down the track waiting to get a shot when the train pulled out. Wyatt tried to get a bead on them in the bad light with his scattergun, but made some noise and they ran. He ran after them and ran across Hank Swilling, who was on our list, but didn't recognize him in a set of city clothes. Lucky for Swilling. Wyatt was through being a Sunday School kid. He ran down Stilwell and let him have both barrels. I put a couple of slugs in him after I got there. I felt like kicking his ribs in for good measure. He was a real low-down, worthless, scum-of-the-earth, back-shooter. Absolutely not worth a cent even to himself."

Doc's voice tells me he still hates Stilwell, even dead.

"We had to get out of Tucson if we were going to run down the rest Wyatt had on his list. Curly Bill, Ringo, Ike Clanton, who we planned to get after he left Tucson, Swilling, Spence, and Behan if we got a shot at him out in the sticks where no one would know. Fat chance. From then on he kept about a dozen of the crowd around him, after he heard how I was looking for him the night Morg got it.

"We hoofed it down the tracks and flagged a freight at Pantano to get back to Benson. The crew kicked till they found out who we were. Wyatt was in tight with the railroad, just like he was with Wells Fargo. At Benson we hired a wagon to get us to Contention, where we picked up our horses.

"We were back to Tombstone before noon and caught some sleep, or at least I did. Wyatt had a lot of business to get out of the way. We knew there'd be a warrant out for us — or at least we thought there would — and sure enough there was. The telegraph man was one of our boys, and didn't give the wire about the warrant to Behan till just before we were ready to leave. I asked Wyatt why we didn't just get the hell out without Behan getting any wiser. The look he gave me answered that. I couldn't believe it, but on second thought I could. He hoped that little piss ant Behan would give him an excuse to kill him.

"The chicken-livered little prick must have damn near died having to make a show of serving his warrant, or else being found out for what he was. He brought along all the deputies he could find, and Dave Neagle too."

(Neagle was marshal, but had been one of Behan's deputies before he was elected marshal.)

"They were all waiting when we came out of the Cosmopolitan onto the street, and looked to Behan to give them their cue. He said, 'Wyatt, I'd like to see you,' and Wyatt gave him a look like he was getting ready to kill a snake and said, 'Johnny, you may see me once too often!'

"Behan never said a word after that. We went down the street, got our horses from Montgomery and left town at a walk, ready to shoot anybody that had any objections. I expect Behan's posse was damn glad Johnny threw in his hand.

"We camped outside town a little ways that

night, planning to go out to Spence's the next day, which we did. Indian Charlie was there — he worked for Spence — he saw us coming too late, and tried to make a run for the rocks and get away. We caught him out in the open and ran him down and sieved him. We camped near town, then rode down past Drew's station and headed out toward the Mustang Hills on a tip Wyatt got earlier that some of the Gang were hiding out over that way."

Doc is quiet awhile, thinking, probably wondering how much to say, or what, in view of what happened.

"We rode up toward a spring along the old army road, planning to camp there. By then most of us were fairly well fagged out and looking for a place to bed down. That sixth sense of Wyatt's was working for him again. He was off his horse and walking with his double barrel in his hand when we popped out right on top of Curly Bill and his boys. Curly was squatted down holding a skillet over a little fire, but he had a scatter-gun leaning on a rock next to him and grabbed it."

Doc is quiet awhile. He's pouring out of the bottle every once in awhile. He starts talking again and says, "The best face I can put on it, I guess, is we cut out of there. I never in the world thought Wyatt hadn't hopped on his horse and pulled his freight with the rest of us, though when I heard the shooting I worried they might have got him. But he didn't run and they didn't get him. He threw down on Curly Bill and damn near cut him in two with buckshot. Curly got a shot at him and tore hell out of his coat. Texas Jack's horse got shot. Wyatt had some trouble getting back on his horse with about a dozen of Curly's crowd shooting at him and the horse jumping around right smart. When he did, he only rode as far as Texas Jack and sprayed the bushes with his Winchester while Jack got his saddle off — a damn fool stunt if you ask me. Anyhow, they ran for it, Jack lugging that damn saddle. Jack had stuck with Wyatt and he was sticking with Jack. They both made it in where we were.

"We felt pretty damn mean about leaving Wyatt in the lurch, but he never said a word about it afterward. I told him we'd go back in and tackle the crowd if he wanted to."

Here Doc laughed, then had another coughing fit. I want to tell him to stop laughing when he talks, that something inside sets him off. He has the ability to laugh at himself and is really pretty funny when he talks. When he gets his breath again, he says, "In case you wondered what I was laughing about, it was what Wyatt said about going back in to shoot it out with Curly's scum. He said, 'I've been.'

"He got the horn shot off his saddle and had a slug in his boot heel that made him think at first he was shot in the foot. He had his nose just above his saddle horn trying to get on when the slug hit it, and he told us it smelled like a rotten egg."

I asked Doc, "Did you see Wyatt shoot Curly Bill?"

"Nope. But Jack Vermillion did. Jack hung in there and got his Winchester out and was backing Wyatt when they dropped his horse. He saw the whole thing."

Doc looks a little rueful, as though he wishes it had been him who stuck. Who can blame him? I never heard Wyatt say a harsh word about Doc as long as I knew him, but it must have made some kind of dent in their relations.

Doc finally takes up his story again.

"We camped that night with a bunch of Mexican wood choppers over in the Whetstones, and the next morning Wyatt met Dan Tipton who brought us some money and information. Johnny Behan had a posse out hunting us, including such rare birds as Ringo. I hoped they'd get within rifle range, but knew they wouldn't with Behan in charge. Tip joined us and never went back to Tombstone. Dan told us he heard that Ike Clanton was going to be leaving Tucson on the train, headed for his ranch over in the Animas to hide out for awhile. It gave Wyatt the idea we ought to look through at least one train headed from Tucson to San Simon, just in case we might catch Ike on it, so we went up to Dragoon and flagged one at the top of the grade. They had to slow down so much on the grade there, if they didn't stop for fear we were pulling a holdup, we could almost walk alongside and get aboard and stop it anyhow.

"Wyatt went through the whole train. If we'd found Ike, we planned to drag his ass out in the desert and do him up. As it was a few mouthy Cowboy-loving damn fools said more than Wyatt was in a frame of mind to stomach and he slapped their faces hard. He wasn't in any mood to take mouth off anyone.

"When we didn't find anyone on the train, we camped for the night, then pushed on up to Colonel Hooker's ranch, planning to rest up. When Hooker heard about the killing of Curly Bill he offered Wyatt the reward the cattlemen had on his head, but Wyatt wouldn't take it. Personally, I would have, but it was his show.

"Behan showed up in a few days with his posse. When Hooker heard he was coming, he offered us his ranch as a fort, and his men to help us, but Wyatt thought we'd better go somewhere else and fort up to keep from getting Hooker in trouble. We went off to a hill about a mile away. Behan didn't seem to be able to find us, for some reason.

"I dropped the papers a love note on the subject.

"We cut out of Hooker's by way of Globe; Wyatt had a tip about someone there that Wells Fargo wanted, but we drew a bum hand there and left Arizona behind, but that wasn't the end of it."

Chapter 23

Doc Holliday On The Ringo Killing

1945

What I wrote way-back-when is copied above, almost word for word the way I wrote it down at the time, but it's obvious I left something very important out of the Tombstone Vendetta. The end of it.

Doc had found a job dealing faro in Denver, so he turned in late in the day (or early, in fact) and slept late. Most gamblers were at work till the wee hours, sometimes almost till daybreak if someone had a hot streak going at the tables. Doc started work in the evening when things first picked up, so I often had supper with him before he went to work.

I wanted to hear what he knew about the death of John Ringo, if anything. It was a mystery around Tombstone when it happened in July 1882, and as far as I knew was still a mystery.

I know more details of that killing now from Josephine Earp's account of Ringo's death but, of course, by the time I read her story I already knew

341

that Doc had been implicated.

When I first asked him about the Ringo killing, I had no idea he or Wyatt might have been involved, so wasn't prepared for the sharp look my question got me.

"What do you know about that?" Doc asked.

"Absolutely nothing."

He studied me awhile with those ghostly blue eyes, probably deciding whether he should trust me or not. By then we were practically pals, or at least I thought we were. Finally he said, "I was one of the main guys in that affair. I'll give you a couple of guesses who killed him."

I thought maybe he was hinting that he had.

"I'll bite," I said, afraid to guess it was him in case it wasn't. Doc was a funny duck. I was never sure what might get him riled. Today I know that's typical of tuberculars.

Doc said, "Maybe I shouldn't tell you this. You're going to have to promise to keep it under your hat."

"O.K. I promise."

"Wyatt Earp killed Ringo."

I was thunderstruck and must have looked it. Everyone thought Wyatt was in Colorado when Ringo cashed in, and that was just the way Wyatt had wanted it.

Doc noticed my stunned expression, of course, and said, "I don't blame you for having your mouth hanging open, but Wyatt sure as hell did beef Ringo. I was along with him." He paused, debating whether to say more, and probably thinking he'd already said too much, because he said, "If Wyatt ever finds out I told you, he'll look me up and wring my neck."

That night I wrote down everything I could remember that Doc said and what follows is just the way it came out of Doc.

He downed a whiskey and poured another from the flask he kept in his coat pocket.

Then he leaned on the table and started talking.

"We didn't get to Colorado till May, after we pulled out of Arizona. We went up the Gila from Globe, sold our nags at Silver City and took a stage to Deming and caught a train to Albuquerque. We stayed there a couple of weeks, then came up to Trinidad. Bat Masterson was marshal there. Wyatt hung around Trinidad, but I never liked Masterson and the feeling was mutual, so I moseyed up to Pueblo where things were wide open.

"You may have heard I had a little trouble in Denver that spring over the Arizona business. That bastard Behan tried to get us extradited, but it didn't wash. Actually, Masterson got me off the hook, but he only did it for Wyatt. Wells Fargo weighed in with us too. They were probably shaking in their boots over what we might say if we squealed on them. Anyhow, 'Haw' Tabor, who was sitting in for the governor,* turned down the extradition. He's a hell of a good old boy.

"After awhile Wyatt wrote me from Gunnison

* H.A.W. Tabor, the Silver King, then Lt. Gov. of Colorado under Gov. Fred Pitkin — **GB.**

343

and said it was the next big thing in Colorado, bigger than Tombstone, so I trotted over to take a look. I expected to find the Earps set up in town, but they were camping west of town. Wyatt, Warren, Dan Tipton and Texas Jack.

"I asked Wyatt what the hell he was doing out there. Living in a tent where it gets cold as a well digger's ass at night isn't my idea of paradise, but he had his reasons.

"He told me he wanted to be out where no one in town would miss him if he wasn't seen around for awhile, because he figured he might have to take a little vacation somewhere. Ringo had got to be the king pin of the gang at Tombstone after Curly Bill and Old Man Clanton got knocked off and some people wanted him out of the way to finally put an end to the organization. Ringo was the only one left with a big enough rep to hold it together. Wyatt said there was a good piece of change in it for anyone who went back with him.

" 'We already got enough warrants hanging over our heads back there,' I told him.

"He said, 'Wait'll you hear how much dough I'm talking about.'

"I'm not going to say how much, or who all paid it, but there were a bunch that wanted Ringo's hide, or actually wanted to be sure that bunch of crooked sons of bitches that had been robbing and killing there for years were killed or run out of the country.

"Wyatt said, 'If Behan happens to get in the way, maybe we can leave him for the buzzards.

Actually, I'd like to string him up and listen to him choke.' That wasn't the old Wyatt Earp talking. You should have seen the look on his face when he said it.

"I had a little pull in Pueblo by then and went back and rigged up an alibi. It isn't hard if you know how to do it.* Wyatt's alibi was leaving his brother and friends behind to drop in town occasionally and be seen. No one would notice he wasn't with some of them. He wasn't that well known there yet. We learned our lesson on alibis with Stilwell. We should have disposed of his body, as you news sharps say.

"We figured if we took a train back to the Tombstone country, we'd have a big problem with our 'phizzes' (faces or physiognomies — **GB**) but by the time we shoved off we were both sporting pretty fair beards. Instead of going on the main line down to Deming and connecting with the S.P., we took the D. and R.G. to **Espanola,** a stage to Santa Fe and on to Lamy where we caught the A. & P. Certain parties made sure there were horses waiting for us near Holbrook and from there we went down through the mountains, almost the same way we went in 1879, only this time to Globe. I had a notion to drop in and see Kate there, but she was apt to get mad at me over some trifle and blab. What a temper!"

---

* He apparently had a bogus charge filed against him, then had his attorney appear for him, which was recorded as "appearing in his own person," whereas only his attorney was there. This pro forma language is not uncommon, according to legal authorities — **GB.**

He laughed and, as so often was the case, ended up in a coughing spasm. After awhile he got his breath back and wheezed again, saying, "I wish she was up here now. She could mother me. And that's not all."

He looked a little sad. She must have been a hell of a woman for all of her temper fits. I think Doc really loved her.

After seeming to be far away there for awhile, he picked up his story with, "We ended up at Hooker's ranch. That whole country was full of spies for the gang, so we travelled mostly at night.

"Plenty of people were watching on our side too. We wanted to get a good bead on Ringo. We knew he moved around a lot between Tombstone and the Chiricahuas, and also knew he was in Tombstone right at the time we got into that country, so we waited for him. I wanted to go into town and get him, just like they did Morg, but Wyatt thought it was too risky. Shit, I'd like to have gone in and pot shot that little piss ant Behan.

"Anyhow, our messenger came in, sure enough, and we cut old John's trail, but it was getting pretty late in the day. He was on the road up to Morse's sawmill. We had our man right on his tracks — somebody he wouldn't have been suspicious of if he saw him because he had to follow him pretty close. He came back and told us Ringo had set up a camp and rolled in to catch some sleep. Knowing Ringo, he was probably hung over.

"It was pretty damn late in the afternoon when we got there. Ringo had started a pot of coffee.

We could smell smoke from his fire. Anyhow, we left the horses a good ways off so they wouldn't give us away, although the road up to Morse's passed right by there and anybody might be passing there with horses. Ringo wasn't over a hundred yards off the trail, but he was out of sight in a little canyon.

"We left one man with the horses and the rest of us split up, three on each side of the canyon, working our way up above him. We weren't aiming to take any chances. Wyatt said, 'I'd like to swing that bastard off on a rope right in the road, but I reckon we'll have to shoot him, because he isn't going to surrender to the likes of us.'

"So we knew what he expected us to do. The first one of us that could get a bead on Ringo was going to cut him down. I hoped I'd get the honor, but I didn't. Something tipped John off and he made a run for it out of his camp. We couldn't tell what was going on over on the other side of the canyon, so we kept moving. I slipped and accidentally kicked a rock down the hill, but that wasn't what spooked Ringo, because from what Wyatt said, he ran a long while before that. I can tell you, they were moving damn careful over on the other side where they'd seen him take to the brush. Even though we didn't have any idea what was going on, we were naturally creeping along like Indians ourselves. Then someone shot. A pistol.

"I thought, 'I hope somebody beefed the son of a bitch!' We stopped in our tracks and waited for somebody to yell over and tell us what was going on, if they got him, but it was quiet as hell. Then I heard another shot, this time a heavy rifle. After awhile Wyatt gave the whistle he used as his personal signal out in the country. He could give the God damndest loud whistle I ever heard by putting two fingers in his mouth to do it. Then he yelled, 'Come on in!' I knew then they had got that dirty son of a bitch.

"Wyatt drilled him in the head with his Winchester when he busted out of the brush. We sat around and drank up John's coffee and waited till it was good and dark before we moved his dead ass down below the Smith's place and dumped it where somebody was sure to find it — not over twenty feet from the road to Morse's.

"I was back up here in less than a week. Wyatt headed for San Francisco." He laughed. "I guess you know why."

I knew why. I helped smuggle Josie out of town when she left. We put her on the train at Benson. At that time she didn't know if she'd ever see Wyatt again. I remember how she looked then, trying to be brave, but her lower lip was quivering when she got on the train. I got up my nerve to give her a squeeze, a real miracle. I think that's when I really started to be her friend, in her mind.

I didn't see her again for a few years, but I kept track of what they were doing through friends, and sometimes in the papers.

This brings me to the end of the Tombstone Vendetta, but its aftermath, for me, is equally interesting.

Chapter 24

The Secret Lives Of Josephine Earp

The extent to which Wyatt was a tool of Josephine, even at Tombstone, has only dawned on me in recent years. I see, in reading over what I've written, that I showed that without fully realizing what I was telling.

Now, I think it's necessary to portray the traits of this woman in her mature years — traits that I saw first in Tombstone. After this the reader will understand more fully, before I end this story, how her strong, calculating nature influenced Wyatt Earp's Tombstone Vendetta.

Josephine Earp herself sometimes became one of my best informants, usually not by intent.

In Tombstone, Josie was still living with Behan long after one would think she'd have pulled out in disgust. Behan's son, Albert was one of the reasons she stuck. He was like her own kid. She loved him dearly, and it was an affection returned in spades. He adored her. I used to drive her over to Yuma to meet him until shortly before she died.

He'd come in from Ajo. Sometimes he'd even come up and meet us at Joe Bush's in Parker. I recall a couple of times he came into L.A. to visit her, but he hated to travel and didn't trust himself on foot in city traffic, since he was hard of hearing. He took a taxi everywhere. I can't say as I blame him — I can still hear pretty well, and even I hate to cross a street in L.A.

Anyhow, it may seem like I'm getting away from my story, but there's a reason. Besides, it's my story and the reader (if there ever should be one) is stuck with it. The main thing is that Josie hung with Johnny a long while after she'd like to have anyone reading her memoir suspect. (I've read, and have copies of, both the earlier and later versions.) It's possible Josie was still in love with Johnny, even after she found him out. He was a Casanova, and she was a damn fool like many women are where that type is concerned. I think she loved Wyatt in time, but not in the same way. She never forgot Johnny, even kept his picture, since we found one in the few things she had in her room when she died. And it was one that had obviously been taken after she left Tombstone. Boy, could that have got her in trouble with Wyatt if he'd found it. He was jealous as hell where she was concerned, even though they sometimes had their fallings-out when he'd pull out and leave her for awhile.

I am probably the only person living who knew so much about Josephine Earp's secretive nature and the several lives she lived in her final years as a result. When she died, Bessie Nevitt and Flood looked for the stuff Josie listed in her skimpy will and couldn't find much.* They found only her radio, which was in her room at Bessie's, her clothes and a few of her latest letters. They asked me if I knew where the stuff was, since it had been willed to her nieces, Alice Cohn and Edna Stoddart. If it had amounted to much I might have put them on its trail, especially if her nieces needed anything, but they're both pretty well fixed, I judge. What I'm leading up to is that Josie chose to lead her life in compartments. I figured she had her reasons, and I saw no need to give her away while the people she wanted to keep unaware of each other were still living. By the time anyone sees this, if they ever do, all those parties will be dead.

The compartments of which I was aware, and I think I knew of all of them, were: (1) her life with Flood and Bessie, (2) relations with Wyatt's relatives, such as his sister, Adelia, and her kids, and even Virg's widow, Allie, though there was no love lost between them, (3) her sisters' families in the Bay Area, (4) the Casons and Ackermans, who were doing her biography; and, you may not believe this, but two more lives. With me, of course, her old faithful chauffeur, which was probably the only reason I knew **all** the others, and

* Her property was actually in the basement of the home of one of her biographers, Vinolia Ackerman, and later unaccountably showed up in a Wyatt Earp Museum in Tombstone, Arizona, and has since sunk from sight. — **GB.**

one more, perhaps the most fascinating connection of all. I'm going to call him only R.J., for reasons anyone can appreciate after they hear his and Josie's story.

R.J. was a fighter pilot in World War I and obviously was a lot younger than us. He met Josie in a most unusual set of circumstances when he was a barnstormer after the war. I can still hear him telling how it happened:

"I was just playing around, chasing clouds with that old Jennie, when I spotted a prospector — or at least what I took to be a prospector way the hell out north of the Whipples on foot; who the hell else would be out there? I never missed a chance to buzz one, so I peeled off and dived down. He heard me coming, only it turned out to be a she. She waved both arms like hell and practically jumped up and down so it wasn't hard to figure something was wrong. I put old Jennie down up the road where it was flat enough to do it and damn near wrecked us at that, then I jammed a couple of rocks under the wheels for chocks and left her idling so I wouldn't have to risk not being able to get the son of a bitch started again. When I got back to the lady she was sitting on a rock about done in. It was Mrs. Earp."

(He never called her anything else as long as I've known him, even when she wasn't around and still doesn't, even with her gone.)

"Naturally I asked her what happened. Her damn mule got away somehow. She was probably taking a leak. Nobody ever found the bastard and you won't be surprised when I tell you what she had the saddle bags full of. Hi-grade. She was so glad to see me, she blabbed out why she was there. She said, 'I've got a mine back there, but please don't tell anyone.' If the stuff she had on that mule was like some of the stuff she showed me since then, a lot of it was almost pure gold.

"She was pretty thirsty and I got some water in her and let her sit down awhile. She told me she was camping with her husband over near the river. Hell, the river was ten miles away. I thought, 'This ain't your average woman.' As we both know, she sure as hell wasn't. She wasn't the least bit scared. Hell, I don't think she's ever been scared in her life. That's all an act she likes to pull on people."

(I'll buy that. I've seen her kill a rattlesnake with rocks and look like she'd have walked a mile to do it, grinning when she was sure it was dead. She always cut off the rattles and saved them, God knows what for.)

"I had a time gettin' her in the plane too; as you know she's gettin' a little hefty. I finally shoe-horned her in and got her tied down. I set down on another damn road near where they were camped, about like the first one. You can bet Wyatt was surprised to see me, and a lot more surprised to see her, though plenty glad. She'd been gone a long while and it was gettin' close to sundown by then. The name Earp didn't mean a thing to me then."

(That would have been 1920.)

"She wasn't a bit scared of flyin'. Loved it that first time and wanted more of it. I gave her some flyin' lessons on and off for years. But she was a helluva damn fool. Woulda killed herself if I soloed her. She just didn't give a damn.

"I could never get Wyatt into a plane. He told me if God intended men to fly he'd give 'em wings. I don't think he was scared of it — just not interested. Besides he never took a chance he didn't have to — I gotta admit flyin' ain't without its hazards; landin' too, come to think of it, especially on roads like that son of a bitch I picked up Mrs. Earp on."

You can see why R.J. is going to have to be just R.J. He may be running around, now that Josie is gone, wondering what to do with a Lost Mine map — probably is. I'm not about to ask him. I can imagine what a target he'd be if word got out, not the least of the reasons I don't want this story to come out until he's gone too. Maybe some of the old timers up around Parker and Blythe suspect anyhow, but they mind their own business. I'd bet R.J. hasn't told anyone (assuming he knows) where the Lost Josephine Earp Mine is located; at least not me, and I never heard that he had any relatives. He's pretty secretive sometimes. Peculiar too. I'll bet he hasn't taken a nickel out of the mine, and never will. Likely one of the reasons Josie liked him was she didn't have to be careful of her money around him. Money doesn't mean a damn thing to him; he's got enough for him and his dog to live on and that's all he cares.

Josie never said a word to me about that bonanza. If she suspected R.J. might have told me, she never let on. I judge the only reason he mentioned it to me in the first place, was he figured I already knew.

Wyatt must have known about it too. But Josie was the "money brains" in their family. He dribbled away the fortune they pulled out of Alaska. He just might have put up a gold mine in a poker game, but he was more apt to lend money to friends or put it in their pie-in-the-sky schemes. She wasn't about to let him pull any boners like that with **her** money. Once was enough. I've heard her get on his case a time or two about piddling away the Alaska money. I can hear her saying, "If you'd had sense enough just to keep it in the bank at interest, we could still be living on it."

It would have made them a couple of hundred a month, which was plenty for them up till the time he died. They could have lived royally on that much, so I never blamed her for lecturing him about it.

Wyatt knew better than to try to find out where she was getting that gold. She wore the pants in the family. Isn't that funny?

Their other bonanza was Josie's sister, Henrietta, who kept Josie and Wyatt on an allowance out of the goodness of her heart. I'll bet dollars to donuts Josie never told her about the gold mine. Of course Henrietta knew about the Happy Day, and learned it wasn't worth much after they tried to work it in earnest. Otherwise she wouldn't have practically kept Wyatt and Josie all those years.

About how worthless the Happy Day was, Joe Bush told me once, "He tried to put their mine up in a poker game against fifty bucks and got no takers. We all knew it didn't have the stuff we wanted."

Anyhow, Henrietta, or Hattie as we all called her, took care of them. She had a restaurant and confectionery shop in Oakland that was the "in" place in town for years. She was a widow. I always wondered if something wasn't going on there with her and Wyatt, since he and Josie stayed with her sometimes for months on end. Maybe that soft spot in her heart wasn't for her sharp-tongued sister.

It was just like Josie to take advantage of her. And, I'll bet Josie didn't have a map around somewhere to pass along to Hattie if Josie died first, though she probably told R.J. if she went before Wyatt, to take care of him, without letting him get his hands on **her** mine. R.J. would have done exactly that, too. He's all man. I'd trust him with my life. I'm not sure Josie wasn't in love with him, though she was old enough to be his mother and then some. But she never knew she wasn't eighteen and beautiful, even after she got fat.

The point of this, after reading it over, must be that I'm trying to leave a record of what Josie was really like, since she was Tombstone's Helen of Troy. I find myself writing in circles, wondering what I started to say, which probably will sound familiar to a lot of old people. I sure learned over the years after I left there that I wasn't as much in the know back at Tombstone as I thought I was, even though it all happened right under my nose.

Nonetheless, no one else living, except Allie Earp, can make a better guess at the pieces still missing from the full story. She tried to tell it, but the fellow she had working on it changed it to suit himself. She threatened to shoot him. Allie's living over with her niece, Hildreth Hallowell (and hating it, if I'm any judge). Allie still likes a nip, and her snuff. Hallowell won't let her have either one if she can help it. There's nothing dead in Allie's head, either, though she's almost a hundred, I'd guess. She's been a widow for forty years, and never wanted another man after Virg died. I can see why.

Anyhow, the rest are all gone now — Scheiffelin and the Girds, who started it all; Morg murdered in Tombstone; the youngest brother, Warren, shot in 1900; Virg, who died in Goldfield in 1905; Behan gone in 1912, drank himself to death; profane old

Jimmy Earp in 1926; Wyatt in 1929; Clum, Parsons and Breakenridge in the 1930's; Josie last year. Pretty soon I'll be joining them. In a way you get so you look forward to it when you've seen all your friends over the divide.

It seems like yesterday I was at Wyatt's funeral, but it's been sixteen years. It even seems like yesterday when I returned to Tombstone after my father's death, but its been sixty-four years. Funny how time slips away and one day, you're old. I don't feel old upstairs, but these ancient bones are getting mighty creaky.

Chapter 25

I Learned About Josie's Past

The Earps were in San Diego and had gotten into horse racing in a big way. I was there laying the foundation for my real estate business. Several others of the old Tombstone crowd such as Albert Fortlouis and E.B. Gifford were also in San Diego, but I was so busy that I hadn't much time to socialize with them. I did try to see as much of the Earps as possible, though, as I considered them special friends.

There was a little Mexican Posada down on the waterfront that had a restaurant — I've forgotten its name — but I used to see Wyatt and Josie there every so often. One night I had a notion I wanted some Mexican food and walked down there. It was early dark. The ocean was slapping on the beach, and the offshore breeze carried that delicious aroma of salt. I was sitting on top of the world with a hefty bank balance and a recent engagement to the girl I was to marry. It hardly seemed possible there was unhappiness anywhere in the world.

I knew better as soon as I walked in and saw the stricken look on Josie's face. She was sitting alone in one corner, and her face was pale and drawn. I went to her table and stood there for half a minute before she noticed me.

She looked up and seemed to recognize me only with a great effort, but when she did she said in a strangled voice, "Ted! Oh, thank God it's you. I need a friend. I think I'm going to kill myself." Then tears streamed down her face.

I pulled up a chair next to hers and put an arm around her. Like most men I didn't have the faintest notion how to soothe a crying woman. And there was nothing of sham in her crying. She wept from the bottom of her heart.

"My God, Josie!" I said. "What's wrong? Where's Wyatt?"

That turned loose more sobs. She bit the back of her hand trying to control herself, and finally gasped, "He's left me."

I couldn't believe it. Like a dunce I said, "Left you?"

She nodded her head, then said quite calmly, "I'm going to kill myself. I already killed our baby."

This stunned me. I knew they couldn't have had a child since the last time I'd seen them. I thought she might be losing her mind and wondered where I could find a doctor at that time of the evening, or whether Wyatt was searching for her after some kind of domestic squabble. I had no idea how bad the situation really was.

Somehow I managed to get her back to the rooms where she and Wyatt had been living. I was hoping we'd find him there, but we didn't. Later I learned that he was far out on the trail to the new Arizona boom camp of Harqua Hala and wouldn't be back for months. Probably he wasn't in a much happier state of mind. The two were meant for each other.

I got Josie to sit on the settee and put my arms around her. Gradually her sobs subsided, and she pushed away to blow her nose and dab her eyes. Then she snuggled back into my embrace.

Thank goodness Wyatt didn't come in at that point, with her face lifted up to mine inviting a kiss! Knowing women now a little better, I realize that a kiss was the medicine needed to heal her battered ego. Josie needed a man to make love to her as completely as his nerve would permit.

The state of my nerves didn't permit at all. I was almost in a panic, my only carnal thoughts being that she was little, and soft and helpless. This was the moment I'd dreamed of for years, and all I could manage was the big brother act.

Besides, I was engaged to Myra, though that wouldn't have mattered to some men. At that moment Josie needed a ruthless seducer, like Behan, the physical kind of man in pursuit of a woman's body, one who will lie like hell to get it. I guess I was a hell of a disappointment to Josie, but I've never been sorry and I don't think she was either. But that — and one other — were the only times I ever kissed her on the lips.

She sensed that I wasn't able to do more than that and straightened a little. "What a mess I've made of things," she murmured. "I wonder what my poor mother would think."

I've noticed that we all tend to think of our "poor mothers" at historic moments in our lives that usually can be summarized as "too late." Josie's turning to her past when she was miserable and feeling sorry for herself is the only reason I know so much of her background. I was there at the right psychological moment.

A few minutes later she said, "I came from a good family, though the way I act you probably won't believe me. My father owns a store up at Gilroy, but we always lived in San Franciso because of the schools and conveniences."

This confirmed at least part of what I'd heard, and I wasn't the least bit inclined to doubt her.

"It must have almost killed my mother when I ran away from home the first time. I was almost eighteen. Myra ran away with me."

Josie had introduced me to Myra, my wife to be, but there had been no discussion of their being childhood friends. Therefore, the question was entirely genuine when I asked, "Myra who?"

"Myra Nagle, of course," she said, looking at me as if I was a fool.

I was thunderstruck. Maybe, under other circumstances, Josie would have kept their secret as she had up until then, but I've thought since that it was her way of being spiteful to me for not responding to her invitation. Josie certainly knew how to be spiteful, as anyone who knew her could attest.

"Myra Nagle," I repeated.

"Yes," Josie said. "We've been friends as long as I can remember. I didn't know she hadn't told you."

I believed her then. I don't now. It's possible she was trying to split us up so she could have me for herself to "show Wyatt." After all, they'd never tied the knot either, anymore than she and Johnny had. That came later.

When I said nothing, Josie continued reminiscing. Talking about her past seemed to make her feel better, so I determined to stay and listen as long as necessary.

"We lived in a big house overlooking the Bay. Everything was so secure and comfortable. I realize that now. I should never have left." She stared down at her hands and seemed lost in the past. "I can still smell how it used to be when I came home from school. There were always spicy cookies and cakes in the pantry and meat roasting in the kitchen. And Mama used to meet us at the door and give us a hug and a kiss and say 'Leibchen,' like we'd been gone for days." Tears threatened to overflow again.

"She had such a big loving heart, and I've come close to breaking it so many times. Mama and Papa spoiled us, me especially. I was the wild one, always getting Henrietta into a lot of trouble."

A smile overtook her tears at this point as she remembered what a headstrong creature she'd been. "There was a Chilena girl sitting in front of me in school, and I always noticed her pierced ears and little gold earrings. I wanted a pair, and Henrietta did, too, so we asked Mama and Papa if we could get our ears pierced. They thought we were too young, but we kept asking. One day I asked the girl where she got hers done, and she said, 'Mi abuela.' So Henrietta and I went to her grandmother's house. The old lady put a cork back of our ear lobes, squeezed, and jabbed a needle through into the cork." Josie shuddered a little. "She put a little piece of silk thread through the hole and tied it, and then we ran home, me hurting and Henrietta crying over the pain. We were scared what our parents would say so we sneaked up the back stairs to our room."

Josie's smile became a mischievous grin. "Mama came looking for us because we came home so late, and we got a good scolding. I did, anyhow, because everybody knew Henrietta only followed where I led. But they forgave us and Papa got us each a pair of earrings.

"They were always trying to keep me busy and out of trouble, but I had too much energy. Finally I took voice lessons from Myra's mother and went to dancing school."

She paused after mentioning that.

"It sounds like a pretty normal childhood to me," I said.

She shook her head. "Maybe up to that point. But remember how **Pinafore** was so popular about ten years ago? Everybody was singing the songs, and I learned the Sailor's Hornpipe at dancing school. Then one of the girls, Phyllis Myers got a part in Pauline Markham's Pinafore Troupe and talked Myra into running away with her when they went on the road in 1879. Myra wanted me to run away, too."

EDITORIAL COMMENT:
Ten Eyck changed the names of all the girls involved except Josie's.

Josie must have known that I had heard none of this from Myra, but if she expected me to be shocked she was disappointed. Myra was already a well known actress when Josie introduced us. She was also beautiful and warmhearted, and I loved her and that was that. I was going to marry her, regardless.

Josie went on. "Myra and I were inseparable. What I wore, she wore. What I liked or disliked, she did. We had the same school girl crushes, and went everywhere together. The thought of Myra far away on the stage was too much for me."

She looked at me, hoping for understanding. "You know what I did, Ted," she said. "I didn't care about anybody's feelings but my own. Mama and Papa were frantic when I didn't come home that night. I got the part of Tommy Tucker in Miss Markham's troupe because I could dance the Sailor's Hornpipe so well."

"How did you run away?" I asked.

Tears came into her eyes again. "The troupe

left us tickets to catch the boat and meet them in Santa Barbara. Can you imagine? We weren't even eighteen, and we didn't have any money. And it was raining, the water was rough. We were both sick all the way to Santa Barbara. And scared. When we weren't sick, we were crying. I wish I'd never left home. By now I'd be married to some nice, respectable man who never fought with me and made me miserable."

She started crying in earnest at the thought.

"Don't be too damn sure," I told her, hoping to take her mind off herself. Then, just as she stopped sniffling, I asked something stupid.

"Do you know where Wyatt is?"

"He went back to Arizona!" She sobbed loudly. "Without me. I know he's never coming back, and I couldn't bear to have our baby without him!"

Love is a funny thing. Josie didn't look like the strong-willed woman she was, but that side of her asserted itself. "I hope he never comes back, damn him!" And her tears dried up as suddenly as they'd started.

"He'll come back," I said, trying to reassure her.

"He can't now," she said. "I had an abortion. He'd kill me."

I'm not sure how I managed to say anything rational in response, but I did. "Did he know you were pregnant?"

She shook her head.

"Then if he comes back, don't tell him whatever you do."

I was wasting my breath, and I knew it. When Josie made up her mind to hurt someone, she did it. She'd ruined Johnny Behan, and he deserved it. I hoped she wouldn't decide to ruin Wyatt, because he didn't.

"It's not the first one, either," she said, defiantly. "I had one in Tombstone after Johnny refused to get married. I told him I was pregnant and he said, 'Whose kid is it? Wyatt's?' " She looked up sadly. "I'd never done more than speak to Wyatt up until then."

By this time, I was sufficiently immune to Josie's charms to doubt her statement. I also remembered that she'd called Doc Holliday "John" the first time I met him. There was plenty of talk around Tombstone about her and other men before she made the complete break from Johnny. But I was surprised to hear about the earlier abortion. In fact, I'd been hoping that when she first mentioned the baby she meant she'd lost the child by accident. Now I knew the worst.

But it was easy to see how a head-strong woman like she was did the things she did. She acted first and then gave way to regret — if regret was needed, but it was hard not to forgive her. That evening, what I felt was compassion. I knew how much she and Wyatt had wanted a child.

"Dr. Goodfellow did it for me in Tombstone," she said, still on the same, dismal subject.

I thought, "My God, how appropriate! The great gunshot specialist doing an abortion for Wyatt Earp's wife."

Poor, impulsive Josie. She kept coming back to the subject because her conscience was bothering her. She needed someone to tell her she'd done the right thing, but I couldn't do it. She'd done the worst conceivable wrong. If she lived to be a hundred she'd never succeed in doing anything that would hurt Wyatt as much, and she knew it.

I'd heard him say a dozen times, "Our first one is going to be a girl. I'm going to call her Sweet Patootie till we think up a name. I think we should call her Sadie, though, because we know she'll be so sweet, just like her mother." He knew Josie hated her middle name, especially shortened to Sadie, and when he wanted to tease her, that's what he called her.

She usually made a sour face when he talked of naming the baby Sadie, and he'd notice and add, "Maybe we'll have to call her Pickle if we name her after her Ma."

Knowing all this, knowing the love that they both felt for one another, I had to ask why Wyatt had left.

She didn't want to tell me, but finally said, "We had a big fight. I was silly."

She kept her eyes averted, then the words burst out. "He was always letting women flirt with him. Finally he was seeing some dizzy blond. So I went out to dinner with Lucky Baldwin and Wyatt found out. He was furious at me. We had a real shouting match. I told him if he went out with other women, I could go out with a family friend.

He said I was jealous over nothing. Ha! He spent the night with her more than once. Is that nothing? I told him he could go to hell, and he packed up and left."

"When was that?" I asked.

"About three weeks ago. I knew he was never coming back, so I went and had it done."

I knew her, and I knew she'd done it on impulse and then was immediately sorry.

"I'm glad it didn't kill you," I said. Abortions were no joke in those days. Women often bled to death.

She put her head on my shoulder and wept. "I'm sorry I did it!" she confessed. "God, if I could only have it back!"

I wished she could, too, but it was done, and all I could do was hold her and sit with her in silence.

A little later she said, "It wasn't like the other time. I still love Wyatt. I'll always love him. I hated Johnny."

I thought I could divert her from her unhappy thoughts and asked, "How did you meet him? I always wondered."

"The Pinafore Troupe was on its way from Tucson to Prescott and met a posse out hunting some bandits. Johnny was with them. They escorted us to Prescott because they were giving up the chase and said it wasn't safe for us greenhorns wandering around. We had two stagecoaches and a prop wagon. They called us "Pinafore on Wheels." It took two days to get to Prescott, and Johnny gave me the big rush all the way. He **could** be charming. And I was young and foolish." She sighed and shook her head. "It seems so long ago now. But I'm still foolish. Anyway, after I got home he came all the way to San Francisco with a diamond, and he proposed. My folks had a fit, but I thought it was the most romantic thing."

A little smile quivered on her lips. "Finally we wheedled an engagement out of my folks. It wasn't easy. We're Jewish but not orthodox, and Johnny's Catholic, but I guess they thought I'd run away again if I didn't get my way. I probably would have."

Knowing Josie, I was sure she would have, and I smiled, myself at the thought.

"So Johnny went back to Tombstone. He'd started the livery stable with John Dunbar by then. And he sent Kitty Jones who was home on a visit with a message. He asked my folks to let me go back with her as chaperone to Tombstone where he could marry me. There was another big fuss, but I got my way and went.

"You know the rest. The only good thing about it was that I was little Albert Behan's foster mother for a year. We still write to each other like I was his real mother."

She was close to tears again, thinking of the two babies that might have been, but she had calmed down a lot and I felt safe in leaving her.

While Wyatt was gone, I saw a lot of Josie, and learned more of her background both from her and from Myra. Myra was with me the night Wyatt came home, not even sure it still was his home. He seemed relieved to have us there, putting off being alone with Josie, but we left as soon as possible. I wondered if she would take my advice and keep the abortion secret.

Later that night I went into Fortlouis'. Wyatt was at the end of the bar. I started over, then remembered that I'd never in my life seen him take a drink. But there he was tossing down a shot with another backed up behind it.

He glanced once my way totally without recognition, and I was shocked to see that his eyes were blinded with tears. He pulled out a handkerchief and wiped them away, then tossed down the waiting shot and ordered a third.

She'd told him all right. She'd had her revenge, such as it was. I left quickly, wondering where she was and what she was doing, and if she was glad.

I'd never loved them more or felt sorrier for them both.

Chapter 26

An Era Ends

One of the most profound terms I've heard applied to California, especially Los Angeles, is that it's the "graveyard of the pioneers."

Wyatt and Josie both died here, although their ashes are buried together at San Francisco, and soon I'll be joining my old friends. It's been a great life, and I have few regrets, but if I don't hurry and finish Wyatt's story, my chief regret will be that I left it unfinished.

I've already written about how Wyatt and Doc got Ringo. That story also came out of Josie on our 1937 trip back to Tombstone, a trip that came about because she had found a new set of biographers to help her with her memoirs.

EDITORIAL COMMENT:
This story, as stated, is in the Ten Eyck papers and is amplified by Josie's story, undoubtedly the same one she told, as above.

The Ackerman's, Harold and Vinolia, were distant relatives on Wyatt's side, and they were having a worse time getting the truth out of Josie than Parsons and Clum did. The problem was that she was trying to appear respectable as she approached the end of her life, whereas, when she was young, she hadn't given a damn what anybody thought.

I'm not sure she did at the end, either. She was making an effort solely for Wyatt's memory, wanting him preserved in the public mind as a lawman who had played a leading role in taming the West.

Maybe that's how he wanted it, too, but I don't know. Actually, I think he only wanted to be left alone while he lived and didn't care what happened after he died. In his later years he was quietly religious, given to reading the bible.

"It's all here in the book," he used to say when I found him reading it.

However, in the spring of 1937, Vinolia and Harold Ackerman accompanied Josie to Tombstone and, by her request I met her there. The weather was raw and chilly, and the warmth from the big stove in the lobby of the Tourist Hotel was welcome.

The hotel was directly across Allen street south of a drug store which had been the Oriental Saloon, and the hotel, itself, was on the site of the Huachuca Water Company building. When Virgil was ambushed in December, 1881, it was with shotguns fired from inside a partially framed building there.

It was sad to see how the historic old burg had gone downhill. Some buildings were tumbling down, and others were in a sorry state of repair. The March wind was blowing dust and trash down those streets that had once been alive with traffic and with the fascinating characters we'd known in our youth. Josie and I both felt as if something had been lost, never to be found again.

One of the few old timers still there was the Chinaman, Quong Kee, living in the remains of his old Can Can Restaurant. He came to the door huddled in a ragged overcoat, a toothless old man, practically broke, with his dog and cat at his heels.

When he found out who we were, and that we wanted to take a picture of him, he insisted on dressing up. He donned a pale lavender brocade jacket, blue corduroy pants, and a brown skull cap. I have the snapshot of me, Josie and Quong Kee taken in front of the Can Can ruins.

In the old days, Quong had staked every cowboy or miner who got to him with a hard luck story. An orphan or two always slept on cots he kept behind the kitchen, and he fed them there, too. But in 1937 he looked as if he were going hungry, and his dog and cat with him. Josie thought I didn't see her leave ten dollars on his old oil cloth covered table as we left, but I did.

She wasn't always so charitable, however. A little later we were at the old Bird Cage theater when some woman found out who Josie was. She came up to her all smiles.

"Would you autograph a copy of your husband's

biography?" she gushed, expecting Josie to be flattered.

She got one of the famous severe looks. "I will not! I'm tired of everyone growing rich on my deah dead husband."

I felt sorry for the woman who looked like she was hunting a hole to crawl into. It called to mind the curse that was supposed to fall on the Bird Cage involving a "toad-in-the-hole." Was Josie the toad? Regardless, I was ready to crawl in a hole myself. And by the time we got back to the hotel Josie had taken some more spleen out on a paper boy who wanted a quarter for a souvenir edition of the famous *Epitaph*.

"A quarter!" Josie stormed. "John Clum who founded this paper got a nickel for one. What's this place coming to?"

At the hotel she observed our shamed looks and said, "I shouldn't have done that, should I?"

We shook our heads in unison.

She laughed. "Wyatt would have said it was the Sheeny in me. He was always teasing me about being Jewish. You know what a tease he could be under that sober pose, Ted. Don't you wish he was with us now?"

"As much as you do," I said.

"Oh, no," she said quickly. "You couldn't. No one could."

Then she turned and went rapidly up the stairs, keeping her head down until she turned away, so none of us could see her tears. My own eyes were a little misty, too. Tombstone brought it all back.

But there was a comic side, too. Harold Ackerman put it nicely after Josie had gone upstairs.
He let out a big sigh and said, "No one will ever
convince me Wyatt Earp was a killer. He lived
with that woman almost fifty years."

But, all in all, the two of us old timers had a
fine time in Tombstone. We even got over to see
Galeyville, the old mining town and cowboy hangout on the East side of the Chiricahuas. There
wasn't much of it left, but the trip was valuable
since it got Josie to tell of what she knew about
the killing of John Ringo.

I am placing here in Josie's own narrative, her
story of the killing of John Ringo:

WHO KILLED JOHN RINGO?

One hot day in July 1882, John Ringo's dead
body had been found by a teamster, sprawled on
a flat rock nested among a clump of live oaks beside the road to Morse's Mill. It was remarked
as strange that one of his cartridge belts was on
upside down and his pistol was hung in his watch
chain, with one fired cartridge beneath the hammer. The watch chain was jammed under the un-
cocked hammer of his pistol so that the weapon
was firmly held by it. A single bullet hole was
visible in John's head. There were no powder
burns, but a coroner's jury conveniently found suicide to be the cause of death. Other peculiar circumstances were ignored or explained away. Pieces
of his undershirt were tied around his bootless feet,

yet he was wearing his shirt. No horse was found near the body. It later turned up ten miles away at the Chiricahua Cattle Company ranch, carrying his boots on the saddle.

Ringo was buried a few rods from where his body was found. The passing of the last of the Rustler leaders created a small ripple, then was forgotten.

Starting early we had a hard hundred-mile drive the next day around the southern end of the Chiricahua range. We took a rough road that wove through Ricker Canyon from the San Simon Valley to the Sulphur Springs Valley. It ascended into an area of green grassy upland meadows studded with pines, their spikes bristling like the spears of an army of giants. A balsam fragrance pervaded the cool air. Early flowers dotted the meadows. In my mind I saw Old Man Clanton and the boys anxiously pressing a herd of stolen cattle through this pass as they undoubtedly had done many times, more than half a century before. Fifty-six years had gone since they laid the Clanton patriarch to rest beneath the iron caliche of the Tombstone Cemetery. It was an even half-century since Ike had been cut down up on the Blue River by the rifle of a range detective. Could it really have been so long ago? Was I really so old now that I had actually been alive here when Old Man Clanton had cashed in? I didn't feel any different inside than I had the day I left home so many years before. Then the age of fifty seemed ancient; now I had more years than that piled on top of my happy, foolish age when I thought fifty was very old.

We passed the place where Camp Rucker once stood. Capt. Hurst's stolen mules from Camp Rucker that Wyatt tracked to the McLaury ranch came to mind. This had been the first time the Earps interfered directly with the Cowboy's affairs. It was the start of the bloody vendetta that only ended when John Ringo was finally hunted to earth.

We turned north along the western foothills of the Chiricahuas. If we were successful in finding the old Smith Ranch in West Turkey Creek Canyon, I would gaze on Ringo's grave before sundown. The story had come to me piecemeal. Thinking about writing this book caused me to recall all that I had ever heard about Ringo's passing. Snatches of conversation between Wyatt and Doc at the Windsor Hotel in Denver during the Eighties came back to mind. The words that I recalled best were Doc's comment, "God, was old John ever surprised to see us drop in for supper."

But who were "us"? The old names came back with difficulty. Wyatt and Doc, of course, but who else had I heard mentioned? Fred Dodge? I knew Fred was still alive. That letter led to my visit to the Dodges in Texas. Before then, one by one the other old names had fallen in place. Charlie Smith who had lived with Bob Winders in Tombstone. His name had always fascinated me — Oregin Charles Smith. But they called him 'Hairlip Charlie'. Nonetheless there was nothing impaired about his bravery or his loyalty to

Wyatt. Then there was Johnny Green, who was in Gunnison with us and went to Dodge in '83 with us. John Meagher, brother of Mike Meagher, the marshal of Wichita for whom Wyatt worked as a policeman in the '70s. And finally Doc's old friend from Texas, Harry Goober. Seven of them. And in addition, three informers were being paid to report to Fred Dodge on the whereabouts of John Ringo. I have already named two of them — Buckskin Frank and Billy Breakenridge. The third was Johnny O'Rourke. Johnny owed Wyatt a favor he was happy to pay off by keeping an eye on the trail to Galeyville. It was an out-of-the-way spot and Johnny was on the dodge, having escaped from the Tucson jail. Johnny was our old friend from Tombstone, Johnny-Behind-the-Deuce, that Wyatt protected at Vogan's from the lynch mob.

The posse entered the country in ones and twos. Wyatt and Doc, sporting beards to disguise their well-known features, traveled west on the Atlantic and Pacific RR., then made their way south through the mountains by horse. The Hooker's Sierra Bonita Ranch was the rendezvous point, but they camped in the hills rather than at the ranch. Otherwise, some curious cowboy would surely have given away their presence by an innocent remark in town. *(The grapevine of the Cowboy Gang in those days cannot be overestimated. A chance remark about a number of strangers would have been certain to bring a spy to see who was infiltrating that country. The spy might have ap-*

379

peared to be a saddle tramp or a merchant traveling by buckboard or a cattle buyer, but someone would have come to have a look for themselves upon the slightest hint that strangers were around — GB.)

By night rides, Wyatt's little group shifted its camp to the Chiricahuas, somewhere in the wilderness north of the Galeyville trail. *(Actually I believe from observation of that country recently that they must have been north of the road to Morse's sawmill, which petered out into a trail some miles farther east — GB.)*

The reader will want to know how I found all this out if Wyatt didn't tell me. Some of it he did tell me, most indirectly by listening to his conversations with old-timers he trusted. But I am proud of my ability as a detective, which led me to suspect how Ringo got his before I found out for sure. One of my informants told me I wasn't only a pretty good detective, but that I'd have made a good hard-boiled cop the way I sweated what he knew out of him. I might add that I'm not talking about Fred Dodge here either, though he certainly was helpful and could have told me the whole story himself if he had desired. Fred, when he discovered that he wasn't protecting Wyatt any longer and, in fact, might be embarrassing to his memory, talked quite freely to me.

Fred also produced another witness who had valuable information but wished to remain anonymous, since his family was ashamed of his past.

Breakenridge got word to Fred Dodge that

Ringo was heading into the Chiricahuas, apparently for Galeyville, but the word came too late to intercept him in a trap. The posse had to take the risks involved in cutting John's sign and following him. The country where West Turkey Creek leaves the foothills is broken by rock-strewn arroyos. Turkey Creek itself has a rocky bottom. The country is relatively open for a few miles where the logging road wound upward on the south side of the creek. Coniferous and live oak trees dotted the landscape. The creek is bordered today, as it was then, with cottonwoods and sycamores and an occasional juniper. As the road penetrates deeper into the hills, the valley narrows and the trees grow progressively closer together until they form a continuous forest.

In the Eighties there was a roadhouse in this area in addition to Morse's Mill and the Smith Ranch. When I visited the place, the Smith Ranch was still there; the Sanders, who I understood were related to the Smiths, were living on the ranch at that time.

Ringo, the day he rode to his death, obviously was not seeking either company or more liquor. If we can believe Billy Breakenridge, John must have had a skinful already and was probably getting a good hangover by then. He passed through the belt of timber along the creek then moved northward up a boulder-strewn canyon. He dismounted, leading his horse up the steep hill to a small open glade atop a low terrace which stood perhaps twenty feet above the canyon floor. There, under the shade of the low spreading branches of a large pine he appeared to have made camp, staking his horse on good grass and stretching out for a snooze.

Some hours later Wyatt arrived at this canyon on John's trail. He dismounted his posse, concealed the horses in the care of Harry Goober, and followed the trail up the canyon afoot, since he suspected John's intention to make a camp. If so, he would come back sooner or later to continue on up the trail to Galeyville. By this time the sun was sloping westward and would dip behind the Dragoons in perhaps a half-hour.

The posse cautiously made its way up the canyon, keeping to the hillsides in order to be above where they expected to find their quarry. Wyatt, Fred, and John Meagher were on the west slope; Doc, Johnny Greene, and Charlie Smith on the east slope.

By a stroke of luck, Wyatt's party spotted the licking orange tongues of flame from a small fire, visible in the deepening shadows. The smoke was barely visible — Ringo was making coffee, but taking the usual precautions observed in Apacheland of using very dry wood. In addition, he knew the country was full of outlaws, many of whom owed him no allegiance. He did not wish to be surprised by anyone.

You may wonder, in view of the condition of the courts, what the posse intended to do with John if they captured him. It may come as a shock to those who prefer the saccharine version of the old west, where knights in shining armor rode, to know that they proposed to hang John at the end of a lariat in a prominent spot where his "taking-off" could not be kept a secret by his followers. They then intended to break up and leave the country as unobtrusively as they entered. *(As a matter of fact, Charlie Smith, Fred, and John Meagher returned to Tombstone afterward —GB.)*

Unfortunately for well-laid plans, something intervened to warn John of their approach. Perhaps it was a jay or a woodpecker that cried alarm to John's wilderness-wise ears; perhaps the keener hearing of his picketed horse caused it to throw its head up, ears pointed and eyes fixed on the woods, searching for potential danger. They did not catch John, as they would have preferred, with his pants down, but they did catch him with his boots and shirt off. Sensing danger, John grabbed his pistol and belt and, pistol in hand, darted for the woods to the left and ahead of Wyatt. The posse froze in their tracks, hoping to lull their quarry into believing he had been startled by a false alarm. There was a tense stillness for perhaps five minutes. A rock unluckily was dislodged by someone on the east slope, since Doc's group kept moving, having no notion of the tableau being enacted by their friends on the other side of the canyon. The passage of the rock to the bottom of the hill must have sounded to the taut-nerved listeners like a freight train. It finally rolled to a stop with one last clack-clack on the rocks of the canyon floor.

What followed was a stealthy stalk of their dangerous prey with the light gradually fading, becoming worse and worse for shooting. Time favored the hunted. It would appear from the manner in which he was found, that John had hastily ripped off his undershirt, after running from his camp, and wrapped his feet as some protection against the rocky ground. He probably planned to quietly make his escape after dark. But it was the light-colored foot coverings that revealed his movements to his stalkers. Wyatt drew a bead on the spot where he had seen John slip into a patch of brush, then traced what he considered would be his path through that clump, holding his sights on the expected exit spot. At that point, someone fired. All of the posse later denied having fired a shot at all. This has remained a mystery to this day. Ringo had to have fired that shot. Why did he do it? What did he shoot at? Did his thumb accidentally slip off a cocked hammer as he lost his footing for a moment in the loose rocks? We'll probably never know. Whatever happened, John broke from his hiding cover immediately following the shot and rapidly ran uphill. Wyatt took a quick careful bead on him with his rifle and fired. John fell heavily without a sound and lay still, never so much as jerking after he fell.

"That was some shot," my informant told me. "In that light, under those conditions there was a lot of luck in it. There was also a hell of a lot of cool skill. If Wyatt hadn't got him then, he probably would have got away. Twenty feet further and he'd have been in the boulders. Then we'd have been in a real mess ourselves."

So the last of the big bugs among the rustlers cashed in his checks.

What about the mystery of how John's body was found? First of all, Wyatt wanted it found. Secondly, the posse could not afford to be seen themselves. Indian Charlie's and Stilwells death had taught them that lesson very well — had they been as sneaky as their enemies about killing, they would never have had to leave the country. When I read *Helldorado* and some of the other books covering the mystery of Ringo's being found as he was, even I conjectured that he must have been packed in from somewhere else to where he was found, most probably in the dark. It appeared to me that he either had been surprised in camp or while asleep; the undershirt on his feet indicated he had been the victim of either surprise or accident and lost his boots, replacing them with something to protect his feet.

I could see Doc's sense of humor in the upside-own cartridge belt — either that or it had been carelessly strapped back on Ringo's body in the dark. The latter seems to have been the case. The posse stayed to finish Ringo's pot of coffee, then packed John out of there. His saddled horse got away during the shooting. His boots, I suppose must have been hung on the saddle.

This closes my case on Tombstone and the Earp-Cowboy vendetta. It was a shame Johnny Behan didn't stumble onto Wyatt's posse in the Chiri-

cahuas about that time. What a sensational head-
line it would have made:

"Sheriff Found Mysteriously Hung!"

The foregoing comprises the whole story that
I reviewed in my mind as we drove up the road
into West Turkey Creek Canyon. I wanted to see
if I could identify the place where Ringo had met
his fate. We drove all the way where the road
petered out into a trail. There the creek tumbled
down out of the hills over the boulders, forming
pretty little pools on the level stretches. The pines
were tall and fragrant here. The wind sighed softly
overhead. Shafts of westering sunlight pierced the
gloom through openings in the trees.

We turned around and retraced our path. At
only one spot did I see a canyon running north
that might have been the one into which Wyatt's
posse followed the outlaw baron. Further back on
the trail, we stopped to ask directions at what the
mail box proclaimed was the Sander's Ranch. I
had asked my friends not to reveal who I was and
they reluctantly kept that promise.

We asked the man who came out if he could
tell us where John Ringo was buried. He pointed
west with his thumb, "Right about 50 yards behind
my shed out there."

"Could we intrude and take a picture?" we asked
timidly.

We certainly could; everybody else did without
so much as asking most of the time.

There, just on the south bank of West Turkey
Creek beneath the spread of an ancient oak, the

last of the outlaw barons slept the long sleep. He and his followers had terrorized southeastern Arizona for half a decade. The grave was marked with a tidy pile of small round boulders from the creek bed. The day had grown too dim to take a good picture. The sun was resting just on top of the Dragoons to the west. The temperature cooled rapidly as it does in the high desert when the sun goes down.

"It must have been like this," I thought, "when the man resting here came to his violent end 55 years ago." /1482 - Currently 1937

I thought of Wyatt then, whose vengeance was finally satisfied by this last killing. It was true, he had not got all the sub-chiefs like Spence and Ike Clanton but he had wiped out the ruling geniuses of the gang. Organized crime in Cochise went to the grave with Ringo. No one was left with the strong personality needed to keep the rank and file in line.

Wyatt seemed somehow very near as I stood there thinking of him. I still missed him desperately. "If only he could be here with me," I thought.

The eerie wind that haunts the Chiricahuas had subtly crept up the canyon as I stood there reflecting on all these sad past events. Its melancholy soughing overhead was a fitting finale to that long-past saga. The wind song would play on over the scene for countless centuries.

"But the wind has no memories," I thought. "I have memories and I'll soon be gone."

That is why I could bring myself to tell even this part of the story, too. In the end, good people must fight fire with fire or evil will rule men's lives. Ringo had not gone out without a chance. His had not been a murder as had been the deaths of those he killed in his life — he had gone out with a pistol in his hand, within a few steps of escaping to continue his evil career.

The last of them had gone; the score was worthy of toting up. Especially since there are persistent attempts to whitewash Johnny Behan and the murdering "Cowboys" that he protected. Doesn't it seem strange that so much bad luck would plague those honest grangers of Johnny's? That is, if they were as honest and innocent as some people would paint them. There was Old Man Clanton shot by Mexicans out in Skeleton Canyon, Dixie Lee Gray killed with him; Billy Clanton gone in the street fight; Ike Clanton shot by detective J.V. Brighton up on Blue River in 1887; Phin Clanton sent to jail for cattle rustling in the late Eighties; the McLaurys shot and killed with Billy Clanton while resisting arrest; Joe Hill killed, falling from his horse, drunk; Leonard, Head and Crane, all shot, the two former by the Haslett Brothers while doing Mike Gray's dirty work, Crane with Old Man Clanton and Dixie Gray; Curly Bill, Stilwell, and Ringo disposed of by Wyatt as I have told; Johnny Barnes dead of a long festering wound received from Wyatt in the Curly Bill fight; Indian Charlie cashing in above Spence's woodcamp in South Pass, shot by Wyatt's posse; and Spence going over the road to the Yuma penitentiary in the late '80s for cattle rustling. A tidy score. It was a shame that the times were so hard that so many honest grangers, misunderstood by the community, were persecuted in such outrageous fashion. Seventeen of the leading lights, all but two dead, the others going in to the pen. Those two were probably privileged guests there since Johnny Behan became assistant superintendent of the Yuma penitentiary in 1887 — that wasn't the way he deserved to get there.

Chapter 27

An Era Ends — Part II

Several years later Josie and I were in Highlands at Bill and Estelle Miller's. It was the day before Memorial Day, and we'd all gone up to put some of Bill's fragrant pinks on the family graves. After the trip to the cemetery we sat down on the Miller's side porch. It was just after sundown, and the scent of the pinks in the big round bed in the yard, and the orange blossoms in Bill's orchards put us all in a mellow mood. That's when I learned about yet another strange facet of Josie's and Wyatt's life.

Estelle had just finished telling us how she was sure that her mother, Adelia, had had second sight and was a bonafide clairvoyant.

EDITORIAL COMMENT:
The family all encountered supernatural phenomena; when Estelle herself died, her daughter LaVonne told me, "The morning after Mom died, I was cleaning in the living room for something

*to do to take my mind off losing her. I was think-
ing if there was just some sign that she was still
all right. She used to go in there every morning
and pull the shade up and then down to just a
certain place and while I was thinking about her
— you may think I'm making this up — the shade
went up all by itself and then down again to just
the spot she liked to keep it. I got a feeling I
can't describe then — I simply knew she was all
right and felt a lot better . . . . . all of my grief
went away, and I said, "I know you're here, mom."*

*Wyatt himself recounted many times that his
'hunches', or premonitions, stood him in good
stead, such as at the time he was approaching
the spot where he met and killed Curly Bill, (mentioned in the Flood Ms.) though he apparently
never told anyone but Josie of real clairvoyance.*

Ten Eyck continues:
   Josie told us, "Wyatt was clairvoyant, too."
   "I never heard that before," Bill said.
   I think it was news to all of us.
   "Wyatt never talked about it, and I've never
told anybody either," Josie said. "He felt embar-
rassed and was almost afraid to tell me."
   She was quiet for a long time, rocking back and
forth in the swing, perhaps debating whether she'd
said too much.
   "Well," Estelle said finally, "go ahead for
Heaven's sake! You've got us all interested now."
   Josie looked at the three of us, and what she
read on our faces gave her courage.

"Well, it was 1883," she began. "We'd been in Silverton, Colorado when Wyatt got a wire from Bat Masterson asking him to come back to Dodge City. Luke Short had been run out of Dodge, and when Bat came to help him they **both** got run out of town. So Wyatt got some mutual friends together, and we all dropped in for a little visit. **They** didn't get run out of town. There were Doc Holliday, Shotgun Collins, and Johnny Green as well as the rest."

At that point the question ran through my mind, "I wonder if Josie knew all the boys called Green, 'Cat House Johnny'?"★ It didn't seem like the time to ask. In fact the appropriate time never presented itself, but I still wonder.

"Anyhow," Josie continued, "they got the trouble straightened out. The governor even sent down a representative — Colonel Moonlight. All I remember about him is his stomach always growled. Wyatt thought it was the Dodge City cooking.

"On the train back to Silverton, Wyatt was quiet for a long time. Finally I asked him what he was thinking about. He said, 'A funny thing happened back in Dodge. Happened twice.' He didn't say anything for a minute, so I told him to go ahead. He wasn't sure I'd believe him. 'You'll think I'm out of my mind,' he said, 'but when I was coming back to the hotel after the council meeting that first night I saw somebody I thought I knew and should talk to passing through the light from a

★ Also Crooked Mouth. — **GB.**

392

doorway. I hurried up to catch him, and just when I figured who he walked like he dodged into an alley. I heard him start running. The hair on the back of my neck stood up, since I knew right then who it was. I peeked around the corner and he stopped, looked back and said as plain as I'm talking now, "Watch out, Wyatt!" Then he ran a ways and disappeared.'

"For Heaven's sake, who was it?" I wanted to know, and Wyatt looked at me like he was trying to decide to trust me. 'It was Morg,' he said. 'Even the voice.'

"Then it was my turn to have the hair on the back of my neck stand up."

Now, neither Wyatt nor Josie had a hyper-active imagination. If Wyatt had told her what he had seen, then it happened. Frankly, while she was telling the story, the hair on **my** neck had been standing up.

We all sat thinking, in silence a minute, then Josie said, "There was more. I asked Wyatt when the second time was that he saw Morg. He said, 'It was the night the boys all got together after the fuss was settled. I stepped out back and was coming in again when somebody came around the corner about twenty five feet away and stopped real quick. I heard the dirt crunch under his boots when he stopped. Then he said, "Wyatt, don't let them get you, too!" and ran just like the first time, and disappeared. That's what he told me just before he died. I've kept my eyes open, believe me, but I still wonder if I'm crazy.'

393

"Wyatt never talked about it again. I don't think anything like that ever happened again, but maybe those warnings saved his life in Dodge. Who knows?"

We talked a little bit about ghosts and the supernatural, but Josie seemed unusually pensive.

Bill finally asked, "What's the matter, Aunt Sadie?"

"I'm wondering whether to tell you **my** story," she said. "Only I'm not sure what happened or if I was only dreaming."

We all urged her to tell what was on her mind, but she swung back and forth a minute before she started.

"It happened when I was in Tombstone with Ted and the Ackermans a couple years ago. I thought maybe I was dying and seeing my past the way they say you do, but I wasn't afraid, just curious to see what was going to happen.

"I was in my room after we'd walked around town, and I sat down in a chair to take a rest. Maybe I dozed off, I don't know, but the stove made the room nice and warm, and I was tired. I'd been thinking that if somebody had told me when I was an empty-headed girl that I'd be back in Tombstone alone and lonely, I'd never have believed them. But there I was, missing Wyatt more every minute.

"And then suddenly I was young again. It was like a huge hand picked me up, turned me over, and set me down again. I thought I'd died and gone back to 1882, and it all seemed so right!"

Her voice and the squeak of the swing chains were the only sounds. It was full dark, and the fragrance of the pinks and orange blossoms were heavy on the air. The whole evening seemed enchanted.

"I knew I wasn't supposed to be sitting there if it was 1882. I was supposed to be looking after Senator Hearst. I'd been nursing him at Mrs. Young's boarding house. But I couldn't move, and that worried me. What if he needed something? So I struggled up and leaned against the window. Then I forgot all about Senator Hearst. Across the street, leaning against a post of the old Oriental, I saw Wyatt. Just the outline of his face under his Stetson." Her voice broke, and she was quiet a minute, remembering her vision.

"Then he took out a cigar and lit it and walked across the street toward me. I thought what if he goes to Mrs. Young's looking for me, and I won't be there! I'm in the wrong place, and I might never see him again! I tried to move, to open the window, to say something, but I couldn't. He looked up then, and waved like he knew I was there, and then disappeared. Suddenly it was all gone."

When she continued I was troubled to hear her words come as though someone else were speaking through her.

"I cried like a child," she said. "I thought, 'I've lost him again! Twice is too much to bear!' "

I knew that was true. I'd been with her the first time, with John Flood and Dr. Shurtleff. She'd almost lost her mind. We finally had to pry her away from Wyatt so they could take the body.

But her story wasn't over yet. She went on in the same strange voice. "I don't know how long I sat there and prayed for God to take me, too. But . . . . . you see, He didn't. Maybe He didn't because I'm supposed to tell Wyatt's story. Tell that he did what he had to do and get justice for it. I pray it's so."

It was a long while before any of us spoke. Her words, the place, the darkness, had cast a spell over us all.

She had been referring to the story that she'd spent so many years perfecting after Wyatt died.*

All too soon, however, she was gone herself.

I received the phone call I'd been dreading from Bessie Nevitt with whom Josie had been boarding. John Flood and I had been taking turns sitting with her.

I haven't said too much about John who was a lifelong friend of the Earps, though younger than us old timers. Flood had been their mining associate since the early 1900's; he was also secretary, confidante, and man of all work. Bless him, he even tried to do Wyatt's biography, but he's no writer and knows it.

That last morning he was arriving at Nevitt's just as I got there. We exchanged looks, not being able to speak. Josie had been almost a sweetheart to me. She'd been more like a mother to John.

The problem was her heart, and Bessie had her

* *I Married Wyatt Earp*, Univ. of Ariz. Press, 1976 — **GB.**

propped up on pillows to help her breathe. She'd combed her hair, and it flowed long and loose over her shoulders.

I took her hand and looked into the still lovely brown eyes. She smiled at me, and the old, youthful face shone out. With her other hand she took John's and squeezed it. We all knew, and how it hurt.

"John," she said, "would you leave Ted and me alone a little while, please? I have something to tell him."

But she didn't have anything to tell me that I didn't already know. There were only the two of us, for the last time. Of all my old friends I knew losing her would be the most terrible blow of all.

She said, "I'm a little bit afraid, Ted. Would you hold my hand tighter?"

I squeezed the frail little hand, still as warm and soft as in her youth. Desperation at my inability to fend off the inevitable rose in me, but I tried not to let it show.

She smiled at me again. "Would you kiss me?" she whispered.

I leaned over and kissed her, and both of us had tears in our eyes.

Then she said, "I'm coming, Wyatt," and love lit her face for the last time.

She died smiling.

Shortly, that look of peace only seen on the dead captured her features, but even in eternal peace it seemed to me that she beheld the world in an ever so slightly imperious fashion — as a great beauty should — down her lovely nose.

I sat holding her hand for a long time, tears streaming down my face.

She had gone to join her one great love.

I hope God wills they are together somewhere forever, crossing great mountains hand-in-hand on their way to their latest boom camp, wherever it is.

Epilogue

So I have lived to finish telling about my old friend's Tombstone Vendetta. Sometimes I wondered if I ever would.

Now I'd like to cross that great mountain in the dusk after them and have a reunion in an old lamplit hotel in some boom camp.

Tombstone would do.

End Note

A majority will recognize that this **is** "the true story of the Earps at Tombstone."

It unavoidably invalidates portions of all the less-than-fully-informed books that have gone before it, which is to say every Earp book to date, including *I Married Wyatt Earp*, which I collected and edited. (This material was not available for my use when that book was published.)

Anticipating the controversy this book may engender, I have, at times, considered sealing my Earp resources (of which this book reveals only the tip of the ice berg) to be opened by later generations who may be less wrapped up in the virulent Earp controversy, since Earpiana is actually a minor area of history, and Wyatt Earp, for all of his magnificent courage, was really a comparatively unimportant figure in the larger events of his own time.

On the other hand, I could not bring myself to turn my back on my promise to Estelle Miller "to try to set straight the picture of her uncles, which had been kicked awry by writers and movies, and try to keep it that way."

So, I have attempted to blend a vast amount of material into one internally consistent document that tells everything pertinent without being ponderous and argumentative, and am making it available to the public.

As Ben Traywick comments in his introduction, I have been victimized in the past by the extensive use of my research without credit. In the case of ethical users, this was probably due in some cases to not recognizing the initial source, after the material had been copied without attribution the first time.

As a convenience to future users, as well as protection for my work, the following disclosures are original with this book (except for a couple of general references I have previously made in articles to the killing of Old Man Clanton, which also were based on my original sources):

> "that Wyatt Earp came to Tombstone as Wells Fargo's man and remained such as long as he stayed there (and for years afterward); that the Kinnear stage holdup was a sham to cover a murder attempt on Wells Fargo's man, Bob Paul, engineered by Johnny Behan, since Paul was about to be awarded the office of sheriff of Pima County by an appeals court, to replace Behan's friend, Charlie Shibell; that there were **eight** killers involved in that attempt, and the identities of the previously-

unnamed other four; that the immediate cause of the so called O.K. Corral Gunfight was that Ike Clanton put his foot in his mouth and blustered to Doc Holliday, in the presence of the Earp brothers, that he and his friends had intended to ambush Doc and the Earps, whereupon Doc hot-headedly told Ike he'd beat Ike to the punch and personally killed Ike's father in a similar ambush, (which was true); that the McLaury boys' brother, Will, hired several murder attempts on the Earps and their supporters, resulting in the crippling of Virgil Earp and the death of Morgan, following which Doc Holliday searched Tombstone high and low for McLaury with blood in his eye, and that Doc so strongly suspected Johnny Behan of being implicated that he also sought him until Wyatt Earp collared him and cooled him down; that the Earp brothers were Tombstone's unofficial, privately financed, police force due to the Town-lot racket, were paid by the big cattlemen as well, and well-compensated by Wells Fargo for everything they did, including Wyatt's return and killing of John Ringo, which definitely wrote finis to the Cowboy Gang. And finally, that Josephine Earp led secret, compartmentalized lives, slanted her memoir to whitewash Wyatt, that she manipulated him at Tombstone and all their lives together, and that she was the strong member of that team; wearing the pants in their family."

403

Appendix

The principal informants who made this work possible are listed by category below:

BLOOD RELATIVES OF EITHER WYATT OR JOSEPHINE EARP:

Mrs. Anna Colclasure and her sister, Mrs. Blanche Weir Shafman (of the Illinois branch of the family); Mrs. Reba Earp Young (of the Lamar, Mo. branch of the family); Mrs. Alvin Greenberg and Mrs. Maynard Wolff (sisters, and grand-nieces of Mrs. Wyatt Earp through Josie's sister, their grandmother, Rebecca Weiner); Mrs. Marjorie Macartney (grand niece of Josephine Earp, through Josie's sister, Henrietta Lenhardt, who was Marjorie's grandmother); Mrs. Estelle Edwards Miller (Wyatt's niece, daughter of his sister, Adelia); Mrs. LaVonne Miller Griffin (Estelle's daughter); Mrs. Florence Edwards Bessant (Estelle's sister); Mrs. Muryl Edwards Hamilton Sullivan (Estelle's sister); George Edwards (Estelle's brother); Jeanne Cason Laing; Dr. Ray Cason Lindsay; Dr. Walter Cason; (the preceding three, all children of Mrs. Wyatt Earp's biographer, Mrs. Mabel Earp Cason, daughter of Wyatt's cousin, William Harrison Earp); Mrs. Martha Chapman Lentz; Mrs. Ada Earp Turner; Mr. Roy Earp; Mrs. Alice Earp Wells; Mr. Virgil Edwin Earp; several others who asked to remain anonymous.

THOSE WHO PERSONALLY KNEW WYATT OR JOSPHINE EARP,
(or both, some quite closely):
Mr. Ted Ten Eyck and his son, Ted, Jr. (both under pseudonyms, as explained in the Foreword); Mrs. Merritt Beeson (daughter-in-law of Wyatt's Dodge City friend, Chalkley Beeson); Mr. John H. Flood, Jr.; (Wyatt's and Josephine's intimate friend and amanuensis on his autobiography); Mrs. Bessie Nevitt (executrix of the estate of Josephine Earp); Mrs. Hubert Thacker; Mr. Bill Miller (whom Wyatt considered a son, and who, in turn, regarded me in the same manner); Mrs. Hildreth Hallowell (grand-niece of Mrs. Virgil Earp, who helped with considerable grumbling, but nontheless helped); Mr. Ernest Cason (husband of Mrs. Earp's biographer, Mabel); Mr. Joe Bush and his wife, Nellie, (years-long intimates of Wyatt and Josephine Earp at Parker, Arizona); Carmelita Mayhew (family friend and a famous character in her own right, who, as she said, knew "where every body in Arizona is buried.").

Again, some remain anonymous, such as the man who appears simply as R.J. in Ten Eyck's diary.

THOSE WHO KNEW MARY KATHERINE HARONEY,
(Big Nose Kate Holliday, Elder, Fisher):
Mrs. Lillie Raffert (niece); Mrs. Hattie Haroney Maddox (niece); Mr. Albert Haroney (nephew); Mr. Theodore Haroney (nephew) Dr. Albert Wm. Bork (her biographer — unpublished); Mrs. Charles Ydeen (related by marriage); Mr. Harold Bruckman (related by marriage); Gertrude Beckwith (grand-niece).

INFORMANTS ABOUT JOHN H. BEHAN:
Mr. Albert Behan (his son); Mrs. Behan Meeker (related by marriage); Mr. John McLean (old friend of Albert's and executor of his estate).

INFORMANTS ABOUT LOUISA HOUSTON EARP,
(Common-Law Wife of Wyatt's Brother, Morgan):
Mr. Bruce Robinson and his sister Eleanor Houston, grand-niece and nephew, who provided me copies of Louisa's letters.

OTHERS WHO WERE VERY HELPFUL:
Mrs. Nellie Seegrist (relative of Magdalena Rysdam, first wife of Virgil Earp); Mrs. Charles Colyn (related twice by marriage to Newton Earp, half-brother of Wyatt); Mrs. Florence Marquis

(niece by marriage of Wyatt Earp's secret second wife, Celia Ann "Mattie" Blaylock Earp); Mrs. Margery Clum Parker (grand daughter of John Clum); Mr. Knolls Ryerson (intimate friend of John Clum); Mr. William Holliday (descendant of Doc Holliday, who laughingly related, among other things, that the Hollidays considered ridiculous the efforts of the McKey's — Doc's mother's family — to garner a halo for Doc); Mrs. Jean Macia Devere (who knew Billy Breakenridge in his later years). Selman McMasters on his great uncle; Ed Godbey, grand-nephew of Texas Jack Vermillion; Dayton Graham; Burt W. Graham of Wise County, Texas (in the Air Force at the time); and many many more (at least a couple of hundred — such as Melvin Jones who knew Wyatt at Nome, Brad and Norm Keene, who did pick and shovel work at the Happy Day, etc.), whom I talked to or corresponded with, some others whose names I failed to record and can't recall, and many I do not record here by their request, and finally, and very importantly, Steve McLaury and his son Shane.

EDITORIAL COMMENTS:

Many of the above people had a unique relationship with the principals in this book, as indicated in parentheses after their names.

My prior article published in *Real West* magazine, entitled "Trailing An American Myth," covers a lot of my globe-trotting activities in pursuit of information on the Wyatt Earps and their cohorts. That article was severely restricted as to what could be said, and — to prevent family squabbling — had to refrain from mentioning the true extent of my relations with various people, such as Mr. and Mrs. Bill Miller, whom I had known since 1943, in fact. A very real consideration at the time was the possibility that items legitimately given to me would be sought by some who had no claim to them, but would — nonetheless clamor to have them. The Ten Eyck connection could not be mentioned at all, yet my relations with Ted Sr. and Jr. dated from the same year, when I was an Aviation Cadet at Santa Ana, California and heard of them all through the base librarian after I drew out Stuart Lake's book, *Wyatt Earp, Frontier Marshal* to re-read it.

During the years following, I spent many Air Force leaves with the Millers and their daughter, LaVonne. Living with them and sitting where Wyatt Earp sat, in his favorite rocker, while I listened to them hark back about him and those who knew him, was an experience that I find indescribable. I was a young fellow who had cut my teeth on Wyatt Earp, especially the Stuart Lake heroic version of him. Even after my eyes were opened, it often raised the hair on the back of my neck to share recollections about my boyhood hero.

Since then I have come to a much-less worshipful view of *Frontier Marshal*, but have no less respect for the man who, with his brothers and Doc Holliday, bravely faced tremendous odds against an evil empire of outlaws and survived — with many lifelong scars, it is true, but survived.

My documentary source material, here in the room where I record this, fills six fireproof safes, with other highly sensitive items in vaults elsewhere. Wyatt Earp has truly been a life work, but I have no sense of being obsessed with him. I have many other interests; have written six Western novels, and am working on other subjects far removed from either the Earps or the West.

For readers who have become acquainted with Wyatt Earp for the first time in these pages, or who simply wish to know more about him, I suggest the following reading list:

The Private Journal of George Whitwell Parsons; It All Happened in Tombstone, by John Clum; Apache Agent, by Woodworth Clum; Tombstone's Yesterdays, by Lorenzo Walters; Helldorado, by William M. Breakenridge; Tombstone, by Walter Noble Burns; Wyatt Earp, Frontier Marshal, by Stuart N. Lake; Tombstone's Epitaph, by Douglas D. Martin; Suppressed Murder of Wyatt Earp, by Glenn G. Boyer; I Married Wyatt Earp, by Josephine Sarah Marcus Earp (collected and edited by Glenn G. Boyer); Wyatt Earp, by Wyatt S. Earp (his autobiography — a collector's item available in some libraries, such as the University of Arizona Special Collections); The O.K. Corral Inquest, annotated by Alford Turner; The Earps Talk, annotated by Alford Turner; many of the books and pamphlets by Ben T. Traywick, whose long residence in Tombstone has made him a magnet for information from the descendants of old time Tombstone residents, which, coupled with his additional documentary research, make his material a rich source of primary information.

The employees of G.K. HALL hope you have enjoyed this Large Print book. All our Large Print titles are designed for easy reading, and all our books are made to last. Other G.K. Hall Large Print books are available at your library, through selected bookstores, or directly from us. For more information about current and up-coming titles, please call or mail your name and address to:

G.K. HALL
PO Box 159
Thorndike, Maine 04986
800/223-6121
207/948-2962

AA
Blakey RG
Dixon

DW

1	31	61	91	121	151	181	211	241	271	301	331
2	32	62	92	122	152	182	212	242	272	302	332
3	33	63	93	123	153	183	213	243	273	303	333
4	34	64	94	124	154	184	214	244	274	304	334
5	35	65	95	125	155	185	215	245	275	305	335
6	36	66	96	126	156	186	216	245	276	306	336
7	37	67	97	127	157	187	217	247	277	307	337
8	38	68	98	128	158	188	218	248	278	308	338
9	39	69	99	129	159	189	219	249	279	309	339
10	40	70	100	130	160	190	220	250	280	310	340
11	41	71	101	131	161	191	221	251	281	311	341
12	42	72	102	132	162	192	222	252	282	312	342
13	43	73	103	133	163	193	223	253	283	313	343
14	44	74	104	134	164	194	224	254	284	314	344
15	45	75	105	135	165	195	225	255	285	315	345
16	46	76	106	136	166	196	226	256	286	316	346
17	47	77	107	137	167	197	227	257	287	317	347
18	48	78	108	138	168	198	228	258	288	318	348
19	49	79	109	139	169	199	229	259	289	319	349
20	50	80	110	140	170	200	230	260	290	320	350
21	51	81	111	141	171	201	231	261	291	321	351
22	52	82	112	142	172	202	232	262	292	322	352
23	53	83	113	143	173	203	233	263	293	323	353
24	54	84	114	144	174	204	234	264	294	324	354
25	55	85	115	145	175	205	235	265	295	325	355
26	56	86	116	146	176	206	236	266	296	326	356
27	57	87	117	147	177	207	237	267	297	327	357
28	58	88	118	148	178	208	238	268	298	328	358
29	59	89	119	149	179	209	239	269	299	329	359
30	60	90	120	150	180	210	240	270	300	330	360